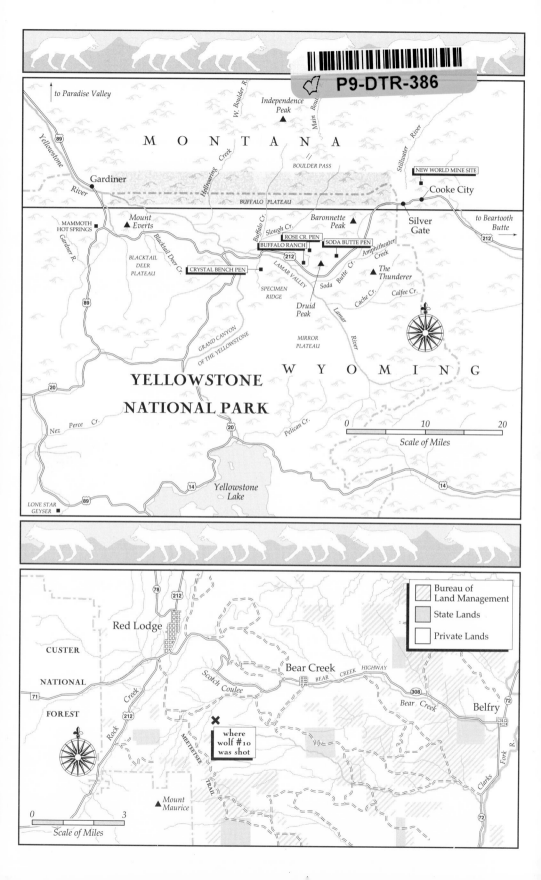

P9-DTR-386

to Paradise Valley

W. Boulder R.

Independence
Peak ▲

Main Boul

Stillwater
River

M O N T A N A

89

Yellowstone

Hellroaring Creek

BOULDER PASS

NEW WORLD MINE SITE

Gardiner

River

BUFFALO PLATEAU

Cooke City

MAMMOTH
HOT SPRINGS

Mount
Everts ▲

Baronnette
Peak ▲

Silver
Gate

to Beartooth
Butte

Buffalo Cr.

Slough Cr.

ROSE CR. PEN

SODA BUTTE PEN

212

Gardiner R.

BLACKTAIL
DEER
PLATEAU

Blacktail Deer Cr.

BUFFALO RANCH

Amphitheater Creek

89

CRYSTAL BENCH PEN

LAMAR VALLEY

Soda Butte Cr.

Cache Cr.

Calfee Cr.

The
Thunderer ▲

SPECIMEN
RIDGE

Druid
Peak ▲

GRAND CANYON
OF THE YELLOWSTONE

MIRROR
PLATEAU

Lamar River

20

W   Y   O   M   I   N   G

YELLOWSTONE

NATIONAL PARK

20

Nez  Perce  Cr.

Pelican Cr.

0                    10                    20

Scale of Miles

14

14

89

Yellowstone
Lake

LONE STAR
GEYSER ■

Bureau of
Land Management

State Lands

Private Lands

78

212

Red Lodge

CUSTER

Bear Creek

BEAR  CREEK  HIGHWAY

NATIONAL

Scotch Coulee

308

Bear  Creek

Belfry

71

Rock Creek

212

72

FOREST

MEETEETSE  TRAIL

✖
where
wolf #10
was shot

Clarks  Fork  R.

▲ Mount
Maurice

72

0                    3

Scale of Miles

# The Return of the Wolf to Yellowstone

## Also by Thomas McNamee

*The Grizzly Bear*

*Nature First: Keeping Our Wild Places and Wild Creatures Wild*

*A Story of Deep Delight*

# The Return of the

# WOLF

## to Yellowstone

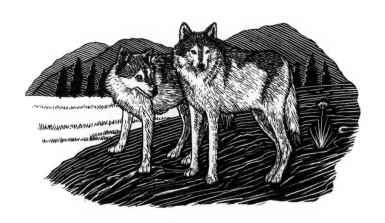

## Thomas McNamee

Henry Holt and Company | New York

Henry Holt and Company, Inc.
*Publishers since 1866*
115 West 18th Street
New York, New York 10011

Henry Holt ® is a registered trademark of
Henry Holt and Company, Inc.

Library of Congress Cataloging-in-Publication Data

McNamee, Thomas
The return of the wolf to Yellowstone/Thomas McNamee.—1st ed.
        p.   cm.
1. Wolves—Yellowstone National Park. 2. Wildlife reintroduction—
        Yellowstone National Park.   I. Title.
QL737.C22M393              1997              96-39702
333.95'9773'0978752—dc21                        CIP
        ISBN 0-8050-3101-4

Henry Holt books are available for special promotions and premiums.
For details contact: Director, Special Markets.

The chapter entitled "Information Lineage" was previously published, in a somewhat
different form, in *Natural History*. The chapter entitled "Drainage Ditch" was previously
published, in a somewhat different form, in *The Oxford American*.

First Edition—1997

*Designed by Michelle McMillian*

*Illustration by Dorothy Reinhardt*

Printed in the United States of America
All first editions are printed on acid-free paper. ∞

1  3  5  7  9  10  8  6  4  2

*For my father, Charles T. McNamee, Jr.*

# CONTENTS

I am drawn to beauty as a tree is drawn to light or an animal to water.

—Andy Goldsworthy, Stone

# TUSCANY

# *Information Lineage*

An austere white stucco house with a roof of ochre tile stands amid the olive groves and vineyards of Chianti. Tight-furled cypresses file uphill along a lane to other villas, other farms. The February sun hangs low in the sky, the icy *tramontana* slices in from Switzerland, but the grass is already green and the trees are in bud. Except for wisps of radio music brought from the house on the transmountain wind, the landscape is silent and still.

Next to the tile-roofed house there stands a copse of trees in which a pack of wolves is sleeping.

Lifting his antenna high, Edoardo Tedesco grins from beneath a slept-in haystack of graduate-student hair. *Tock,* goes the receiver, *tock.* He has found his study wolves.

This is the ancient place of the wolf in our world: nearby, unknown.

"Excellent," says Tedesco. "The shepherds do not kill them yet."

In a swale of green shorn to velvet, a man smoking a pipe watches his sheep. A big white dog lies at his side, also watching. "This is the very old guard dog of Italy, the Maremma," says Tedesco, "but these shepherds come from Sardinia, where there are no wolves, and they don't know how to train the Maremma, and when the wolves come, the dogs run away."

But surely wolves prefer their natural prey? In Minnesota and northern Montana, hardly any livestock is lost to wolves.

Tedesco gives a sardonic smile. A graduate student in wildlife biology at the University of Rome, he has been studying this pack in Tuscany for two years now. Wolf range has been expanding steadily for the past twenty years from the province of Abruzzo in central Italy, a hundred and fifty miles from this pasture in the legendary winemaking region of Chianti, twelve miles from the city of Siena. These wolves are newcomers. "In the beginning, they stayed in the gorges—dense shrub vegetation, very good habitat for wild boar, roe deer, red deer." (The gentle-looking landscape here is riddled with vertiginous, almost people-proof slashes.) "But there were not so many wild prey, because of the poaching, and soon the wolves killed most of them, and then they began killing sheep."

Not many, surely?

"Two or three thousand last year, killed in the province of Siena only. This alpha male, Alvio, is very clever, very hard to find. Now we have a radio collar on him, and also on a subadult, a male, we call him Fulvio. Thirty, forty sheep this pack alone has killed in two years."

The shepherds tolerate this?

"In Italy the wolf is protected absolutely. The owners are compensated, ninety percent of the value, but this does not satisfy them. They tell me, 'We are going to kill your wolves.' "

But the law!

That thin, sardonic, so Italian smile again.

The guard dogs go untrained, the shepherds oil their guns and trade forbidden poisons, the whole country has a long tradition of wildlife slaughter, there is agriculture nearly everywhere, the human population has been dense for hundreds of years, many laws are deemed no more than wishful guidelines, there is not one speck of what an American would call wilderness—yet Italy *has wolves.*

Yes, the gray wolf, the wolf of lore and gore, the wolf that pulls down moose in the Yukon, pounces on ptarmigan in the Siberian taiga, prowls for incautious goats at the edge of bedouin camps—*Canis lupus* is alive and well not twenty miles from the Piazza Campidoglio, where the bronze wolf-mother of Rome suckles Romulus and Remus through the centuries.

In the half century since World War II, there has been a prodigious flowering of education, industry, and prosperity in Italy—*Il Boom*, it is called. Italy is now one of the world's great industrial powers. Among the Boom's effects has been an exodus of Italians from the villages and farms to the cities, and among the effects of that exodus has been reforestation of the land left behind.

Reforestation has made possible the recovery of remnant populations of the small roe deer, the large red deer (a cousin of our North American elk), and the wild sheep known in French and Italian as *mouflon*. In a few high-mountain refuges there are growing populations of chamois and ibex. There have also been reintroductions—of native deer, exotic deer, mouflon—with varying success, depending on how extravagantly the local populace flouts the game laws. Wild boar, with their stupendous reproductive rate (up to ten young per annual litter) and their adaptation to a wide range of habitats, are flourishing. All these are good wolf prey, and more prey has meant more wolves.

New national parks and nature reserves have been designated. A contemporary map of Tuscany, to take just that region as an example, shows an extraordinary patchwork of protected areas—the Parco Naturale delle Alpi Apuane, coastal wetlands, great forests, wild rivers.

An increasingly urban and well-educated citizenry has insisted on enforcement of anti-poaching laws, especially in the more law-abiding north of Italy. Many younger Italians have taken up the banner of conservation. Habitat loss has also been slowed by the declining birth rate of the Italians, which is among the lowest in the world.

The contemporary wool and lamb industry is dominated by gigantic operations in New Zealand and Australia, where predators are largely nonexistent. Sheep production in Italy has been in decline since the Industrial Revolution began. More recently, the decline has been accelerated by the spread of universal mandatory education. In former times, the son of a Tuscan shepherd had little choice in life but to be a Tuscan shepherd. Today he may be a banker, a computer programmer, a builder of Fiats in Turin, a waiter in Beverly Hills. A Tuscan country girl is still likely to devote her adulthood to home and family, but she too will probably do so far from where she grew up. Only in the remotest pockets of Italy do the ancient ways survive with any real vitality: in Sardinia, some places high in the Apennines, the far south. These are also, by no accident, often the places where wolves have persisted through the centuries.

The wolves of Italy are astonishingly adaptable, and their adaptability may be the direct result of human persecution. Centuries of trapping, poisoning, and gunning down have been tantamount to intense selective breeding. The wolves with the slightest inborn recklessness are quickly removed from the population, the survivors being wolves who can outwit their persecutors. Such non-natural selection may be why Italian wolves are smaller than their American or Russian cousins, less dependent on cooperative hunting, and much less picky about their diet.

I have seen photographs of Italian garbage-can raiders with their fierce mouths trailing strands of spaghetti. In the fourteenth century, wolves dug up the shallow graves of European plague victims. In the Middle East, wolves cower outside the towns, stoned by boys, with little more than the occasional outcast dog for a square meal. Wolves are survivors.

If in a given patch of habitat there is enough prey to feed only one wolf, one Italian wolf will live there alone. If there is only enough for two, two there will be, sending their young to find better work elsewhere—another old Italian tradition. Large packs are rare. Howling is rare. The modern Italian wolf can be as furtive, skulking, and cunning as the ancient wolf of legend.

There are wolves in Italy from the heel of the boot to the Alps. Some live in populations large enough to be self-sustaining. Many live in habitat sufficiently rich to support the traditional pack structure, in which an alpha male and alpha female preside over an extended family that hunts cooperatively, maintains an enduring territory, and howls in the night—but human killing keeps that luxurious style of life rare.

The wolves of Italy form what is known as a metapopulation, a population of populations. Simple size is a critical factor in the long-term survival of any population of living things, and a network of small populations can be just as viable as a single large population; interconnection is the key.

The Apennine mountain chain and other forest corridors have allowed the wolf populations of Italy to remain interconnected. The wolf's reproductive rate is high, and young wolves forced out of their families with the arrival of new litters manage to find one another readily, probably owing to their extraordinary sense of smell and their habit of scent marking, mainly with urine, wherever they go. A wolf can breed at the age of two, and in Italy the typical litter size ranges from four to seven pups. A few subordinate, non-reproducing adults may be allowed to stay with the pack to help in the rearing of pups—and these may hope for a vacancy at the top of the pack hierarchy. Generally, though, there is a steady supply of dispersers leaving home every year to join other packs or form new ones.

Since 1976, when legal protection began, the wolves of Italy have spread from a few mountain enclaves into a wide range of habitats. There are wolves in the shrubby coastal *macchia* of the south, some of them living on little more than garbage scavenged from village dumps. There are wolves in the mountain forests all along the Apennines, some of them hunters of game, some of them raiders of livestock. There are wolves in national parks, wolves on farms, wolves in suburbs. Although their most preferred habitat is remote forest, Italian wolves occur in habitats that make a mockery of the commonplace American presumption that the wolf is a creature only of the wilderness. Wolves have been seen, captured, or killed on the outskirts of Florence, Siena, Milan. From a low of perhaps a hundred in the early nineteen-seventies, the wolf population of Italy may now exceed five hundred individuals. Wolves overflowing out of Italy have even colonized the Provençal Alps of southeastern France.

One of Italy's two largest centers of wolf population occurs in relatively lightly settled country—the central Apennines east of Rome, including the Abruzzo National Park. The other is in the heavily peopled landscape of Tuscany and the Emilian portion of Emilia-Romagna. Small populations dot the rural landscape, appearing and vanishing like will-o'-the-wisps. Yet even where wolves are abundant in Italy, they can remain largely unknown. Ask a villager at the foot of a mountain where a wolf pack is living, and he may well stare at you in astonishment. Wolves? Here? No, signore. Tell a housewife picking out her fava beans and spring lamb in the Campo dei Fiori marketplace in Rome that she is standing within a half hour's bus ride of wolf country, and she may indulge you with the condescending Roman smile reserved for bad children and idiots.

Extermination has been the lot of wolves in France, Germany, the Low Countries, Switzerland, Scandinavia. Yet wolves have survived in Italy,

Spain, Portugal, the Balkan states, and Greece. In western Europe there is a north–south gradient of doom.

Why?

Luigi Boitani, of the University of Rome, is Europe's leading wolf scientist, and also Edo Tedesco's faculty adviser. Boitani has been studying wolves in Italy and around the globe for more than twenty years, and he has found that wherever wolves occur, with the sole exception of a few Arctic islands devoid of human settlement, the principal determinant of wolf life or death is the behavior of the people living nearby. Boitani believes that that behavior is the product less of present necessity than of ancestral culture.

For many centuries before the nineteenth century, from the British Isles across to Russia, from Scandinavia down to France and Germany, most northern Europeans were nomadic herders. Resources were scarce in the cold north, and unevenly distributed. The herds had to keep moving. Human numbers were small, villages few. The distances the herds had to cover were so great that it was impossible for any herder to know the landscape in detail or to predict the movements of predators. Wolf attack could come anywhere, at any time. There was not much to be done but to kill every wolf you could.

By contrast, in the rich, warm south, herds could be maintained on a small year-round patch of pasture. Sedentary herding was the rule. Here people have lived for centuries on small farms or in villages adjacent to grazing land—also almost always near rugged, densely forested mountains where wolves can take shelter. The flock grazes year after year in the same places, and the herder knows every spring, tree, and thicket. He knows where the wolves live: up there in the winter, down here come spring.

There are patterns, habits, stability. The people share their information. The wolves move across the upper meadow in the early summer evenings. The shepherd keeps his flock away from there. He gathers them close to the house at night. He listens for trouble in his sleep. If you come, Mr. Wolf, I will kill you.

And the wolf replies: I leave you those places at those times, for I can hunt elsewhere or at night.

Generations pass. The patterns hold. The understandings endure. In time there forms in both the wolf population and the human community what

Luigi Boitani calls an information lineage, an intimate knowledge of their world and its rules, passed down from families to their young through time.

"One of the commonplace names in Italy is Passo del Lupo," says Boitani—Wolf Pass. "A thousand years ago, the wolves crossed the road at this point. I can take you there today and you will see their tracks still."

So what has happened in Tuscany?

"Disruption of the information lineage," replies Boitani. "The Sardinian shepherds, who are new to Tuscany, and the wolves, who are also newcomers, do not understand one another. That is the critical factor in wolf survival in human habitat: mutual understanding."

FEBRUARY 25, 1994

The yearling Fulvio lies dead beside the Via Cassia, run over by a car in the night.

MARCH 20, 1994

Alvio, the radio-collared alpha male, suddenly goes off the air. The wolf team drives the entire province of Siena in their battered Land Rover, rotating the tracking aerial out the window, listening for hours from the highest points, morning, evening, night. Nothing. They fly back and forth over all of southern Tuscany. On Alvio's frequency there is only silence.

The researchers follow wolf tracks, they howl, they scan the landscape through telescopes. Nothing. But the shepherds are still complaining of losses. The surviving members of the pack begin killing sheep in broad daylight, in full view of the shepherds. Edo Tedesco knows that if Alvio were still alive, he would keep them from taking such stupid risks. The alpha female is probably dead now too.

JUNE 15, 1994

No! She is alive, and so are two of the yearlings. Not only that, she has six new pups. The pack remains insanely visible. The wolf team watches them kill a roe deer. Several times they see wild boar face the pack down. They see the mother and the subadults regurgitating food for the pups.

JULY 31, 1994

The wolf team badly needs to get a radio collar on one of these wolves, but three weeks of attempted trapping go by in vain. The wolves continue killing sheep. The shepherds are enraged. They believe that the wolf team is not studying wolves but importing them; they know that these kids are under the control of the archvillain Luigi Boitani, who is putting wolves all over Italy. One shepherd claims that the wolves killed two hundred of his sheep in one night. The research team is evicted from the house they have been renting, and nobody else in the area will rent to them. Their funding is not renewed. The Siena wolf project is over.

The blur of American time—from wolf-packed wilderness to strip mall in the blink of a Roman eye—tends to obscure the methodical deliberateness of the American wolf's destruction. Control was never the object of the American crusade: only annihilation would do, first with simple atavistic fervor and ultimately by government fiat. It is surely no coincidence that the extermination of the wolf in the United States was carried out by descendants of Europeans of the north.

Imagine the incredulity with which an earlier American generation's bounty hunter would greet the idea that the United States government would someday spend millions of dollars to restore the wolf to its ancestral range. Many old-timers in the American West today are dumbfounded by the largely urban sentiment in favor of the wolf's return to Yellowstone.

Once upon a time, the object of our identification was the placid grazer, the vegetarian victim, the sheep, the deer. Now, the savage predator, the carnivorous victor, *Tyrannosaurus rex*, the wolf, is our self-projection—and this in a world in which meat eating (by humans) edges ever closer to the category of sin, a world in which the victim is otherwise the image of our compassion and often of ourselves.

Could it be that our newfound love of the wolf is as irrational as our forebears' hatred? Could it be that the wolf wolf lovers love and the wolf wolf haters hate are both falsehoods?

Tuscany whispers to Yellowstone, "You must find out for yourself."

# CHEYENNE

# Two Opposed Ideas

The Cheyenne Cattle Company restaurant at the Hitching Post Motor Inn specializes, fittingly, in beef. For hundreds of miles in all directions from Cheyenne, Wyoming, the principal use of the land is the growing of cow meat. There are a few towns, and a handful of nature reserves from which livestock is excluded, but those are tiny islands in an ocean of cattle.

The Greater Yellowstone Coalition, with which I have been associated in one way or another for ten years, was founded on the idea of a Greater Yellowstone Ecosystem, a vast complex of wildlands with Yellowstone National Park at its center and also including Grand Teton National Park, seven national forests, a couple of national wildlife refuges, part of an Indian reservation, various state holdings, and private lands. The ecosystem is centered in the northwest corner of Wyoming, and extends into eastern Idaho and southern Montana. The Coalition promotes the G.Y.E., insistently, as "the largest remaining essentially intact ecosystem in the temperate zones of the earth." We also have known all along that the phrase "essentially intact" shrouds a lot of not-quiteness.

For one thing, no gray wolf: *Canis lupus* used to be the top predator in this ecosystem and is the only missing member of Yellowstone's native fauna. For another: within the roughly 18 million acres of the Greater Yellowstone Ecosystem, only the 2.2 million acres of Yellowstone National Park are off limits to *Bos taurus*. In the hundred or so years since the

domestic cow's introduction to the ecosystem, that one species has drastically altered this supposedly natural landscape. Find yourself a sylvan
creekside spot to camp somewhere in Greater Yellowstone's designated
national forest wilderness, and you may be twenty miles from the nearest
human dwelling place, but what's that stinking, fly-blown, squishy,
greeny-brown heap on your nice flat tent site?

Nearly all of Greater Yellowstone is high, cold, and dry. Most of the
precipitation comes in the form of high-mountain snow, which melts
with a great symphonic roar in the spring and pours off the central
plateau in torrents. The narrow bands of verdure along the creeks, rivers,
and lakes are the only habitats where moisture is abundant year-round,
and in these green bands, known as riparian zones, there is a wide range
of soils, topographies, and microclimates. Because of that habitat diversity, the riparian zones harbor a wide variety of leafy plants. The variety,
abundance, and sheer density of plants in turn provide shade, food, and
visual cover for a panoply of birds, mammals, and invertebrates. Yellowstone's riparian zones, therefore, are home to much of the ecosystem's
species diversity.

Come out of the savage summer sun of the grasslands or the monoto-
nous shade of a lodgepole pine forest, come into the cottonwoods and
willows along a foaming mountain stream, and you feel yourself
instantly engulfed in life. The air is cool and humid, full of bugs and birdsong. Listen, and you hear living things creeping around all around you.
The grass turns green here first, and stays green here all summer while
the treeless uplands parch. Worms and arthropods and insect larvae
writhe in the riparian humus. Predators stalk their prey in the under-
brush. The clear water is richly oxygenated by its tumbling over the
rocks, highly mineralized by its intense friction with the earth, and alive
with gravity's energy.

The stream is a thronging ecosystem in itself. Cutthroat trout scour
the riffles, gobbling up aquatic insects, shrimp, little fishes. Bald eagles,
ospreys, herons, mergansers, kingfishers, otters, and grizzly bears thrive
on the trout. Moose browse the willows and doze in the shade. This is
where elk come to die, and thereby feed ravens, foxes, and beetles.

Cattle also love the riparian zone. They love it above all other kinds of
land. They love the shade and the water and the lush sweet grass and

the nice soft place to lie down. Given half a chance, they will love it to death.

All over the West, cattle have trampled streamsides to bare mud. They have grazed the deep-rooted bunchgrasses down to stunted nubs, making way for the non-native plants—often noxious weeds—that thrive on disturbed soils. They have stomped out the shrubs and rooted up the ferns and devoured the sprouting young trees.

The old dead cottonwood where the eagle builds her nest falls down in due course, but no new ones rise to replace it. Nor, with the forest under-story trampled flat, are there nesting sites for songbirds. Silt washes into the spawning beds and clogs the gills of the trout. If a grizzly bear dares to show up, some cowboy will probably reach for his rifle.

It was the cowboy, of course, who tamed the Wild West. It is commonly said that the bison were killed off to deprive the Indians of food, but was it not just as much to make way for cows? It certainly was for cows' sake that the West was fenced. From the sparse and patient grasses of the desert to the spongy tundra at ten thousand feet, from the middle of Kansas to the middle of California, from the Mexican border to the Canadian, cattle dominate the landscape of the rural American West. It was on the cow's behalf, of course, and the cowboy's, that the wolf was extirpated even from cow-free Yellowstone.

I live on a ranch in southern Montana about five miles north of the Absaroka-Beartooth Wilderness, at the foot of the Absaroka Mountains, near the northern edge of the Greater Yellowstone Ecosystem. (Absaroka—pronounced "ab-SOR-ka"—is the name of this region's indigenous people, known in English as the Crow.) We own cows, though I don't like them much. They stink, they bawl, and for sheer stupidity they have no peer in the animal kingdom.

I also want wolves back. You may call me hypocritical. I prefer to think that I embody a paradox, one captured in the famous remark of F. Scott Fitzgerald, "The test of a first-rate intelligence is the ability to hold two opposed ideas in the mind at the same time, and still retain the ability to function."

This duality of identity—conservationist and rancher—makes possible for me a kind of stereoscopic vision. If I may escape the label of hypocrisy, I am, I believe, in a position to be especially fair. I also believe I should be held especially accountable for fairness. I can see, for example, that while cattle grazing has done great damage to the grasslands of the West, cattle ranching is still the best means available of keeping the West's open space open and its prairies unplowed. Ranches can simultaneously be elk range, bear pastures, mountain lion hunting grounds, waterfowl refuges, rare plant sanctuaries, eagle habitat. Subdivisions cannot.

Think of cows, then, not just as riparian stompers but also as nonviolent protesters holding back the bulldozers. And think of the cowmen not only as truculent bullies but also as members of a diminishing tribe that conserves in its folkways and values and skills a wealth of time-tempered knowledge.

*But—but—but but but*, I hear my conservation colleagues sputtering: Look what they've done to your own valley, McNamee!

Alas, that is true too. Overgrazing has badly damaged the pasturelands of our ranch, making possible the invasion of a European plant called leafy spurge, which looks sort of like tarragon and acts like prairie cancer. Unless we fight it aggressively—with herbicides and, more recently, with spurge-eating beetles—leafy spurge could eventually replace the rich diversity of our grasslands with a monoculture of itself. This has already happened not far downstream from us, and it is chilling to behold.

If leafy spurge were allowed to take over, our place would no longer serve as elk winter range, for elk cannot stomach the stuff. We would lose our sharptail grouse, our meadowlarks, our antelope, our deer, our mountain lions, our gophers and mice and the magnificent raptors that swoop down on them. Nothing native to our region will eat leafy spurge. Only sheep raised on the stuff will touch it—and sheep, with which we have experimented, bring their own set of problems, notably, spreading the seed that survives the journey through their guts.

When two partners and I bought this ranch, in 1989, cattle had been grazing the riparian zone along our stretch of the West Boulder River for nearly a century. The banks in many places were bare. Each spring, when high water came, the river would eat away at the denuded banks, and whole chunks of sod would fall into the current and be washed away. Year by year, the riverbed had been growing wider, shallower, more exposed—providing less and less habitat for aquatic life. What had once been a broad bottomland forest of cottonwood and spruce, some earlier rancher had cut to the last tree, and it had never grown back because the cows stomped down every sapling that dared to show its head. Where willows should have grown along the banks there was raw dirt. Weeds—Canada thistle, hound's-tongue, burdock—crowded the river margins, and native grasses were disappearing from the riparian zones.

Then we fenced the cows out. We left them a couple of places to go down to the water to drink, and these remain to this day bare, bug-plagued, and noisome. But all along the rest of the stream the recovery has been so fast and so lavish it seems downright magical. Young willows are dense along the banks, and the beavers and deer are evidently pleased. The first moose in memory showed up recently. New river banks are abuilding, in some places six or eight feet out from the old cow-crumbled ones. The river is getting narrower and deeper, and the fishing is markedly better. Warblers, minks, otters, snipe, owls, a dozen-plus species of ducks, and many previously absent native wildflowers have found a home.

Big cottonwood trees—full of holes and rot, their dead crests perches for eagles, their high limbs deep-shaded cover for songbird nests—are the emblem and the heart of a Rocky Mountain riparian zone, but ours had been destroyed. Cottonwoods spread mostly by underground runners, so to *get* cottonwoods it helps to *have* cottonwoods. For a cottonwood tree to sprout from seed requires a very narrow set of conditions: a spring flood just so high, a deposition of silt just so sandy on just so moist a soil, and a whole bunch of other stuff. In our fenced-out riparian zone, cottonwood saplings have at last begun to appear.

So. The damage cattle do can be mitigated. We are not running any fewer cows because we fenced them out of the river. As we slowly get control of our leafy spurge, and the vigor of the native vegetation returns, the land will sustain more cows, whose grazing patterns can be managed to combat non-native plants. Someday, maybe—this is my dream—we will get together with our neighbors and tear down all the fences except on the ridges defining our watershed and we'll all sell our cows and buy a communally owned herd of bison. Um, possibly not very soon. Cowmen don't like buffalo.

The cowmen displaced the bison for cattle and replaced the Indians with themselves. Now the cowmen have become the Indians. There is another wave of invasion across the American West—of people like me, and worse.

The worse want every last cow off the range. They want wolves not only back but protected no matter what. They don't eat beef. Some of them won't wear leather shoes.

As I do my bit of justice to a T-bone at the Hitching Post tonight, and the cholesterol races to its final clotting place, I'm thinking, *No wonder the cowmen are angry.* Many of them see the return of the wolf to Yellowstone—carried out by their government, at very considerable expense, and at *their* expense, particularly—as the symbolic end of the cattle culture's hundred years of hegemony. And unless the cowmen succeed in federal district court here in Cheyenne tomorrow, the return of the wolf to Yellowstone will be under way.

The wolf opponents' sole and last hope is the suit known breezily as *Wyoming Farm Bureau Federation; Montana Farm Bureau Federation; American Farm Bureau Federation; Mountain States Legal Foundation, Plaintiffs,* vs. *United States Department of the Interior Secretary, also known as Bruce Babbitt, in his official capacity; Assistant Secretary, Fish and Wildlife and Parks, Department of the Interior, also known as George T. Frampton, in his official capacity; United States Fish and Wildlife Service Director, also known as Mollie H. Beattie, in her official capacity; United States Fish and Wildlife Service Regional Director, Region 6, also known as Ralph O. Morganweck, in his official capacity; Director of the National Park Service, also known as Roger Kennedy, in his official capacity; United States Department of Agriculture Secretary, also known as Michael Espy, in his official capacity; United States Forest Service Chief Forester, also known as Jack Ward Thomas, in his official capacity; Department of Interior; United States Fish and Wildlife Service; National Park Service; Department of Agriculture; United States Forest Service, Department of Agriculture; United States of America, Defendants.*

This is a last-minute, last-ditch attack. The U.S. Fish and Wildlife Service, the National Park Service, and their Canadian counterparts are poised to begin the capture of wolves in Alberta and their immediate transportation to central Idaho and Yellowstone National Park. Everything is in place. Professional trappers in Alberta, paid two thousand dollars (by the U.S. government) per live wolf trapped, have already caught, radio-collared, and released seventeen "Judas wolves," so called because they will betray their families. The minute the judge says go, biologists and sharpshooters will radio-locate the Judas wolves and, hence, find the packs of which they are members. Canadian trappers will set leghold traps or wire snares in the packs' principal travelways. Tranquilizer darts shot from low-flying helicopters will immobilize as many as possible of the wolves that elude the traps. The goal is to capture three entire family groups. As soon as the three packs are in hand, they will be sent straight to Yellowstone. Each pack will be held in a pen for six to twelve weeks and then turned loose. Another fifteen wolves will go to central Idaho and will be immediately released to the wild. There will be wolves in the West again, and the cowmen will have lost the most desperate struggle they have fought since they first conquered the land.

I know what most of them seem not to understand: the fact of the wolf will be far less bad than the fear. Wolf depredation at its worst will have only highly local economic effects. The government in its plan has sworn to control all depredating wolves, and the owners of killed livestock are to be compensated at market value.

Then I remind myself that the Wyoming Farm Bureau Federation and its co-plaintiffs represent not the average, peace-loving rancher but the farther fringes of rancher paranoia. So do their lawyers. Remember Ronald Reagan's shiny-pated, widely hated, and finally incarcerated secretary of the interior James Watt? The Mountain States Legal Foundation, whose attorneys will open the proceedings tomorrow morning, is none other than James Watt's "public-interest" law firm, dedicated to saving the West from pointy-headed tree huggers and their wolves. The M.S.L.F.'s particular specialty is cultural paranoia.

The fear ranchers feel—not of wolves, but of losing their own august place atop the world of the West—is dark, deep, and real. Making a living, modest as it tends to be, is not often a cowman's sole preoccupation. Myth and style and glory and honor permeate the ranching life. When you go into a restaurant in midtown Manhattan, you cannot necessarily tell the lawyers from the bankers from the publishers, but the minute you walk into the Stockman's Café in Anywhere, Wyoming, you know who's a stockman: it is not just the hat and the boots and the shirt and the scarf and the Wrangler jeans and the big bright silver belt buckle and the faded outline of the Copenhagen snuff can in his back pocket; his bearing, his taciturn dignity, his low voice and thin smile all proclaim his calling and his honor in it.

The reality of the ranching life can pretty much be summed up as long hours, poor money, guaranteed uncertainty, and unending, brutally hard work. It is no wonder that the cowman needs a rich mythical dimension—and no wonder that his way of life has inspired such powerful emblems and folklore for Americans who don't know which end of a cow is north.

The physical objects themselves, after generations of burnishing by movies and stories and songs, take on a mythic hue: the beautiful horses, the beautiful leather, the sun-crinkled squint toward the distant horizon. The yearly progression of calving, branding, breeding, gathering, and shipping assumes the stateliness of ceremony. The larger world, through its image-hungry entertainment industry, then transforms these small and practical simplicities into epic and spiritual ones, and finally the cowmen reconsume the recycled images in all their magnification of magnificence. Rodeo fashions these days, even in the remotest small-town arenas, owe more to Hollywood than to history. The cowman knows, sometimes not quite consciously, that it is not from him and his brethren that the symbols have been extracted for mass distribution, but rather from those who have gone before them. The image factory doesn't need him anymore.

The cowman knows, too, that beneath the movie-costume clichés of the ranching life is an ethic of open-hearted decency. You do not consider not attending barn raisings in ranch country. When old So-and-so goes bust or needs expensive surgery, as often as not a collection is quietly taken up. Peruse the personal ads in the Billings *Gazette* and see how many of the "gals" are looking for a "cowboy type." That's because he's a fellow you can count on.

And they do love the land. It is not cowboy-kosher to gush, of course, but a stockman on his horse in the middle of the prairie on an autumn afternoon, pushing sleek mama cows and their fattening calves down out of the mountains toward the shipping pens, will look across at the aspens quietly rattling their yellow leaves and beyond them to the early snow on the peaks, and down at his good rich grass, and his heart will swell with *glory*. Not many people in offices or on factory floors have had much of that. It makes a cowman *proud*, feeling so much.

Much of the reward of the ranching life rests on such feelings, such images (or illusions) of continuity, such fragility. It is no wonder, all in all, that an occasional cowman gets to feeling paranoid.

With a belly full of Cheyenne Cattle Company beef and baked potato I am headed for my room when I espy tomorrow's entire defense lineup dining together at a long table. At the far end is a busy heads-together whispering among the lawyers—two young women, an older one, and a guy, none of whom I've seen before. Everybody else at the big table is a longtime pal of mine from the years of effort that have led us to this moment. There are companionable howdies all around.

Here is L. David Mech, widely considered the world's leading wolf biologist. David Mech (pronounced "meetch") is lean, soft-spoken, watchful, *attuned*—like a wolf. From Mech the judge will be getting the straightforward facts of wolf biology, naked of sentiment, based on years of solid field research. Mech always takes care to express uncertainty where it exists. He is pretty certain, however, that wolf depredation on livestock in Greater Yellowstone will amount to very little.

Here is Hank Fischer, of Defenders of Wildlife, the father of the put-your-money-where-your-mouth-is fund that will compensate ranchers who lose livestock to wolf depredation. Among all the conservationists in the long campaign to return the wolf to Yellowstone, Fischer stands pre-eminent. He has been at it for fifteen years, and has probably put more hours into this than anybody else alive. Whenever and wherever there is any kind of wolf powwow, it's like, "Oh, hi, Hank"—of course he's here.

Tom France, the National Wildlife Federation lawyer who will appear as an amicus curiae, as usual looks simultaneously movie-star handsome and as if he has just been worked over by some police-state police. France, like his longtime friend Fischer, has endured some tough times from his fellow conservationists for supporting the final reintroduction plan, which allows ranchers to kill wolves under certain circumstances.

Steve Fritts, small, bald, bespectacled, and earnest, the U.S. Fish and Wildlife Service's lead scientist on the wolf project, is to be in charge of the trapping of wolves for Yellowstone and Idaho in the faraway boondocks of Alberta—if the Feds win this case. Fritts is the numbers guy, the one who has calculated standing prey biomass, predation rates, wolf population growth curves, projected effects on huntable game. If a question of biology arises, Fritts is the guy who can reel out the data.

Ed Bangs, the wolf project leader, has his customary ironic twinkle in his eyes. Bangs has sat in the hot seat through the endless public hearings, has steered the Environmental Impact Statement between the implacable ire of the wolf haters and the implacable outrage of the cow haters, and has had his life threatened several times for his trouble—a circumstance under which he has kept up the most extraordinarily buoyant humor, which he attributes to a philosophy of profoundly not giving a shit whether we get wolves back or not, or indeed about much of anything.

Carter Niemeyer, a blond giant, describes his role in life as "reformed gopher choker." Niemeyer is the chief wolf catcher for the Animal Damage Control unit of the Department of Agriculture, and so will be the one to see that depredating wolves are taken care of—whether trapped and moved, or killed. He has seen the wolf population of northern Montana grow in the last decade to some seventy or so animals, and he has been notably successful in keeping both wolves and ranchers out of trouble.

Wayne Brewster is militarily dapper even out of his National Park Service uniform, military of bearing too, blue eyes narrow behind thick glasses. Though a biologist by training, Brewster is the master strategist, the field marshal. As I take a seat, peppering the gang with questions, it is Brewster whose glance darts downtable in response to a sharp peremptory "*Shhh!*"

The shush has come from the older woman lawyer. "She doesn't want us talking to the press," says Brewster. "You'd better take it up with her."

I move down to the lawyer end of the table and pull up a chair. The woman will not look at me. I meet Christiana Perry, in from D.C., the lead attorney for the Department of Justice, and Carol Statkus, the assistant U.S. attorney for Wyoming, and Kim Cannon, a private attorney who is helping out. The shusher continues to ignore my existence. Finally I maneuver myself into her line of sight, stick out my hand, and say, "Hi, I'm Tom McNamee."

She looks at my hand and gives it a hesitant shake, as one might touch a dead fish of doubtful provenance. She does not introduce herself.

"What's your name?" I ask brightly. "And what brings you to Cheyenne?"

She turns away from me without speaking.

I persist. "I'm writing a book about the return of the wolf to Yellowstone?" I say cheerfully to the back of her neck. "And of course this trial kind of brings the whole story together? I didn't get your name."

She turns slowly back toward me with a look of exasperated disdain. "My name is Margot Zallen."

"You're one of the attorneys, right? What's your role?"

"You can look up my title in the court papers."

Well, onward. "This trial is really one of those defining moments, isn't it? I mean, you win this and the wolves hit the ground."

"I don't talk to the press."

"I'm not press, Margot. My book's not going to be out for a year and a half—at the soonest. Besides, I've devoted years of my life to getting wolves back into Yellowstone. My magazine pieces helped get this thing moving. I've testified before Congress. I've raised money. When I was president of the Greater Yellowstone Coalition, I made sure we came out for wolves. Ask any of these guys. I'm not going to go blabbing your trial strategy to the newspapers. I don't even want to know what your trial strategy *is*. I just want to talk to these people. History is being made here, Margot, and I'm writing it."

As my reward for this uplifting peroration I receive a cold, hard glare.

I am rigid with rage and hurt. Why should I let myself get so upset about this? One of my friends takes me aside in the hallway and reassures me that I shouldn't take it personally, she's like this to everybody.

Finally, in bed, it comes to me. All these years I've been doing smug armchair anthropology on the wolf haters, about how their hatred has so much less to do with any fact of wolf reality than with their own tribal identity, and now I have experienced tribal repudiation and am mortified: *I'm one of you,* I tried to say tonight, and *No, you're not,* said a priestess of the tribe. Sleep will not come. I'm a wreck, all reason lost. So great is the power of social belonging, and of the fear of losing it.

# Canis lupus irregardless

You can tell the players without a program. The Mountain States Legal Foundation lawyers probably wear suits to work every day in Denver, but here in Cheyenne they manage not to look it. If passing for a good old fence-fixing feller stuffed for this formal occasion into a stiff disguise is their subtle intention, they are subtle indeed. As he opens the Farm Bureau's case against the assembled might of the United States, Richard Krause tugs at his tie, clumps back and forth before the bench, fumbles with his papers. His delivery is halting, his elocution murky, his manner pure hayseed.

But he obviously knows the four requirements for the granting of a preliminary injunction: the wolf reintroduction must be shown to cause irreparable harm to the plaintiffs; the plaintiffs must be likely to prevail in the full trial to come; an injunction must cause less harm to the American people than not granting it would cause to the ranchers; and the granting of the injunction must have no adverse effect on the public interest.

By ten o'clock, the five reporters and twenty-one members of the public in the pews are half asleep. My head lolls forward, then snaps back, and I try to remember that this is important stuff going on.

The setting is basic, boring federal courtroom: bland wood paneling, acoustic-tile ceiling, burnt-umber synthetic carpet. Judge William F. Downes, despite an unfortunate mustache and his young years, projects an air of grave authority. As Krause mumbles on, Downes kneads his chin in impatience.

Some of what Krause says is undeniable—for example, that there is no question of imminent extinction of the gray wolf. There are, as he says, sixty to seventy thousand wolves in Canada, seven thousand in Alaska, two thousand in Minnesota, Wisconsin, and Michigan. When he says that wolves surely will not confine themselves to Yellowstone Park, he is right. They will also inhabit cattle country, both public and private.

Some of what he says, however, is preposterous—such as his claim that wolves prefer livestock to all other prey. He claims also that there are already wolves in Yellowstone. It is true that there have been occasional visits by far-wandering wolves, but extensive surveying has shown zero resident wolves. Krause insists that the original Yellowstone subspecies of the gray wolf, *Canis lupus irremotus*, is extinct and therefore cannot be reintroduced. (Nineteenth-century hairsplitting did divide wolves into twenty-four subspecies in North America alone, but contemporary tax-onomists, focusing on genes in preference to body measurements, have pretty much concluded that a wolf is a wolf is a wolf. "*Canis lupus irre-gardless,*" cracks Carter Niemeyer across the aisle, sotto voce.)

Chrissy Perry's prim French braid and knee-length skirt proclaim Washington, rectitude, adulthood. When she starts talking in her small high voice, however, I cannot help hearing a little kid—albeit one who has already decided to be a lawyer when she grows up. I am soon enough disabused of my shallow prejudice: this woman has done her homework. She knocks the four injunction underpinnings down like midway ducks, and all but dusts her hands.

The parade of plaintiff's witnesses begins. Up first is Larry Bourret of the Wyoming Farm Bureau Federation, a former state commissioner of agriculture and a veteran of years of battle against the Feds on wolves, grizzly bears, predator poison restrictions. Bourret's chiseled face and up-right bearing are perfect, but his information is not. He is supposed to be the cool head with the hard data, but when U.S. Attorney Carol Statkus bears down on him on cross-examination, he pretty much crumbles:

Does Mr. Bourret believe there are already wolves in Wyoming?

He does.

How many?

No idea.

Are his members reporting livestock losses to these wolves?

No.

What scientific studies can he cite to support his contention that the Wyoming livestock industry will be devastated?

He names one, can't quite remember the others.

Asked to substantiate his members' fears, Bourret can cite only well-worn anecdotes—wolf stories from ninety-odd years ago, when the populations of wild wolf prey such as elk and deer were at their lowest ebb.

Judge Downes interjects that if he is to decide the question of irreparable harm, he is going to need more than anecdotal evidence. Bourret is unable to dispute the data from Minnesota showing very low depredation rates there. Having maintained that he and his organization have been inadequately consulted, he is forced to grant that they have testified throughout the public hearings, written many letters, and submitted stacks of documents backing up their position.

An indication of the tension behind these proceedings comes in a complaint by the Mountain States lawyers to the judge, alleging that one of Downes's clerks had a friendly, and highly improper, conversation with one of the defense lawyers last night at the Hitching Post.

Downes plays it down: "For those of you who aren't accustomed to Wyoming, it's always good manners in Wyoming to say howdy. You have to understand that this court doesn't operate in a vacuum. I walk down the street to get a haircut, I go work out in the athletic club, and somebody has an opinion on wolves. You can guarantee it. They have been offered to me in rather incongruous places, from social occasions, Christmas parties, to the shower room of the athletic club. And people are not neutral on this subject."

Well, and it turns out to have been a case of mistaken identity anyway. It seems that J. T. Cummins of the Montana Farm Bureau Federation, sitting in the Hitching Post coffee shop, mistook the judge, from the rear, for Tom France of the National Wildlife Federation. In other words, where Cummins believed he was seeing an associate of Judge Downes improperly conferring with wolf lovers, what he was actually looking at was the judge talking to his own clerk.

Cummins is the next witness, and a hot-headed one. To his claims that the wolf plan was shoved through without adequate consultation, Statkus responds with withering, rapid fire. Did the Montana Farm Bureau comment at the E.I.S. hearings? Did they also submit written comments? Did they participate in the hearings on the implementation rules?

Yes. Yes. Yes.

How many livestock operators in northern Montana have gone out of business owing to wolf depredation?

Don't know of any.

And what about the plaintiffs' declarations regarding danger to children?

Little girl lost her arm in Missoula, Montana, to a wolf-dog hybrid two years ago.

Is he aware of the scientific literature showing minimal livestock loss?

Depends on whose science you read.

Does the Montana Farm Bureau retain the services of a scientist to do authoritative work on these questions?

"We don't need one. We have Mr. Bourret."

Next comes an elegant, proud-postured rancher named Kathleen Sun, whose family has raised livestock in Wyoming since 1872, the year of Yellowstone Park's creation. That year was also the dawn of an era of disgrace: the first decades of the world's first national park saw a massive slaughter of wildlife. Elk and bison by the thousands were shot by market hunters for shipment to the eastern states. Every year hundreds of wolf pelts were handed in for bounty. With their wild prey all but wiped out, the few but wily wolves still alive turned to livestock, and by the turn of the century, wolf depredation was a genuinely serious problem for the likes of Kathleen Sun's forebears.

She has some fine family stories. Her father-in-law killed the last old lobo, in 1913. The pelt, six feet from head to tail, is in the county museum. The jaw was ten inches across. The wolf and his mate killed thirty-five yearling cattle in a month.

Statkus again demands hard information supporting irreparable harm. How big is the Sun ranch?

Not sure. Maybe a million and a half acres.

How far is the ranch from Yellowstone?

Two hundred miles.

If she loses stock to wolves, will she apply to Defenders of Wildlife for compensation?

Certainly.

A young rancher, Regan Smith, describes his hardscrabble sheep operation on the Beartooth Plateau. He has had bad predator problems, it seems, including a dog that got into his sorting pen one night. The dog killed only two or three sheep, but some fifty of them died—smothered by one another. Now he's got these Great Pyrenees guard dogs, and his predator problem has gotten much better.

The Farm Bureau lawyer asks Smith what percentage of loss would put him out of business, and suddenly Smith is in tears. Something about his way of life; he is almost sobbing. "I don't need to lose that many more to lose that way of life."

The room is silent, stunned. Smith pulls himself together and stands down.

More ranchers, more old stories. The plaintiffs' case dribbles to a close. This is the best the dread Mountain States Legal Foundation can do?

# A Fierce Green Fire

December 22, 1994

The only thing that could make Ed Bangs look more casual in the witness box this morning might be a can of beer in his hand. As head of the U.S. Fish and Wildlife Service wolf recovery team for the northern Rockies, he has answered all these questions over and over and over, and the closer the actual reintroduction of the wolf has come, the more repetitive the objections and complaints have been.

The history that has brought Bangs here today is a long one.* Like most of American history, the story of the wolf is also a bloody one.

At the beginning of the nineteenth century there were many thousands of wolves in the West, but with the booming of the fur trade, which penetrated into even the remotest corners of the Yellowstone wilderness, the populations of all fur-bearing animals plunged. Throughout the eighteen-sixties, the American Fur Trading Company was shipping five to ten thousand wolf pelts a year from the upper reaches of the Missouri River drainage. The beaver, also an important prey animal for wolves, was nearly extirpated.

The eighteen-seventies brought the greatest sustained wildlife slaughter in the history of the earth: the massacre of the American bison. In the wake of that slaughter, cattle and cattlemen (often backed by

---

*For a detailed accounting of the extermination of the wolf in the West and of the hard, slow climb back toward this moment, I enthusiastically refer you to Hank Fischer's book *Wolf Wars*.

empire-minded Wall Street speculators) spread across the Plains with astonishing speed, stocking the ranges far beyond their carrying capacity.

Wildlife dependent on grazing suffered accordingly; the bison was gone, and now deer and elk grew scarce. Many wolf packs turned to preying on cattle. Traps, bullets, and the most effective wolf killer of all, poison, made short work of the naive predators. Soon only the remotest mountain wilderness, such as Yellowstone, still held viable populations of wolves and their wild prey.

Then came the market hunters. Undeterred by the creation of Yellowstone National Park in 1872—for it was scarcely patrolled at all—they slew Greater Yellowstone's elk and bison by the thousands, always sure to leave behind a few carcasses laced with strychnine to poison wolves (and any other meat eater that happened by—eagle, coyote, raven, bear). By 1886 the carnage in Yellowstone had become a national scandal, and the U.S. Cavalry was sent in to protect what was left of the park's "good" wildlife, a category that definitively did not include wolves.

Wolves undoubtedly benefited from the rise in their wild prey populations occasioned by the military protection, but the benefit was brief, for cattle were nearly everywhere, and then as now the cattlemen cried out for government relief, and then as now they were well connected. In 1914, Congress declared war on predators in the West, turning the National Biological Survey, which had previously been devoted to gentle research, into an army of death squads. Beginning in 1918, even the newly created National Park Service took up arms against the wolf, trapping, shooting, and poisoning the adults, and torching the pups in the dens.

In 1923 the last known wolf den was destroyed in Yellowstone National Park. The last photograph of Yellowstone wolves was taken in 1926—two adults on a bison carcass in the valley of the Lamar River. Then they were gone.

It was Aldo Leopold who seems to have been the first to broach in print the notion that maybe this was wrong. In his essay "Thinking like a Mountain," published in 1944, Leopold describes the moment of his conversion. He has just shot a wolf in New Mexico:

> We reached the old wolf in time to watch a fierce green fire dying
> in her eyes. I realized then, and have known ever since, that there

was something new to me in those eyes—something known only to her and the mountain. I was young then, and full of trigger-itch; I thought that because fewer wolves meant more deer, that no wolves would mean hunters' paradise. But after seeing the green fire die, I sensed that neither the wolf nor the mountain agreed with such a view.

It took another thirty years before that green fire began to glimmer in the minds of conservationists. I do not know how it happened in the world at large, but my hunch is that the revolution in public attitude toward wolves is probably rooted in experiences like my own.

I grew up on the Tennessee-Mississippi state line just south of Memphis, Tennessee. When I was little, we were surrounded by forest and swamp and wildlife. By the time I had graduated from high school, however, it had all been cut down, drained, graded, roaded, subdivided, built on, channelized, sterilized, the forest and swamp and wildlife forgotten. I suppose that every American now alive has experienced the diminishing of nature and known firsthand the wanton vandalization of natural beauty. It is instructive that the time when people began to love wolves coincides with the paving of America.

In 1972, President Richard Nixon issued an executive order banning the use of predator poisons on federal lands. In the same year, Nixon's assistant secretary of the interior, Nathaniel Reed, called the first official meeting to discuss restoration of the wolf to Yellowstone—the meeting that began Dave Mech's long-playing role in this story. In 1973, Nixon signed the Endangered Species Act, which set in motion the process that has brought Ed Bangs to the witness stand in Cheyenne today, twenty-one years later.

The gray wolf was among the first species listed under the Endangered Species Act as being in danger of extinction. It is a peculiarity of the Act, and perhaps its greatest strength as a bulwark against the trashing of the natural landscapes remaining to us, that species are considered state by state. Hence the abundance of wolves in Alaska, Canada, or Russia has no legal bearing on the question of their endangeredness in Idaho, Montana, or Wyoming.

It was simple and clear from the beginning that the wolf could be restored to the northern Rocky Mountains very easily—all you had to do, really, was go get some wolves in Canada and push them out of the truck down here—and the law called for restoration of endangered species wherever possible. Simple, and clear.

I wonder now whether the authors of the Endangered Species Act even half foresaw the tumult that would ensue from government programs to restore species like grizzly bears, alligators, and wolves. It is a tough enough challenge to try to stop a dam for the likes of the snail darter or the Furbish's lousewort; it is a task on quite another scale to rejigger the management of millions of acres for the sake of the griz or to have gators snatching poodles into the bayou behind Aunt Minnie's patio.

In accordance with the Act, a recovery plan for wolves in the northern Rocky Mountains was duly written. In accordance with political reality, it took seven years to do so—just in time for Ronald Reagan and James Watt to stifle conservation efforts at every level of government. The 1980 plan did not call specifically for Yellowstone reintroduction, but the seed had been planted. People were excited, and talking. Support for wolf restoration was growing.

By 1983 there was a revised recovery plan, and this iteration specifically asserted that the only way to get wolves back into Yellowstone was going to be to put them there. In 1985, a poll by Stephen Kellert of the Yale School of Forestry showed that a wide majority of people in Minnesota, where wolves were recovering strongly, like having wolves in their woods. In a survey conducted in Yellowstone Park, 60 percent of park visitors agreed with the statement, "If wolves can't return to Yellowstone on their own, then we should put them back ourselves."

Also in 1985, Hank Fischer of Defenders of Wildlife and his fellow wolf advocates persuaded Yellowstone National Park to provide space for a splendid exhibit called "Wolves and Humans," which had been five years in the making at the Science Museum of Minnesota, in Minneapolis. Two hundred and fifteen thousand park visitors came to see "Wolves and Humans." In one of this story's nicer ironies, so did President Reagan's good friend William Penn Mott, director of the National Park Service.

Mott fell in love with wolves—and with the idea of reintroducing them to Yellowstone. He was one of those elderly people who draw fervor from having ambition behind them, and he threw himself into the political challenges. Mott quickly saw that the main obstacle to wolf restoration was the livestock industry. His solution was simple and elegant: Why not pay them for their losses?

Hank Fischer seized on Mott's idea. I remember announcing the establishment of the fund to the annual meeting of Defenders of Wildlife that November in New York: people were crowding up to the podium after my talk, all but waving their checkbooks. Soon the reintroduction of the wolf was Defenders' number one issue—not only, I believe, because it was good conservation but also because it was by now a very popular idea.

Wolves were already returning naturally to northern Montana, and it seemed only a matter of time before they would find their way to Yellowstone. The biologists believed that a natural recovery in Yellowstone might take a very long time, but the politicians did not want to take chances. A naturally recolonizing population would be entitled to the full protection of the Endangered Species Act wherever wolves occurred, whether in a national park or a sheep corral. It would be illegal for anyone to kill any wolf under any circumstances.

Senator James McClure of Idaho, chairman of the Senate Energy and Natural Resources Committee, and long an opponent of wolves in any form, saw something that most of his colleagues had failed to consider, namely, that a narrowly restrictive reintroduction would be less bad for the livestock industry than an unrestricted wave of natural immigration. He also recognized the burgeoning of popular enthusiasm for the wolf, and he knew that in the end the livestock interests were going to be outnumbered.

With McClure's advocacy, it seemed that wolf reintroduction was just around the corner, and in January 1986 I published an article in *Audubon* magazine blaring just that message. "The army of the wolf," I wrote, "is ready to advance. The livestock lobby's power is ebbing year by year."

Let's just say I was a little premature. For one thing, the new director of the U.S. Fish and Wildlife Service was Frank Dunkle, formerly the director of the Montana Department of Fish and Game, an agency with little relish for wolves. Dunkle let it be known to the conservation community that when it came to wolf reintroduction, please not to bother him. When he came to visit the "Wolves and Humans" exhibit, Dunkle was pointedly sporting a maroon silk National Rifle Association jacket and cap.

The wolf partisans gave as good as they got, bombarding Dunkle with letters, petitions, and in due course a threat to sue the Fish and Wildlife Service if he did not sign the recovery plan. Finally, in August of 1987, taking nearly everybody by surprise, Dunkle pulled the now four-year-old wolf recovery plan down from the shelf, dusted it off, and, unwilling to sully his own hands, had his assistant regional director sign it.

That very same month, with exquisitely bad timing, a newly established wolf pack in northern Montana lit into a flock of sheep near the town of Browning, killing eight adults and a lamb. A short time later, they killed three steers. Worst of all, the sheep and the cattle all belonged to one family of ranchers.

Wolf advocates had long claimed that depredation on livestock would be so infrequent and so widely scattered that it would not pose an economic problem for any individual rancher. Here was vivid proof of the opposite case: this family was suddenly three thousand bucks in the hole. While the Fish and Wildlife Service and Animal Damage Control tried to catch the wolves, they killed again. By the end of August the pack had taken ten sheep and four cattle.

The story was in all the local papers week after week, and the ranchers made sure to make plenty of noise. While the conservation groups argued among themselves about whether the wolves should be killed, moved, or left alone, the anti-wolf groups worked the phones, and Washington listened.

In the end, some of the Browning wolves were killed, some were captured and kept in captivity, and Defenders of Wildlife quickly compensated the stock owners. But the damage had been done.

Maybe it was Dunkle's intention all along to approve the plan and then not enforce it—thus neatly ducking the lawsuit and also appeasing his livestock industry buddies. Maybe the outcry from the stockmen after the Browning depredations helped him change his mind. In any case it was less than a month after Browning that Frank Dunkle went before first a Montana timber industry meeting and then the Wyoming Wool Growers Association to assure them that wolf reintroduction—recovery plan be damned—was doornail dead.

Another funny thing happened that summer of 1986. A freshman congressman from Salt Lake City spent a week at the Yellowstone Institute, an education center in the national park's Lamar valley. Representative Wayne Owens of Utah took a course in wolf ecology, and, like Mott, he fell in love. His office chair was hardly warm before Owens had introduced a bill calling for reintroduction of the wolf to Yellowstone within three years.

Congressional old-timers laughed up their sleeves. You simply do not do local legislation without the support of at least some of the local legislators. Much of the Greater Yellowstone Ecosystem, and all but two narrow slices of Yellowstone National Park, are situated within the state of Wyoming, and Wyoming's Congressman Dick Cheney and senators Alan Simpson and Malcolm Wallop—the state's entire congressional delegation—considered wolf reintroduction the moral equivalent of germ warfare. Owens's bill did not stand a chance, and everybody knew it.

But it did keep the wolf advocates' pot boiling. Most conservationists figured that anything that irritated Simpson and Wallop this much had something to be said for it. Most conservationists in those days had little interest in the messy backroom realities of the political process, little taste for making deals. Theirs was a world of battles, and they had gotten used to losing. Maybe, just maybe, this one was winnable.

Even Frank Dunkle saw the rising of the pro-wolf tide. He recognized that for all his public bluster against reintroduction, his department was going to have to manage the natural recovery of wolves in northern Montana. Not to do so would be a violation of the law, and he could be sure that the conservation groups would hold him to it, in court if necessary. And so, as 1987 waned, Dunkle quietly allocated two hundred thousand dollars to start up a U.S. Fish and Wildlife Service wolf recovery team for the northern Rockies.

The man hired to head the team was Ed Bangs. Bangs knew well that the bitter cultural conflict underlying the wolf debate was making this into perhaps the most controversial issue in American conservation history. He knew that politics, not biology, was going to determine the outcome. And indeed, under Bangs's stewardship, no conservation issue has ever involved as much public participation as the gray wolf reintroduction program.

From the moment he began to run the wolf recovery effort in Montana, Bangs was knocking on doors, shoving his foot in, and talking. Long before the official reintroduction proposal was making its laborious way through the labyrinth of the National Environmental Policy Act, Bangs was talking to Kiwanis Clubs, ranger stations, local conservation groups, rod and gun clubs, and anybody else who would listen.

By the time there was finally a directive from Congress to start work on an Environmental Impact Statement, Bangs knew that listening to the public was the most important thing he could do to make wolf reintroduction happen. And he knew that far more people loved the idea than did not.

Bangs knew also, however, that the greatest political power would be wielded by those who had something to lose or thought they did. As general public enthusiasm for the wolf was rising, so was the pressure brought by livestock interests on their congressional delegations to scuttle the proposal.

Idaho's senator McClure was thinking toward his retirement, and perhaps toward his historical legacy. Maneuvering skillfully between the warring factions, McClure wanted the government to be as thoroughly prepared with information as it could possibly be. It was primarily thanks to McClure that the National Park Service produced the two-volume report *Wolves for Yellowstone?*, published in 1990 and 1992—a massive compilation of scientific studies, computer modeling, and social and economic analyses, embodying virtually everything known about wolf biology and attempting to forecast how the return of the wolf was likely to affect both human concerns and natural processes in the Greater Yellowstone Ecosystem.

*Wolves for Yellowstone?*—note that question mark—was also a way of putting off the bureaucrat-scaring decision to proceed with the Environmental Impact Statement that the wolf advocates were clamoring for. By delaying the E.I.S., McClure was able to give the wolf opponents the impression that he was looking out for their interests—which he was, with considerably greater foresight than the stockmen's own professional advocates were capable of. The Wyoming Farm Bureau Federation and nearly every other livestock industry group had apparently convinced themselves that they could stop the wolf bandwagon cold, no matter what the biological facts and no matter how great the pro-wolf momentum.

At the same time, McClure was also setting the stage for wolf reintroduction, for he knew that the two things the opposition most dreaded—drastic reduction in game populations, and severe damage to the livestock economy—were not going to come to pass. The computer-modeled projections of *Wolves for Yellowstone?* showed only mild effects both on hunting and on the ranching business. In the spring of 1990, McClure announced that he would not run for re-election that fall, and on September 19 he introduced the Northern Rocky Mountain Gray Wolf Restoration Act of 1990, calling for wolf reintroduction in Yellowstone Park and the wilderness of central Idaho.

The pro-wolf forces could hardly believe it. The hearings on the bill before McClure's Energy and Natural Resources Committee, in September 1990, featured strange bedfellows indeed. On behalf of the Greater Yellowstone Coalition, the Idaho and Montana offices of the Wilderness Society, the Montana and Wyoming chapters of the Sierra Club, and the National Parks and Conservation Association, I testified—and watched, and listened—in a kind of goofy delirium. Could this really be happening? Had McClure put some sort of spell on Malcolm Wallop? Wallop, in the United States Capitol, was actually lecturing the livestock industry witnesses for not supporting the McClure plan.

It was all too good to be true, of course. In a welter of late-session wrangling, the McClure bill dropped dead. In its place, Congress appropriated another big chunk of money—$375,000—for that classic Washington refuge of pusillanimity, a committee. The Wolf Management Committee was to start afresh, write a new plan. Take your time, boys.

From day one, the committee was a snakepit. There were five pro-wolf members, five anti-wolf members—the usual antagonists, livestock interests versus conservationists. They came close on one occasion to a compromise, but in the end, under pressure from the organizations behind them not to give ground, they got nowhere.

One good thing had happened nonetheless. Although the politicians had intended delay, they also wanted an eventual solution—a deal. Many of the conservationists were bending over backward to make concessions to the livestock industry. The wolf advocates knew, after all, that depredating wolves were going to be controlled, legally or otherwise, and they knew that wolf recovery was perfectly possible even with quite high wolf mortality. The livestock lobby sneered at what they saw as the weak-kneed accommodation of the pro-wolf forces, but they failed to realize that the pro-wolfers' flexibility and reasonableness were gaining them increasing credibility in the corridors of power. Capitol Hill now knew that it was the livestock people who were unwilling to deal.

The improved effectiveness of pro-wolf strategy was due in no small part to a woman named Renée Askins, who in 1990 founded an organization called simply the Wolf Fund, with the single goal of returning the gray wolf to Yellowstone. The minute the wolf was back, Askins said, she would shut the Wolf Fund down. Askins's combination of personal charisma, political intuition, and raw intellect gave a formidable boost to the whole campaign. She aligned herself with Defenders of Wildlife's Hank Fischer, who held that allowing the killing of depredating wolves by ranchers themselves was the best way to buy enough political oomph to get wolves on the ground. Askins learned Washington realities quickly. She found out who needed what in a deal, who was willing to take a risk and who wasn't, where there was wiggle room in some congressman's bombast and where not.

Although some hard-line environmentalists were aghast at what they also saw as weak-kneed accommodationism, it was in direct response to the prospect of a plan accommodating livestock interests that in November 1991 Congress appropriated $350,000 to fund an Environmental Impact Statement on wolf reintroduction.

Ed Bangs was hired to lead the project. He began, in the spring of 1992, by soliciting the involvement of about twenty-five hundred individuals and groups in a series of "scoping sessions." These were meant to be easygoing, informal get-togethers—open houses, Bangs called them—where people could voice their concerns and know that the Feds were listening *before* they started writing plans. There were twenty-seven of these scoping sessions in the three states with territory in the Greater Yellowstone Ecosystem—Idaho, Montana, and Wyoming—and seven others in major cities around the country.

These hearings elicited over four thousand comments, the great majority of them pro-wolf. The livestock groups were stunned, and they whined for help from their friends in Congress. They wanted another shot, another entire round of twenty-seven hearings—a second chance to pack the halls with their troops. Pressed hard from above, Ed Bangs capitulated; he scheduled twenty-seven "alternative scopings" in exactly the same twenty-seven cities. The anti-wolf forces prepared to mount their greatest show of force yet.

The livestock groups were vastly outnumbered, and the pro-wolfers knew it. Nonetheless the wolf advocates were going to have to prove that public support for wolf reintroduction was now insurmountable. By fax, phone, hand-holding, and an occasional hinted threat, Hank Fischer, Renée Askins, and their fellow wolf lovers galvanized the conservation world. They pleaded with organizations that had had scant interest in wolf reintroduction or had been afraid of the political risks of supporting it. Now, the pro-wolf activists insisted, *now*, this August of 1992, now was the critical time, the great moment—a chance for the greatest conservation victory of the century. Having botched the first round of hearings so badly, the anti-wolf forces were poised to put every last ounce of their strength into this second round.

Defenders of Wildlife, the Wolf Fund, the National Wildlife Federation, the National Audubon Society, the Greater Yellowstone Coalition, the Sierra Club, the Environmental Defense Fund, the Idaho Conservation League, the Wilderness Society, and dozens of smaller groups raised a mass cry for help, and soon this second round of twenty-seven scopings was taking on the romantic mass appeal of the civil rights and anti-war days of the sixties and early seventies. It was chic, it was exciting, it was time, it was *right*.

To Boise, Cheyenne, Helena, Seattle, Salt Lake City, Denver, Washington, the greens poured in by the thousands. There were thunderous demonstrations in the public squares, impassioned orations, embarrassing songs, kids dressed up in wolf suits, long lines of witnesses signing up for their two minutes of glory. Armed officers guarded the hearing rooms.

The livestock crowd had its speakers, singers, and passionate witnesses too, but they were overwhelmed by the pro-wolf multitude. The Farm Bureaus and their allies had miscalculated badly. When Bangs added up the comments—some seven thousand, both oral and written—a good 80 percent favored the return of the wolf to Yellowstone.

Bangs and his team spent the winter boiling down the issues into a Draft Environmental Impact Statement, or D.E.I.S. Here at last was the distillation of everything: the legal justification under the Endangered Species Act; a history of the extirpation of the wolf, and of the proposals to bring it back; the specifics of wolf recovery under various possible scenarios; analysis of the likely effects of wolves on the ecosystem; guidelines for the humane treatment of transplanted wolves; the size necessary for a wolf population to be viable over time; characteristics of travel corridors; habitat and range requirements; the spiritual, the cultural, the social considerations; the methods for control of depredation on livestock, and provisions for compensation of the stock owners; a strategy for minimizing illegal killing of wolves; the impacts on huntable big game, on tourism, on other animal populations, on local economies; which agencies would do what, and when; possible restrictions on land use to protect wolves; the areas appropriate for wolf recovery; the timetable; and of course the cost.

It was a massive job, and thorough. The D.E.I.S. weighed over three pounds. Every ounce of it, by law, was subject to public review. That meant more hearings.

On July 1, 1993, after a news conference in Washington, Bangs sent out five hundred copies of a press release to the media, soliciting their audiences' comments on his D.E.I.S. To public libraries in Idaho, Montana, and Wyoming, to the affected agencies, to the whole panoply of pro-wolf and anti-wolf groups, and to anybody else who half hinted at wanting one, he sent the entire document—seventeen hundred copies plus. There were forty-two thousand people on the wolf-reintroduction mailing list by now, and a summary of the D.E.I.S. went to all of them. That summary and a schedule of still another round of public hearings were combined into a full-page insert that ran in six newspapers in the Greater Yellowstone region two July Sundays in a row—280,000 inserts in all.

In August and September came the hearings. There were four in Idaho, in Boise, Coeur d'Alene, Idaho Falls, and Lewiston; four in Montana, in Bozeman, Dillon, Helena, and Missoula; and four in Wyoming, in Cheyenne, Cody, Jackson, and Riverton. There were also four national hearings, in Denver, Salt Lake City, Seattle, and Washington.

I will never forget September 1, 1993, in Cody, Wyoming. Cody, just east of Yellowstone Park, prides itself on being a cow town, an oil town, a boot-wearing, ass-kicking town, and the anti-wolf crowd figured that a pre-hearing rally in the city park would be a good place to show what they were made of. Placards, contributed by the local logging company, read:

**THE REAL ENDANGERED SPECIES THE TRUTH**

**WYOMING IS NOT A ZOO**

**ENVIROS ARE A *PACK OF WOLVES***
**OUT TO DESTROY THE WEST**

**WOLVES DON'T PAY TAXES**

**HEY ENVIRO GROUPS HOW MUCH $$**
**HAVE YOU MADE OFF THE WOLF?**

**MORE THAN THE WOLF IS AT THE DOOR**
**WHAT'S THE REAL AGENDA?**

**WYO. CAN'T AFFORD WOLVES**
**LESS ACCESS, LESS WILDLIFE, LESS HUNTING,**
**LESS JOBS, LESS HOPE**

Copies of a "public opinion survey" were handed out, with a request to circle your responses to statements like the following:

There are 1,500 to 2,000 gray wolves in Minnesota, 7,000 to 10,000 in Alaska and 40,000 to 50,000 gray wolves in Canada, according to wildlife biologists. This means wolves are not endangered. They should be removed from the Endangered Species Act.   YES   NO

A $100,000 fine and a mandatory prison sentence for killing a wolf that is killing your pets, horses, or livestock is another reason to stop the reintroduction of the gray wolf.   YES   NO

The Environmental Impact Statement on the wolf has been national in scope. Folks in Seattle, Denver, Washington, DC and across the nation have commented at public hearings and/or submitted written comments. Holding national hearings confirms the lack of support at the local level. I believe local states', counties' and individuals' comments must have priority over far removed city folks who often have romantic ideas of wolves and who don't have to live with these highly efficient predators.   YES   NO

At the podium beneath the cottonwoods a man named Jerry Kysar recited a cowboy poem recounting his shooting of a wolf south of Yellowstone Park in 1992, and waved the black pelt over his head. That carcass had provided the first physical proof of a wolf presence in Yellowstone since the nineteen-thirties. The dead wolf was shown by DNA analysis to have been a far-wanderer from the northern Montana population.

Speaker after speaker fulminated that the wolf reintroduction plan was really a gigantic conspiracy to deprive Westerners of their property rights. Paul Hoffman, executive director of the Cody Chamber of Commerce and a former staffer for Senator Alan Simpson, had by far the best material: "This," he thundered, "is a battlefield in a new civil war—the bicoastal areas against the West. Our battles are not Antietam or Gettysburg but the wolf, grazing, timber. This is a war on our culture, our way of life. And in this war the wolf is the nuclear weapon!"

Inside the hearing hall, Ed Bangs gazed placidly out over a crowd that in earlier days would happily have seen him hang.

The chairman of the Park County (Wyoming) Commission wanted Mr. Bangs to know that his, the commissioner's, constituents' human rights were being denied by "reintroduced grizzly bears." He predicted that the county infrastructure would collapse as local companies pulled up roots and fled the onslaught of the wolf.

A man named Ed Livingston, seizing the microphone in a death grip, predicted widespread rabies, attacks on humans, wolves in town. He said den-area restrictions would lead to closure of the region's national forests and national parks to all human use. Tourism would come to an end. Wolves had never lived anywhere near Park County, he said. Finally, just about staring a hole in Ed Bangs, Livingston assured him that he, Ed Bangs, would be held personally accountable for it all.

David Flitner, president of the Wyoming Farm Bureau Federation, said the wolf plan reduced the state of Wyoming to "serftitude," and promised, "We will do everything to oppose this, *both legally and otherwise.*"

Norm Bomer had come all the way from North Carolina to bear witness. "I am a Christian," he testified. "The Bible says we are to subdue the earth and fill it. Man got rid of wolves because they were part of a curse."

It went on like this for hours, culminating in three drunken cowboys threatening personal violence against Bangs. Through it all, he nodded, thanked each witness politely, and wrote down God knows what on his pad.

Cody having been such an embarrassment to them, the pro-wolf forces made a particular effort to ensure that at the next Wyoming hearing, in Cheyenne a few weeks later, the composition of the crowd would be different. And it was. They had placards now, too:

**WOLVES RESTORE THE BALANCE**

**BRING BACK THE WOLF**

**ANSWER THE CALL OF THE WILD**

**WHO APPOINTED RANCHERS JUDGE, JURY & EXECUTIONER?**

A college girl in a scruffy wolf headdress and fuzzy fake-fur booties led a bunch of other college girls in a chant:

> *"One, two, three, four,*
> *we want wolves in ninety-four!*
> *Five, six, seven, eight,*
> *wolves just want to procreate!*
> *Wolves are great!*
> *We can't wait!"*

There was a lot more wolf support at the Cheyenne hearing than there had been at Cody, but basically you could sit for an hour at any of the hearings and hear the same things over and over. You could nearly always predict just from looking at the person approaching the mike which side he or she was on.

Neohippiechick in granny glasses and Birkenstocks? The one who refers to the wolf as *"Cannabis lupus"*? Guess.

Gray-suited, wingtip-shod, straight-parted spokesman for Republican congressman?

Brillo-bearded, steel-rim-spectacled, flannel-shirted granola eater?

Gristly, gimlet-eyed old rancher lady smoking unfiltered cigarette outside?

I found the whole thing at once funny and sad, in roughly equal measure. Then, just when my cynicism was about to launch me over the pale of caring, I heard an elderly man named Bill Tallbull, a Cheyenne Indian, the founder of a multitribal coalition called the Medicine Wheel Alliance.

This is a very emotional time for me. . . . The night I was born, January 21, in a little valley, the medicine men were coming down the valley to see my mother, and they heard wolves. The wolves were talking, and the men understood that the mother had lost one of her young. They knew then that something powerful was happening in that valley that night. I had just been born. They said, "Maybe this is the wolf that that mother was looking for—Other Wolf." My name is Other Wolf. My father's name was Little Wolf, and he predicted that in forty years, wolves would come to talk to me. Coyotes came, but I ran them off. Three nights, the same thing happened. Now it's forty years more, and still no wolf. The coyotes jumped at the opportunity to deceive me, play tricks on me. I fed them, and I said, "No, don't deceive me. Tell me the truth." The coyotes stayed four years with me, and then they were shot, for their hides. I want to reconnect with the wolf, and see him, and talk to him, and see what he has to say. I know what it means to be an animal who doesn't know where to go, like the wolf and the grizzly bear. Now, I live on the reservation. It's my sanctuary. Let's let Yellowstone National Park be the sanctuary for the wolf.

No one seems to talk about the spiritual quality of this land. It has strong spiritual people in it—the wolf, the buffalo, the grizzly. When my son turned forty, the coyotes came to him, and they continue to talk to him. You all have spirits. Every animal has a spirit. We have spirit religion since the beginning of time. I hope the spirit you carry with you connects you with the powerful spiritual nature of this land. Thank you.

From my point of cultural vantage I could easily have heard all this as the not quite coherent ramblings of an old man, but I knew that Tallbull was speaking to us from across a chasm, of culture and of time. And I knew that it was over there, with him, that the wolf actually lives.

The last few hearings were an anticlimactic bore. In Denver, after not one single anti-wolf person had testified all day, I gave up at four o'clock. In Washington, D.C., neither press nor politicians bothered to show up. Bangs sat at the desk on the stage, occasionally examining his ballpoint pen or chatting with the stenographer, and waited till the timekeeper told him it was over.

Seven hundred and fifty thousand documents had been distributed. Seven hundred witnesses had testified. Letters had come in from all fifty states and more than forty nations. There were 160,000 written comments, about 60,000 opposing wolf reintroduction and 100,000 favoring it ("Most of them, on both sides, misinformed," says Bangs). It was the biggest official citizen response to any federal action ever.

The Final Environmental Impact Statement was released in July of 1994, and to no one's surprise it called for reintroduction of the gray wolf to Greater Yellowstone and central Idaho under the so-called "experimental population" rule, which allowed the killing of wolves under certain circumstances, even by ranchers.

The experimental-population question had opened a bitter rift in the conservation community. The Sierra Club Legal Defense Fund, the Sierra Club, and the National Audubon Society were opposed to allowing any wolves to be killed under any circumstances, and they threatened to file suit against the federal government to stop the very wolf reintroduction that conservationists had dreamed of for twenty years. The principal wolf advocacy groups—in particular Defenders of Wildlife, the Wolf Fund, and the National Wildlife Federation—pleaded that this was the best that could be done in the sublunary world and would suffice. The others remained determined to sue. Dialogue died, succeeded by furious silence.

Bangs and his team had a very busy time ahead of them. First they had to complete what is known as a "rule-making": the "rule" is a highly detailed document that specifies the processes and procedures for implementing a federal law. Upon approval of the rule by the executive branch, it is published in the Federal Register and thereby takes legal effect. This particular rule was to set the reintroduction in motion and to govern the specifics of wolf management thereafter.

A draft of the rule was released to the public on August 15, 1994, to be followed by yet another period for public comment, of sixty days, and still more public hearings, and finally the final rule. Without waiting for the now-inevitable results of all that, the Wyoming Farm Bureau Federation announced its intention to sue to stop the reintroduction.

Under ferocious pressure from their erstwhile allies, the Sierra Club Legal Defense Fund and its clients decided not to try to stop the Yellowstone reintroduction, but at the same time they announced that they *would* sue to stop the Idaho program.

From my point of view, the differences between the Idaho and Yellowstone situations were all but invisible, but a momentum was at work familiar to anybody who has ever had a boss or parent who cannot bring himself to change his mind despite any amount of evidence. There had been increasing reports of wolf sightings in both Yellowstone and central Idaho, and while some of them were doubtless dogs, coyotes, hoaxes, or hallucinations, some of them doubtless were wolves. Extensive surveys of both areas, however, had shown that there were no resident breeding wolves. None. And the definition of a "population" arrived at for the E.I.S. by a consensus of the world's wolf experts was a minimum of two breeding pairs. Yet the belief in phantom-wolf populations persisted— among both friends and foes of the wolf.

We live in a world in which marble Blessed Virgin Marys burst into tears, in which dinosaurs live at the bottom of lochs and never come up for air, in which yetis and sasquatches prowl the mountain heights—in which, in short, empirical non-verifiability is frequently not accepted as proof of non-existence. The need to believe in invisible things is an ancient characteristic of our species.

Besides their belief in invisible wolves, there were other, only dimly recognized factors in these groups' refusal to accept the compromise. One was an inchoate horror of letting wolves be killed just for being wolves. Another was the presumed sanctity of the Endangered Species Act, which for some conservationists has achieved the sort of fierce infalli-bility claimed for papal bulls. There may also have been an element of reciprocal hatred of the livestock groups, who have so long regarded environmentalists as agents of Satan.

Still intending to trap and move thirty wolves from Canada to Yellow-stone and Idaho in November, the wolf team had many difficult logistics to arrange—trapping areas to define, permissions to obtain, airplanes to book, holding pens to build, jurisdictional conflicts to reconcile—and still more witnesses for Ed Bangs to hear out, most of them old familiars by now.

At the rule-making hearing in Helena, only thirty people showed up, and only eight made comments. In Cheyenne, Boise, Salt Lake, Denver, and Seattle it was much the same.

The last hearing took place in Washington, at the Jefferson Audito-rium, deep inside the echoing marble mausoleum of the Department of Agriculture. When the hearing began, there were three officials present, including Bangs sitting at a desk on the stage and trying to look attentive; four witnesses, who gave short statements and then left; and me, doo-dling on my pad. Bangs was required to keep his store open all day whether he had any customers or not, and he had none. A certain "Elvis Presley" had signed up to testify, but in the event did not.

Late in the afternoon, two witnesses showed up, both pro-wolf and both brief, and then silence returned, and then it was over. Ed Bangs had squeezed the last blood from the turnip of public opinion.

The final rule was signed by Secretary of the Interior Bruce Babbitt and Secretary of Agriculture Mike Espy on November 18, 1994, and was pub-lished in the Federal Register the following Tuesday, November 22.

The Canadian trappers started setting their traps the next morning. There was a flurry of protest in both Alberta and British Columbia, along the lines of "How dare these Americans take our wolves?" Then Indian tribes in B.C. got into the hoorah.

Most Canadians, however, realized that they had plenty of wolves; indeed the wolves to be sent live to Yellowstone would otherwise have been sent skinless to the cat food factory. Moreover, many of the elk of the Canadian Rockies were the descendants of Yellowstone elk shipped north long ago to redress Canada's own nineteenth-century mass slaughter, and those Canadians who remembered that reintroduction were glad to spare us a wolf or thirty. The trappers in Alberta captured and collared a half-dozen "Judas wolves" in short order, but dealing with the fracas in British Columbia took a few more days, and the date for the return of the wolf to Yellowstone was postponed until December 7.

Those few days were long enough for the American Farm Bureau Federation and its Idaho, Montana, and Wyoming affiliates to file suit against Bruce Babbitt, his Interior Department, and just about every other federal agent and agency in sight.

Senator Conrad Burns of Montana wrote a letter to Babbitt demanding that he suspend the reintroduction until the lawsuit was resolved—which could easily take another year. Senators Al Simpson and Malcolm Wallop, Senator-elect Craig Thomas, all of Wyoming, and Senators Larry Craig and Dirk Kempthorne of Idaho co-signed.

Babbitt ignored Burns's letter, but the Fish and Wildlife Service agreed to delay the importation of wolves just a little longer—until January 1, 1995—so that the Farm Bureaus' motion for a preliminary injunction could be heard in federal court.

Which brings us to Christmastide, 1994, and Ed Bangs, the leader of the wolf reintroduction project, lounging in the witness box. The case that the Wyoming Farm Bureau and its co-plaintiffs have brought to Denver has been pretty wobbly, and almost incomprehensibly argued; it is small wonder that Bangs is wearing something of a smirk.

Judge William F. Downes sternly insists that all the testimony today must address the question of irreparable harm, and he interjects his own questions often, which tend to be clear and straightforward: "Can you give me a statistic as to losses associated with predators?"

"In Montana," Bangs replies, "we did a study looking at predator-caused losses. Of the cattle that were lost in Montana, I think it was two point four percent of all losses were due to predators."

Chrissy Perry of the Justice Department continues her examination: "How many livestock losses are expected to result from the introduction of wolves into the Greater Yellowstone area?"

Bangs's reply, drawn from the Environmental Impact Statement, is also straightforward and clear. The recovery goal—the population size at which wolves in the northern Rocky Mountains will be removed from the endangered species list—is ten breeding pairs of wolves, for three years in a row, in each of three areas: northern Montana, central Idaho, and Greater Yellowstone. When you add in the nonbreeders, ten wolf pairs represent about one hundred wolves. On the basis of data from other places where wolves and livestock live together, the E.I.S.'s expectation is that one hundred wolves will kill about nineteen cattle and sixty-eight sheep per year in the Greater Yellowstone Ecosystem. In the early years of the reintroduction, Bangs avers, there may well be no depredation at all.

To determine the likelihood of immediate harm, the judge is going to have to look at the likely effects of the first phase of the reintroduction. To decide on the likely outcome of a full trial on the merits, he will have to consider the effects of a fully recovered population, and decide whether or not an annual loss of nineteen cows and sixty-eight sheep represents irreparable harm to the regional livestock industry.

Bangs observes, with his trademark who-cares shrug, that the total expected loss of livestock to wolf predation is approximately one tenth of one percent.

Bangs is also familiar with the study that Larry Bourret was unable to remember yesterday, in which the effects on cattle of a totally uncontrolled wolf population were measured. Wolves that begin to kill livestock tend to get worse as time goes by, Bangs tells the court, and he discourses at length on the provisions in the reintroduction plan for control of depredating wolves. Modern control tools such as helicopters, radiotelemetry, and immobilizing drugs, he testifies, can be very rapidly effective.

Richard Krause's cross-examination is a dense thicket of double negatives and malapropisms: "Can you state as an unequivocable fact that none of our clients in the experimental-population areas will not be severely impacted from wolf predation?"

This is Krause's ninth consecutive iteration of that impenetrable construction and that nonword. "Better run that one by me again," drawls Bangs. "The 'unequivocable' is getting to me."

Krause, rattled, refers to his own Exhibit One as "Restoring Plaintiffs to the Northern Rocky Mountains of the United States."

"Restoring wolves?" tries Bangs, helpfully.

Judge Downes grows exasperated. "Well, ladies and gentlemen," he says, "I have a lot of questions of this witness that I don't think either the United States or the plaintiff adequately addressed. It was a disappointing morning in terms of getting information, and I need information and I need it in a hurry." He then proceeds through a succession of crisp, quick queries leading to the question of imminent irreparable harm.

Bangs is equally quick and clear. "If we let wolves loose this year, is anybody going to be severely impacted? The odds are high that there will be no livestock depredations. But if I was a prophet, I'd be living in a penthouse in Las Vegas."

Hank Fischer is next up. He has the smooth, deep voice of a professional announcer (in fact, he has his own program on public radio). His posture is formal, his manner businesslike. He affirms the continuing success of the Defenders of Wildlife compensation program in northern Montana: no one who has been offered compensation has yet turned it down. He assures the court that because the fund is fully endowed, it can continue indefinitely in Greater Yellowstone and Idaho.

Mountain States attorney Steven Lechner's tone is rough, but Fischer does not give him much to work with. "What happens," demands Lechner, "if the fund or the Defenders of Wildlife goes out of business?"

"I don't know."

Referring to a statement Fischer made in 1989, Lechner bears down: "Did you state that the purpose of the compensation program isn't to make ranchers happy or gain their support, but the purpose of the program is to develop enough of a political and economic comfort level with the public so as to allow wolf recovery to proceed?"

"Yes."

"Did you say that?"

"Um-hm. Could I explain that?"

"No."

The judge wades in eventually to Fischer's rescue, but he remains concerned that a private fund may not be as trustworthy as a legislatively mandated program.

Fischer is ready for this one too. "Congresses come and go. Times change. They could decide that spending money on this wasn't a priority anymore either."

Wolf biologist Dave Mech is the next witness. His voluminous curriculum vitae and bibliography are entered into evidence.

"Yesterday," says Perry, "we heard argument or testimony that wolves prefer livestock to other kinds of prey. Based on your experience, do you agree with that statement?"

"No, I do not."

As for a claim by a Farm Bureau witness that in Minnesota, "the dairy operations were gone and the deer were gone and the wolves were now eating dogs off their chains"?

"Well, we've got two thousand wolves in Minnesota, and this past fall has been one of the most successful deer-hunting seasons on record. We have between three hundred and four hundred thousand deer in wolf range in Minnesota. So, I mean, if you call that the deer being gone, I mean, I don't—and we have about two hundred and thirty thousand cattle in wolf range in Minnesota, and about sixteen thousand sheep. We have about eight thousand to nine thousand moose in wolf range.

"It is true that wolves are killing some dogs. That's a perennial thing. You know, wolves kill something on the average of maybe five or six dogs a year that are reported to the government. So that part of it is true. And sometimes they do kill them on the end of the chain, I guess."

Richard Krause tried to impeach Mech's testimony by reading quotations from his book *The Wolf*, in which he wrote that livestock were likely to be more vulnerable to wolf predation than wild ungulates were.

Mech is ready. "I've learned probably ninety percent of what I know since I wrote that book. I wrote that book in 1968. Since that time, I've watched wolves, and I've seen that, you know, they don't just go to a farm and prey on the livestock. I mean, an excellent example is right here in Montana, where a wolf pack raised a litter of pups in the middle of, I think, five hundred cows and calves. In the middle. Walked through them every day. Raised a litter of pups for a year without touching a cow or a calf."

# The Balancing of Harms

DECEMBER 23, 1994

Carter Niemeyer kills wolves and loves wolves. Those of you who are hunters will recognize this tender paradox. Of those who are not, I ask a less abstruse recognition: simply, that in the American West, whose landscape and politics are both dominated by the livestock business, livestock-killing wolves are going to be controlled, either by law or by outlawry, no matter what wolf lovers wish. The latter means would be less discreet than the legal, and more lethal.

Therefore, to save wolves we kill wolves. That is, to save wolves as a species, we must kill some of them. Carter Niemeyer is the man on the ground, the man who must race to some mountain pasture and find and measure the fang marks on a mangled carcass, tease hair and bone out of turds, sit with the enraged ranch family face to face across the kitchen table. He is also the man who must track and trap the guilty wolf, and sometimes pull the trigger. He looks not only ranchers in the eye but wolves too.

Niemeyer probably knows as much about catching and killing wolves as any other human alive. He knows that with radio collars and cleverly placed traps, it is not, in the end, very difficult.

The Animal Damage Control unit of the U.S. Department of Agriculture is reviled by many conservationists. In times not long past, A.D.C. has in fact been responsible for heedless overkill of predators. Some critics say that the agency still overdoes its job. Some ranchers want more. Increasingly, A.D.C. is trying to control predators by nonlethal means. The general perception—on both sides—is that if a rancher thinks he has a predator problem, A.D.C. will be there to solve it.

Which is precisely what makes Niemeyer so powerful a witness. He has been choking gophers for A.D.C. for twenty-one years, and has been the chief wolf catcher in the West for four. Of the carcasses of predator-killed livestock he has investigated in that time, fewer than 10 percent have been wolf kills.

"In the short term," demands the judge, "do you believe this plan puts in place sufficient safeguards to protect stock growers from depredation due to wolves? And I mean by that the next two years."

"I think in the short term we can deal with wolves," replies Niemeyer evenly. "I have no way of predicting what the long term will bring."

If three years is "the long term," what is fifty, a hundred? Will the middle of the twenty-first century see wolves restored along the Rocky Mountain chain from Canada to Mexico? Will the West still be blanketed with cattle pasture?

Given the pace of life in the United States at the end of the twentieth century, I find it impossible to think that far ahead. If you stabilize the growth of the earth's human population at its 1990 rate and just let it perk along until the year 2150, it grows from five billion to *three hundred billion* people. There will not be much room for wolves on that kind of planet.

Krause and Lechner close, setting forth how they believe their case has met the requirements for a preliminary injunction. The judge jumps into the midst of Lechner's remarks: "You recognize, of course, that the burden is on you to show irreparable harm in these proceedings. And what proof have you presented to me that satisfies that burden? My biggest problem with your case, Counsel, is that it relies a lot on anecdotal evidence."

That is precisely the weakness of Wyoming Farm Bureau Federation et al. They have cited no modern situation, no scientific study, that supports their case. The corresponding strength of the government's case lies less in the history of public consultation than in the stacks of studies gathered for the Environmental Impact Statement, all showing low rates of wolf depredation on livestock. "What they're talking about is speculative," says Perry, "and what we have is predictive."

But as the day winds down, Judge Downes keeps turning to the question of harm to individuals. He seems almost haunted by the possibility that Regan Smith could go out of business on the Beartooth Plateau. "This is the first time in my professional life that I've addressed this issue," he says quietly as he adjourns.

In the hall outside, neither side dares to predict an outcome.

# *Decision*

JANUARY 3, 1995

## IN THE UNITED STATES DISTRICT COURT
## FOR THE DISTRICT OF WYOMING

WYOMING FARM BUREAU
FEDERATION, et al.,
Plaintiffs,
*vs.*
BRUCE BABBITT, Secretary,
Department of the Interior, et al.,
Defendants.

The Court appreciates the anguish of Plaintiffs' members, and particularly that of the witnesses who testified on Plaintiffs' behalf. Yet expressions of fear and trepidation, however genuine, cannot be accepted as proof of immediate and irreparable harm. . . .

THEREFORE, it is ORDERED that Plaintiffs' Motion for Preliminary Injunction is DENIED.

# HINTON

# *Wolfward*

Hasting north for the capture and conveyence of our heroes, my Nissan Pathfinder and I trail a plume of cloud across the snow-pied prairies of the Blackfeet Indian reservation. We skirt the jagged, scarcely peopled East Front of the Rockies and plunge into a blizzard gusting down the fjords of Glacier Park. The road goes to dirt, and then ice. Veils of powder swirl out of wind-stunted aspen and settle on the narrowing road. This is as wild a place as a motor vehicle can come south of Canada, a place of grizzly bears and, recently, of wolves.

At dusk an ice-fog rises from the earth, haloing the customs-house lights, glazing the day ice with night ice. The borderlands stretch lightless west and east to a lightless horizon. North, a town at last appears in the blackness. The Pathfinder steams, and sighs; the motel has plug-ins for block heaters. Bad pizza. Bed.

# *Via the Mall*

Dawn shatters any childish delusion of the Wastes of the Frozen North. Where we statesiders quail at the bone-jolting cold, Canadians simply put on more clothes and build cities. From the international boundary north, the road is smoothly paved, two lanes wide, then four, then freeway through wheat fields and farm towns till Calgary rises gleaming like Oz on the horizon. This is cocker spaniel country, not wolf.

Three hundred kilometers more of ice-fogged, ice-greased freeway brings only Edmonton, home to 850,000 people and the West Edmonton Mall, the biggest indoor shopping experience in the world.

World Waterpark

world's largest indoor wave pool

full-size replica of the Santa Maria

Deep Sea Adventure

submarine rides
(four submarines, more than the Canadian Navy has)

dolphin shows

Sea Life Caverns

The Beach Hut

Ice Palace Skating Rink

Europa Golf Course

Chinese Pagoda

replica of the British Crown Jewels

Fantasyland Hotel
(including Roman, Arabian, Polynesian, Victorian Coach,
African Safari, Truck, and Igloo theme rooms)

Turbo Ride Theatre

Below the Belt

Pumped Actionwear

Luv N Stuff

Wild Gravity Bungy Co.

House of Knives

Virtual Reality

Yuk Yuks Komedy Kabaret

Galaxyland Amusement Park

aviary

chapel

doctors

dentists

lawyers

nineteen movie theatres

two McDonald's

106 other restaurants

800 stores and services

15,000 employees

325,000 light fixtures

How is it that these people have wolves and we don't?

West of Edmonton begins the boreal forest that stretches north unbroken to the Arctic. The land rises, dips, rises, and dips. The dips are muskegs, spiked with skinny black spruce; the rises, are white spruce, poplar, and rock.

Giant trucks blast by, laden high with tree trunks no fatter than fence poles: plywood, pulp, a Japanese city's worth of shoji screens, a Sunday *New York Times*'s worth of words. Mule deer mince across a clearcut littered with slash, then spring away at the ice-crack of my opening door. The air is hard as glass.

The Pathfinder's trip odometer, set at zero at my mailbox in Montana yesterday, scrolls to an even one thousand miles as we roll into Hinton, Alberta. Sulphurous smog from the local particle-board plant yellows a pallid setting sun and wreathes the motel neon. On the table at Smitty's Family Restaurant sits a plastic placard listing the appetizers, each of which has a superfluous paragraph of description except the only one that needs describing, a thing called *poutine*. A Canadian specialty? Indeed it is, the waitress confirms. Poutine is French fries with melted mozzarella and brown gravy.

Some seventeen Judas wolves have been trapped for the Yellowstone and Idaho projects since last November, representing thirteen packs. Trappers in the Alberta Rockies are accustomed to getting two or three hundred dollars Canadian for a wolf, dead of course, but for these precious dynasty founders, alive, the U.S. Fish and Wildlife Service is paying two thousand dollars apiece.

Animals with prettier fur than wolves are the usual quarry of trappers. The money is better, and the trapping is easier. Yet wolves, in the end, are not really all that hard to trap, at least until they have had experience of trapping, after which they may become impossible to catch. They are not stupid.

The basic routine for trapping our wolves alive is this. Road-killed game meat is placed in the midst of dense brush cover through which there is only a narrow passage to the bait. Nothing can be touched by a bare human hand, which to a wolf would reek of peril. In each passage is set a snare of quarter-inch steel aircraft cable, at wolf's-head height. Ravens and magpies tend to find the baits first, and the wolves follow the birds to the trap. A string of these setups is called a trapline.

Steel leghold traps catch wolves more easily than snares do, but in this savage depth of midwinter a trap would quickly freeze a wolf's leg, by cutting off the blood supply, and give you at best a three-legged wolf.

Wolves caught in snares are usually caught by the neck, so the snare has an anti-slip stop on the cable to keep it from hanging its client.

A U.S. Fish and Wildlife Service agent will run the line with the trapper at least once every day. The agent will carry what is known as a jab stick—basically a broom handle with a tranquilizer-filled syringe duct-taped to the tip. When they find a wolf in the snare, it's one quick stick and good night, Charlie. For each new wolf caught this way the trapper gets another five hundred bucks.

Today has already yielded one adult male and two pups from one pack and another adult male from another. Tomorrow a Bell Jet Ranger helicopter will arrive from Alaska carrying two experts in aerial dart-gunning.

All the "fur on the line"—meaning, rather coldly, every wolf caught on a registered trapline—is by law the property of that trapper, so for each wolf darted, whether from the air or on the ground, Mr. Trapper will be paid another three hundred dollars, even though he may be smoking his pipe by his fire at home.

Beyond the edge of town the night is black and hard, and wolves are moving in it.

# *Love and Bondage*

The sun hangs at treetop at noon, veiled in pale gray. The snow squeaks loud underboot. Numb cold shortens breath, blunts fingers, burns toes like hellfire. It is thirty below.

Lost in the overcast to westward rise the peaks and glaciers of Jasper National Park. To north, east, and south the forest rolls in waves to an indistinct gray horizon. Squares of bright white clearcuts here and there patch the black-green quilt of conifers.

In a little clearing stands a compound of drab stamped-metal buildings, and amid the buildings stand a stamping, sneezing, freezing assortment of journalists, videographers, veterinarians, rangers, and miscellaneous hard-core wolf groupies. A long row of long-lensed cameras stand ready on their heavy tripods. The ink freezes in my pen. This in normal times is the maintenance headquarters of the William A. Switzer Provincial Park. Today it is wolf central.

I lived for some years in the path of incessant helicopter flights, in New York City. I don't think one of them ever passed over that failed to occupy my entire attention. It is not that I have a particular interest in helicopters; it is just that below a certain altitude, they are so goddamned loud that I can do nothing but pay attention. I could cram blasé fingers in my ears when the A-train shrilled past, and choose whether to curse or ignore the bowel-wrenching deep-bass bleat of the world's loudest fire engines, but all my New-Yorkerly habituation to noise was for naught against low-flying helicopters.

How, then, must a wolf in these quiet woods feel as this glittering red *tchwing-tchwing*-ing monster howls down out of the sky fast as a stooping falcon and a man in a helmet and mirrored sunglasses leans out of its backside with a Palmer gun and fires a dart into *your mother* and she slows, stumbles, and dreamily falls into the snow and lies still, and the monster wheels against the magnesium-white sun and drops back toward *you*?

The moment of terror is short, but how long will its memory be? From the moment the tranquilizer takes effect and the wolf falls unconscious, in any case, all is gentleness and care. Men and women race across the clearcut toward the figure crumpled in the snow. Soft mittened hands lift her onto a blanket, rolling her tight for warmth. A neatly tailored ripstop nylon blindfold shrouds her dilated eyes from searing snowdazzle. A stethoscope seeks her heart. The pilot throttles hard for Switzer, skimming above the pointed trees.

The noise descends in a cloud of snow. The terrible blades slow, stop, and droop, and the door slides open. Two men hurry forward with a canvas stretcher.

Raised with dogs, and with dogs therefore as my graven image of canidity, I am always surprised by how long wolves' legs are, how big their feet. The stretcher jounces past the cameras, the long white legs protruding from the blanket-bundle and flopping over the side.

In the borrowed equipment shed that serves as their temporary wolf clinic, the veterinarians gently unwrap the wolf. She is almost pure white, heavy-chested, dense-furred, healthy. The people move softly, their voices hushed. The assumption is that the anesthetized wolf, lying swaddled in an old down comforter on the stainless steel examining table, can hear us perfectly well. One does not want to disturb her. This mercy seems a little self-serving, considering what she has just been through and all that still awaits her; yet the love of the doctors and handlers is palpable in their low voices.

An oxymeter clipped to her tongue takes the white wolf's temperature, her pulse, her respiration rate, and measures the concentration of oxygen in her blood. The vets pull back her soft black lip and examine her teeth:

the extent of wear is an index of age. This wolf is probably five or six. She weighs ninety-two pounds.

The veterinarians measure every possible body dimension. (The males even get their testicles calipered.) Blood is drawn, to be sent to a lab in Vancouver and analyzed for rabies, brucellosis, parvovirus, distemper. They squeeze feces out of her colon, to be checked for parasites such as echinococcus—tapeworm, to us civilians. She is surveyed for external parasites as well. This wolf has lice. She gets a shot of penicillin to ward off infection from all this human handling, a big fat pill of worm medicine, and a lice-killing dusting. A plug of flesh is punched out of each of her ears and slipped into a glass tube for DNA "fingerprinting"; this material may ultimately be used for analysis of her mitochondrial DNA, which can trace the ancient ancestry of any animal through the maternal line. Yellow plastic tags are bradded through the holes in her ears, each bearing a provisional identification number. (Shortly, the yellow tags will be replaced with either blue, for wolves bound for Idaho, or red, for Yellowstone wolves.) Out of the sight of the reporters, quite secretly, a "personal identification tag," known as a P.I.T. is inserted through a little incision in each wolf's skin. This is a tiny electronic device that can be scanned by a non-invasive bar-code reader, so that any one of these wolves may be unmistakably identified in the future—a valuable secret for future prosecutors.

Throughout the examinations, while the wolves sleep under the mild and shallow anesthesia of Telezol and Xylazine, Yellowstone Park veterinarian Mark Johnson insists that the animals be touched as little as possible, and that when they must be handled they should be touched "gently, respectfully, and with love." The nylon blindfolds will spare the wolves, should they begin to wake, the terrible sight of humans.

The Canadian trappers stand by in a diffident cluster, perhaps a little amused by all the fuss but awed as well. One of them comes forward to listen to the wolf's heartbeat through Johnson's stethoscope, and his eyes light up in what looks to be joy.

The shipping crates are lined up at the back of the building. They are beautiful objects, in their industrial way. Each is handmade, of gleaming polished aluminum. They are essentially perforated boxes, about four feet deep by three high by two and a half wide, with a vertically sliding solid front door and, behind that, an inner door of vertical square bars. The floor is made of closely woven steel mesh. Carry-handles slide out of tubes at the four corners: the white wolf will proceed to her new home like a royal personage in a sedan chair.

Once examined and medicated—"processed," the vets and biologists call it—each wolf is carried to a chain-link enclosure to await assignment and transfer to Idaho or Yellowstone. The blindfolds are lifted. To minimize the social stress of seeing their fellow prisoners, the wolves are placed in cells lined with opaque tarpaulins. The concrete floors are densely covered with insulative straw. If the wolves show signs of agitation, Valium is available, though so far, in the opinion of the watchful veterinarians, none has been needed.

A solid coal-black wolf is drawn into the tightest possible coil at the farthest possible corner of his enclosure. His only movement is the steady, rapid rise and fall of his flanks. His nose is tucked behind his paws. This is a posture for sleep, but the wolf is not asleep. In the moment before I blink away from his unblinking gaze, his amber eyes are watchful, cold, and cognizant.

# Not a Good Day

This entire operation is predicated on snow. Deep snow restricts the distances wolf packs can travel and makes individual wolves easier to hit with a tranquilizer dart. Deep snow is a commodity that in central Alberta in January tends to be abundant, but Alberta is not cooperating. Tracking conditions are lousy and getting worse. It has not snowed for a week, and the wildlife-rich forests around Hinton are densely crisscrossed with animal tracks. From a rattling, shuddering helicopter, moose, elk, and wolf tracks all look alike.

Flying conditions are lousy as well. Thirty below is brutally cold even for 53 degrees of latitude above the equator and six thousand feet above sea level, and when the marksman must ride perched in the wide-open back door of a helicopter while trying to steady a heavy gun, he does feel the chill. The light remains misty, gray, and shadowless. The U.S. authorities are grumbling about the astronomical and still mounting helicopter costs. Today they will bring in a fixed-wing aircraft, which can range farther and faster than the choppers can. When this Super Cub spots a pack, its crew will radio in to headquarters at Switzer Park, and the Jet Ranger crew will take to the air. Pilots and gunmen pace up and down in the maintenance yard, clapping their mittens together.

There are only seven wolves in custody so far, of the thirty required—fifteen for Yellowstone, fifteen for Idaho. The Idaho operation is going to be what is known as a hard release: the wolves will be ear-tagged, radio-collared, and then flown to sites deep in the wilderness, the doors of their shipping kennels will be opened, and from then on it'll be up to them.

Each year as pups born the previous spring begin to mature, some of their older packmates are expelled from the pack and forced to make their own way in the world. For a hard release, those dispersers are the wolves you want—old enough to hunt and make a living on their own but young enough to be still unattached and on the lookout for a mate.

Wolves are supremely social animals, and when expelled from their natural pack, they are supremely lonesome. If you have ever owned a dog and left it behind when you went on vacation, you have seen the look on your dog's face that expresses how the lone wolf feels.

It is helpful to remember that a wolf is not a dog at all, but a dog in many ways is a wolf. A Labrador retriever, an Afghan, a Shih Tzu is only a hundred thousand years down the evolutionary road from wolfhood, whereas wolflike wild canids of one sort or another (including some horrific sorts, such as the wonderfully named dire wolf) have been around for some twenty million years.

They have been around people all that time. Modern wolves and modern humans evolved in the same era. You could probably even say that they co-evolved. So, though most of you have probably never seen a wild wolf, you know wild wolves in your bones. I am sure that that partly explains why *Canis lupus* is so popular. Wolves are familiar to us. In fact, the domestic dog's scientific name is *Canis familiaris*. The Latin adjective *familiaris* means "domestic," "family," "household." The family wolf.

Therefore you dog owners understand the intensity of loneliness that is the motivating principle of the hard release: the biologists know that within a year or two, at least some of these lonely wolves will have found one another, formed pair bonds, and taken up traditional family life. And they will have done so with a maximum of naturalness, a minimum of human interference.

As of this morning, two of the wolves at Switzer have had blue tags clamped through their ears, meaning that they have qualified as Idaho wolves. In their eyes I see, foremost, incomprehension, but also wariness, watchfulness, apprehension, loneliness, and, most remarkably, a kind of calm. The veterinarian Mark Johnson confirms that the best way to evaluate a wolf's relative peacefulness or agitation is just to look at the wolf's eyes and facial expression and use your good sense. What you know from dogs will be just as true in a wolf: wide-open, shifting eyes and raised brows mean agitation; a peaceful gaze means peace. There is something going on in a wolf's eyes, however, that touches on a realm far beyond anything dogs know. I know no name for it, but there is a composure, a dignity, a *selfhood* about these wolves, which even in this chain-link ignominy clutches at my heart and stirs awake a mysterious envy.

Another fifteen wolves of the same sort—young, healthy, and of dispersal age—are to be brought to Idaho at this time next year, and again the next, perhaps for as long as five years. There are very few cattle and sheep in central Idaho, and therefore few armed wolf haters, and there is wild prey aplenty, so the population is expected to grow fast. The official recovery goal is ten mated pairs of wolves in northern Montana, where natural recovery is well under way, plus ten in central Idaho and ten in Greater Yellowstone. Each population must then maintain itself at that level for at least three years. If things go as hoped—if, that is, there is no epidemic of wolf killing, and if the wolves do not go running home across the prairies—full recovery could come to pass within a decade.

The biologists' greatest worry under the hard-release system is homing. Even though these young wolves bound for Idaho may not have come from established packs in Canada and therefore may not be as tied to home as territory-holding pack-member wolves would be, there is no assurance that they will not streak straight north the moment the boxes are opened. They will be emerging into a world inconceivably devoid of wolf smell, wolf sign, wolf howling from over the hill. The hard-released wolves' first response to such desolation may well be to set off in quest of familiarity, of company—and there is a considerable body of research evidence that wolves are expert navigators, even after the disorientation and trauma of drugging and translocation. Certainly the Idaho wolves are likely to wander before they settle down, and wandering may bring them into the proximity of firearms and people bearing them.

But this is an experiment! And a glorious one—a superlative symbol of the young science of restoration ecology. Top predators are known to influence ecosystems very strongly. Therefore their removal has certainly changed both central Idaho and Greater Yellowstone in unknowably many and profound ways. Restoring wolf populations there may tell us things about ecology never yet dreamed of. And having wolves for neighbors certainly will be a good test of our willingness to get along with our fellow creatures on this ever more anthropocentric planet.

Two of the wolves in the holding pens at Switzer are brothers, either one or two years old, one gray, one black, weighing about seventy-five pounds apiece; they are members of a pack named for a lake named Petite by the Voyageurs. The Canadian trappers who managed to snare these two and another young male have seen the tracks of the rest of the Petite Lake pack, but those seven wolves are almost certainly wise to the game and will be virtually impossible to trap. Aerial darting is the only way to get them now.

The packmate of the two captive wolves has been released wearing a radio collar and has rejoined the pack. Today the traplines have been shut down, and the aerial gunners are sweeping the Petite Lake pack's territory, listening for the telltale beep of the Judas wolf's radio collar.

The plan is that among the fifteen wolves to be sent to Yellowstone, there will be at least three already mated pairs. The rest, ideally, will be members of their packs—most likely, their offspring. The typical wolf pack is basically an extended family, made up of the alpha male and alpha female, who are usually the only wolves to mate and who generally lead in the hunt; several subordinate (or beta) adults or subadults, who help hunt and whose most important social role is as "aunt" or "uncle" to pups born the previous April or May; and finally, of course, the pups, of whom there might be anywhere from one to ten.

The hierarchy is rigid, and absolute loyalty is demanded, and yet, of course, as in our own species, stability often breaks down. A young Oedipus ousts his dad. An interloper takes control and tosses out her predecessor's offspring. Packs split into two, packs disintegrate. Two separate packs may decide to merge.

Pack sizes vary widely. Some may be as small as a young pair just starting out in life. Dave Mech, in *The Wolf*, cites an observation of an Alaskan pack with thirty-six members. Here in the foothills of the Alberta Rockies, six to eight would be typical. The Petite Lake pack, at ten, is a big one.

The hope has been to capture more than three whole packs and then to pick from among them the three pairs and their packmates who seem fittest. Those who fail to make the cut would be released back to the wild. The loss of three packs should have only a modest and short-lived effect on the existing wolf population, for wolves are so abundant here that there will be plenty of young dispersers available to colonize any vacated territories. This wolf population sustains losses on this scale year after year.

The Yellowstone component of the experiment is to be a soft release: each of the packs will be held for six weeks or more in a secure enclosure, smelling the smells of their new home, and, it is hoped, forgetting their old one. Various versions of the soft-release technique have been tried elsewhere, most notably in the restoration of a red wolf population in coastal North Carolina, a project that was led by wildlife biologist Mike Phillips, who is now the leader of the Yellowstone wolf project. The North Carolina operation and most other soft releases have tended to involve much longer periods of captivity than six weeks, but for a number of reasons—not least the danger that some anti-wolf politician might hatch a scheme to prevent the wolves' release while they are still locked up—the Yellowstone wolves cannot be held so long, and no one knows if they may streak for home or wander into trouble.

A stack of red ear tags and radio collars in the processing shed awaits the capture of suitable wolves for Yellowstone. All we have so far are the two cowering brothers—certified by further tooth examination as pups of the year, that is, born in the spring of 1994—who have half buried themselves in straw in their holding pens.

Late in the day, the Jet Ranger clatters along just above the treetops, homing in on the location given by the helicopter crew to the crew of the Super Cub. The chopper's global positioning system consults a satellite far above, which informs them that they have arrived at their target. They hover. Sure enough, a wolf breaks into the open, running truly for dear life. The gunner leans out the open back door, draws a bead, and shoots.

The wolf skids to a swirling-powder stop, nose plowing the shallow snow. By the time the helicopter has landed and the crew has reached her, she is dead. The tranquilizer dart has pierced her chest cavity. This has not been a good day in Hinton.

# A Pack of Wolves for Yellowstone

JANUARY 10, 1995

Doom comes screaming out of the sky. The helicopter skims the ground not ten feet up, across a clear-cut and straight toward a wall of trees, with the gunner halfway out the door—this is very dangerous flying—and *blam!* a Petite Lake wolf falls. The chopper lands just long enough to scoop up the tranquilized wolf, then returns instantly to the air. It hovers just over the forest where the biologists know the wolves are, pounding them with brain-scrambling noise.

One wolf, a big black one with a silver streak down the front of his neck, breaks out of cover. *Blam!* Two down—but no, he's still running. The helicopter lands. Two men leap out and give chase through the trees. Gradually the drugged wolf slows. Confused, he turns back toward his pursuers. He sits down, waiting for them, looking straight into the face of what he must know to be imminent death. One of the men raises a jab stick, the other a pole with a wire noose at the end. The black wolf snarls weakly, too sleepy to run anymore, or too hopeless. One man tightens the noose around his neck. The wolf snarls again, yet more weakly, and lies down, his mind clouding over. The other man jabs a second dose of tranquilizer into his flank.

This tough, brave wolf, with the big balls of a breeder, must surely be the alpha male—half the prize.

Again the helicopter squats on its noise above the wolves, and again one breaks free and—*blam!*—falls.

Again, with the same result.

And again.

Back at Switzer, the veterinarians and biologists examine the wolves from Petite Lake. Two are pups of the year, both male, brothers of the two in hand. The testicle calipers confirm that the big black wolf is the alpha male. The sixth is the only female. Her nipples are swollen, her vulva is turgid and bloody, she is decidedly ready to breed: the alpha.

We have a pack of wolves for Yellowstone.

In the McLeod River country, another Judas wolf unknowingly betrays her mother. This collared pup survived a disastrous snaring operation last fall, in which three of her packmates were strangled. The alpha male and alpha female of the McLeod pack were not caught that night. Now the male has disappeared. It seems likely that he has only recently been killed, which would mean that his one pup and her mother are the only members of the pack left alive. The adult female shows every sign of rich, ripe estrus.

She is so beautiful, solid black, and so healthy, just under a hundred pounds, probably four years old, and so ready to breed—and wolves are so hard to come by lately—that Steve Fritts, in his role as the leader of the Canadian operation, makes a quick decision to send her down to Yellowstone immediately, with her daughter and the six members of the Petite Lake pack.

Perhaps the trapping crews may yet find the alpha male. Maybe they will catch two more whole packs. Then Fritts can send her back to Canada to be turned loose. Maybe he will have to try to force a new mate on her—a highly uncertain proposition, since unrelated wolves who are introduced in captivity may well choose violence over romance. But an alpha female wolf as perfect as this black beauty, and in heat, is just too good to let go.

Good news also on the Idaho front: two more unrelated young adults are in hand, for a total of four.

Fritts telephones the U.S. Forest Service in Missoula, Montana, to send the plane. In the stinging, acrid, God-knows-what-below-zero morning darkness, the Pathfinder starts up faithfully, and we race south for Yellowstone.

# Noncomedy of Errors

The twin-turboprop Shorts Brothers C-23 Sherpa sits in the hangar at Missoula. The runway has iced over, and the airport is closed.

At the Hinton airport, preparations continue apace. The eight wolves bound for Yellowstone, each with a numbered red tag in each ear, and the four wolves for Idaho, with blue ear tags, lie unconscious in a neat row beside the runway. They get a thorough preflight medical check, and then are gently slid into their glittering shipping containers.

The sky over Hinton is clear, but flying conditions elsewhere have been terrible. The Sherpa finally gets out of Missoula and heads for Canadian customs at Calgary, but Calgary is socked in. Pilots Eldon Askelson and Eldon Hatch—the Eldons, as they are cleverly known in Missoula—go on to Edmonton, for customs, gas, and a bite to eat. There they discover that their U.S. government credit cards are not accepted by the Canadian telephone system, so they can neither call in to Hinton nor report back to Missoula. They learn that the weather halfway to Hinton, at Edson, Alberta, is "zero-zero," meaning zero ceiling and zero visibility, and they conclude that Hinton must be bad too.

Meanwhile, Steve Fritts, Mark Johnson, and the rest of the wolf team, under Hinton's blue skies, are coming to a rolling boil. Fritts is frantically calling the Calgary airport, the Edmonton airport, the Forest Service in Missoula, everywhere he can think of, trying to find his airplane. The

Eldons, who have been up since four-thirty this morning, are having lunch at the Edmonton airport café.

Eventually the steaming Hintonians get through to the Eldons, and in a voice Eldon Askelson later describes as "strained," Steve Fritts desires them to get their asses to Hinton *now*. The Eldons had been planning to go up and take a look at the weather in any case, and the plane is gassed up and ready. About three in the afternoon, they touch down at Hinton.

Fritts, Johnson, and their team get the wolves loaded; Johnson will ride with them all the way to Yellowstone. The wolves must pass through Canadian customs, and so the Eldons head for Calgary, which is reported to be open now, but as they approach the Calgary airport it fogs in again, and the plane diverts toward Edmonton. Then they hear that Calgary is back open, so they turn around to try it again. Under a low ceiling, they manage to land, and the Canadian customs officials helpfully rush the wolves through. From Calgary they are to fly to Great Falls, for U.S. customs, and from Great Falls to Missoula, toward which a caravan of Yellowstone Park rangers is now racing—seven cars and two big horse trailers (one for backup, or perhaps a decoy?). But Federal Aviation Administration regulations stipulate that a pilot may work only fourteen hours straight, whether flying or not, and the Eldons have maxed out at Great Falls. They beg for an extension of just one hour, which is all it would take to get to Missoula, but their Forest Service supervisor turns them down. Exceptions, he tells them, are made for matters of life and death only—human only. The Yellowstone caravan actually has a cellular phone in one of the cars, but nobody seems to know the number. So the trailer that is supposed to carry the long-suffering wolves to Yellowstone is headed for the wrong city—168 miles wrong.

This might be funny were the wolves' lives not at stake. The drugs have long since worn off, and you cannot keep administering them indefinitely. The wolves have been handled with all the tenderness their handlers can muster, but think about it: darted, drugged, blindfolded, poked, prodded, caged, hog-tied, boxed up, trucked, loaded, pitching and yawing for hours inside some roaring machine, bounced, jounced, unloaded, reloaded, bombarded by the voices and noises and smells of their one great source of terror—humanity—these wolves are under inconceivable stress. It is not unusual for wild animals in the stress of no more than ordinary captivity just to drop dead.

Eventually, however, the rangers reach Missoula and learn that they must drive on to Great Falls. At three o'clock in the morning, they arrive at the hangar where the caged wolves await. Mark Johnson and crew, exhausted, load the four wolves for Idaho onto a truck, and then the other eight into one of the horse trailers.

The caravan sets forth for Yellowstone. The rangers are packing a good amount of armament, for anywhere along the way there could easily be some crank who would love to put a hole in a wolf tonight, or a wolf-loving G-man.

# YELLOWSTONE

## Captivity

# *Arrival*

The wolf returns to Yellowstone amid jubilation worthy of a Caesar. There is even a triumphal arch—the doleful dark gray basalt monument dedicated by President Theodore Roosevelt in 1903 to commemorate the creation of the world's first national park thirty-one years before.

Beneath the Roosevelt Arch in summer there flows a mighty stream of the motorized People for whose Benefit and Enjoyment, according to the concrete tablet above the keystone, the park exists. Sealed inside the arch is a time capsule containing, among other treasures, the minutes of a meeting of a Grand Lodge of Masons; some coins; the writings of one Cornelius Hedges advocating the creation of the park; editions of two local newspapers, the Livingston, Montana, *Enterprise* and the Gardiner, Montana, *Wonderland*; a photograph of President Roosevelt; and some postcards featuring views of the park.

Beneath the Roosevelt Arch this frigid morning proceeds a giggling line of Gardiner children freed from school to be eyewitnesses to history, flanked fore and aft by hectoring teachers. From the arch to park headquarters five miles on, throngs await the jubilee. Years hence will these kids be telling their children and grandchildren that they were here this day?

Beyond the arch, across the snow-patched flat where antelope graze on more placid days, and up the hill past the cliffs where bighorn sheep are wintering, and lining the ridgetops along the little tumbling Gardner

River,* are hundreds of cameras—the tripod-mounted, long-lensed thirty-fives and four-by-fives of the still-photo pros, the tiny point-and-shoots and jiggling camcorders of the masses, the brightly logo-emblazoned, hundred-thousand-dollar video cameras of the television news teams who have descended on Yellowstone from all over the world. Several dozen broadcasting trucks aim their big white dishes at relay satellites far above. TV crews are shooting video of other TV crews. Part of the coverage is how much coverage there is.

Beneath the arch, at eight thirty-five A.M., come a half dozen ranger patrol cars flashing red and blue, with a gray horse trailer behind them. There are eight aluminum boxes inside the trailer. In one is the black female wolf from the McLeod pack, henceforth to be known as Number Nine. In another lies her yearling daughter, reddish-gray, seventy-seven pounds, now Number Seven.

Another container holds Number Four, the ninety-eight-pound alpha male of the Petite Lake pack, black with the silver streak on his neck. The alpha female, now denominated Five, is light gray and weighs exactly the same as her mate. Their four yearling pups—born in the spring of 1994—are all males: Two, black-and-silver, weighing seventy-seven pounds; Three, all black, eighty pounds; Six, also black but without the silver, seventy-five; Eight, gray, at seventy-two pounds the runt of the litter.

The drugs having long since worn off, the wolves are fully conscious, but they are perfectly quiet and still. All of them are lying silent and wide-eyed in their metal boxes, disoriented and exhausted from twenty-three hours of travel, loud noises, unidentifiable smells, and fear.

As the wolves come through the Roosevelt Arch, a cheer—a roar—goes up from the crowd. In many eyes burn tears of joy.

The wolf trailer and the patrol cars continue up the hill to the lovely old stone buildings of the former cavalry post below Mammoth Hot Springs, originally known as Fort Yellowstone and still the national park's headquarters. Here others join the convoy, including Yellowstone Park's new superintendent, Mike Finley (the park's chief executive officer), U.S. Fish and Wildlife Service director Mollie Beattie, and Secretary of the Interior Bruce Babbitt. The biologists are waiting at the ready:

*Nineteenth-century spelling has bequeathed us the *Gardner* River running through *Gardiner*, Montana.

Mike Phillips, the project leader; Doug Smith, who will coordinate the field research; Steve Fritts, of the Fish and Wildlife Service, just arrived from Canada himself. Veterinarian Mark Johnson, who still has not slept, remains with the wolves to make sure they continue breathing.

The caravan makes its processional way some twenty miles to the south and east of Mammoth, to the lower valley of the Lamar River, where the last wolves of Yellowstone perished.

The Lamar and the rolling high-elevation grassland savannas below its confluence with the Yellowstone River and on down a few miles past Gardiner constitute what is known as the Northern Range. The Northern Range is one of the world's great places for wildlife: its biological productivity equals that of the Serengeti Plain of east Africa, despite the long cold winters and relative aridity. The Northern Range this winter is home to perhaps eighteen thousand elk, about two thousand mule deer, five hundred bighorn sheep, several hundred antelope, two hundred moose, a few white-tailed deer, a few mountain goats, and five or six hundred descendants of the last wild bison left alive in the United States in the eighteen-eighties.

In summer, most of those numbers roughly double. And the Northern Range is only part of what will soon be wolf habitat in Greater Yellowstone. There are seven other herds of elk besides the huge Northern Herd. The wolves will have enough to eat.

The wolves, biologists, and bigwigs come to a stop at a roadside pullout. It is much too small to park the whole caravan on, but parking in the road is not a problem, for the entire valley has been closed to unauthorized entry. Even the press is shut out, except for a handful of press-pool designees acting on behalf of the impatient horde stuck back at Mammoth.

The snow here at sixty-two hundred feet is about a foot deep, the wind raw as a whip. A truck-sized sled drawn by two sly-looking mules waits at the trailhead. On the rough board seat sit two impressively hatted mule drivers, Wally Wines and Bob Blackwell. The biologists lash three wolf containers to the bed, and the sled lurches forward. It proceeds slowly over the uneven ground, up and over a steep-sided shoulder known as Crystal Bench, and then up the drainage of tiny Crystal Creek, nearly dry this dry winter. The humans trudge along behind, the lowlanders gulping the thin mountain air.

A little more than a mile in, the sled arrives at a sparsely forested hollow of aspen and lodgepole pine, in which there stands a roughly round chain-link enclosure, one acre in size. The fence is ten feet tall with a further inward-slanting two feet of chain link at the top and an apron of chain link beneath the soil extending inward three feet. The wolves can neither climb out nor dig out. The pen cannot be seen from the road. This is where the Petite Lake wolves are to spend the next two months, becoming the Crystal Creek pack. Rangers will be guarding all three acclimation enclosures around the clock, living in tents nearby.

For the last hundred yards to the pen, the biggest wigs, Beattie and Babbitt, take the forward handles of the box containing Number Five, the alpha female. Automated shutters click and whir, tape rolls silently, pool reporter Angus Thuermer scribbles. Superintendent Finley and the park maintenance foreman, Jim Evanoff, bring up the rear. It is a media moment par excellence, as the evening news tonight and the front-page photographs across the country tomorrow morning will attest.

"I hope this is a one-way trip," growls the secretary of the interior—for this is as far as the wolf project can go. The boxes may not be opened; the wolves may not unbend their creaking legs. This has all been for the cameras. The return of the wolf to Yellowstone is on hold. Indeed, these wolves may have to be returned to Canada, or put to death.

The Mountain States Legal Foundation has mounted a last-instant sneak attack: yesterday morning, with the wolves already in the air, the M.S.L.F. lawyers were at the U.S. Court of Appeals for the Tenth Circuit, in Denver, asking for an emergency stay of both the Idaho and Yellowstone reintroductions. It is rare for a higher court to countermand an order of a lower court in advance of consideration of the full case on the merits, but this one has done it. The appeals court judges say they need forty-eight hours to study the Farm Bureau's arguments and decide whether to block the wolf reintroduction altogether.

By the time the appeals court had ordered the stay, the wolves were already in transit. The clerk of the court immediately telephoned Alice Thurston, the Justice Department attorney who had made the government's case earlier in the day, to tell her that the judges had decided to suspend the reintroduction. The written order mandating the stay would not be ready till morning, but the court's order was to be enforced as of now.

Thurston pleaded that the wolves could be let out of their traveling kennels and into the pens without actually being "released." They could still easily be loaded back up and returned to Canada, if the court should so command. But the clerk was not so sure, and checked with the judges. The judges said forget it, keep them in the boxes. And indeed, when the paperwork arrived this morning, the court order had had three new words added to yesterday's version: ". . . The release of wolves into Yellowstone National Park and/or central Idaho, *in any manner*, is hereby temporarily stayed . . ." (italics added).

Forty-eight hours more in these two-by-three-by-four-foot boxes will be ruinous, says the park veterinarian, Mark Johnson, perhaps fatal. The only way to get water to them is to squeeze ice cubes through the interstices in the grid of bars across the one small window.

"These are boxes that were not made for anything other than transportation," a spokesman for the U.S. Department of Justice, Bert Brandenburg, tells the *New York Times*. "There's no provision for taking care of feces or urine. The boxes are enclosed on the inside, so it's dark. There's no light coming through."

The Idaho wolf team, similarly stymied, finds a place for their four wolves in a quiet local kennel in Missoula, Montana. Two Nez Perce elders, Horace Axtell and Allen Pinkham, of Lapwai, Idaho, come to bless the wolves, pray for them, and sing to them. (The name first given to their people by European Americans was *Nez Percé*—French for "pierced nose"—but it has come to be pronounced "nez purse" and spelled without the accent mark.)

The Nez Perce happen at the moment to be proposing to the United States government that the tribe serve alongside the U.S. Fish and Wildlife Service as comanager of the Idaho wolves, to the tune of some two hundred thousand dollars a year. This may or may not have something to do with the arrival in Missoula of three Lemhi Indians (pronounced "LEM-high") to protest the Nez Perce blessing. The wolves are supposed to be released in their own *Lemhi* valley, they say, near the town of Salmon, Idaho, in *Lemhi* County, and if any Indians are going to do any wolf blessing they damn well ought to be *Lemhis*.

Interior Department attorneys are at the appeals court in Denver at this moment, filing their own emergency appeal, begging for a quicker decision. At least let the wolves out of the boxes and into the pens, they implore the judges.

The biologists bring a second sledload of caged wolves to the Crystal Bench pen and then move on to the one at Rose Creek, to leave there the boxes containing Nine, the mateless alpha female, and her daughter, Seven. Nine's muzzle is bleeding where she has been biting at the bars of her kennel. So is her vulva, for a different reason: this wolf is near the peak of her once-a-year-estrus. She is obviously uneasy, anxious, and depressed. With every passing hour, this stress becomes more likely to end her fertility. Bruce Babbitt, Mollie Beattie, and Mike Finley head grimly back to Mammoth to meet the press.

The interior secretary is visibly agitated. "The Canadians," Bruce Babbitt explains, "have said no returns, no refunds. They can't go back to Canada."

What, then, if the court decides to forbid their release?

Wild adult wolves are unlikely to survive captivity. The only course left will be euthanasia.

The wolf advocates are walking the halls of park headquarters in a leaden daze. The Fish and Wildlife Service director is afire. "This is going to be wolf heaven," fumes Mollie Beattie, "if we can just get them out of purgatory."

Looking harried and solemn, wolf project leader Mike Phillips takes a seat at the end of the big table in the park's executive conference room. Microphones are thrust into his face. The room is hot, and jammed. Phillips squints into the blazing TV lights. "When wolves are extremely stressed," he says, very slowly, "they have a tendency to slip into a stupor of sorts. These wolves have certainly done that. They are not doing well."

The evening wears on. Dread steadily mounts. Then a call comes in from Denver. The court has lifted the stay.

Mike Phillips and his boss, Wayne Brewster, jump into a truck and speed to the Lamar to join Doug Smith at the Crystal Bench pen. In the darkness, the biologists draw up the guillotine-like sliding door of each box in the enclosure and secure each so that it will stay open. It is ten-thirty P.M. The wolves have been caged for thirty-eight hours. The people leave a road-killed elk on the ground nearby and hurry away as fast and as quietly as they can, locking the pen gate softly behind them. All six Crystal Creek wolves cower in their kennels, drawn up as far to the rear as they can scrunch. Not one emerges.

At Rose Creek, as soon as the door slides open, young Seven steps cautiously out of the kennel. Her mother remains within, withdrawn.

# *A House Call*

JANUARY 13, 1995

Through the milky light of winter dawn, the ranger guarding Crystal
Bench peers through his spotting scope and sees the ivory arcs of elk ribs
gnawed clean. Half of the elk hindquarters is also gone. He rushes to his
radio.

The rising sun reveals wolf after wolf, six of them, running around the
pen perimeter, around and around and around. They have already worn
a circular trail of bare black soil in the snow. There has been, apparently,
no social conflict, and all six are moving well.

The exulting wolf team arrives. As they approach, the wolves stop circling but not moving: now they pace the fence at the farthest remove
across the circle from the gate, fifty yards this way, seventy back, back
and forth, racing past each other, whirling, then racing the other way,
occasionally stopping to try to dig beneath the fence, not in panic but definitely with ardor. They will not look at the oncoming men. They want
out, and away.

The men come on. They open the gate. The wolves are moving faster
now, really scared. Mark Johnson notices that the black pup Six is
bleeding from the mouth. The men herd him away from the others and
close in as he trembles, shrinking into the earth, uncertain whether to try
to dash between them or just keep still. They cast a net over Number Six,
and he thrashes in panic, but only for a moment. The men push him flat,

carry him to the small enclosure next to the gate, and hold him down firmly as the net is peeled back.

This young black wolf's mouth was injured at Hinton, probably when he tried to chew his way to freedom, and his sutures have pulled out. Mike Phillips jabs a hypodermic behind his shoulder, and the wolf sinks to the ground. Mark Johnson rapidly cleans and restitches the wound. They lay the unconscious pup out in the pen and withdraw. Soon Number Six is racing up and down with his packmates, good as new.

# What Humans Call Freedom

The fog and rain over Idaho have not abated, and the four subadult wolves remain stuck in Missoula. The plan has been for them to go to two sites accessible only by helicopter, well inside the Frank Church River of No Return Wilderness, but the poor animals have been in transit and captivity for four days, and no one knows how long their health will hold out. The wolf experts confer. Okay, enough is enough. They will truck the wolves to the end of the Salmon River Road, stopping in the town of Salmon along the way so the Lemhis can add their blessings.

In addition to their official numbers, these Idaho wolves have been given names by schoolkids in a statewide contest. The first wolf, a ninety-pound black male, wears a radio collar that the kids have painted with the name Moon Star Shadow, each letter a different color. The snapping of shutters is the only sound as he steps from the kennel, peers around at more people than he has ever seen in his life, and pees on the ground. This may be taken as the universal gesture of canine self-assertion, or maybe he just had to go. The wolf then lopes away, not particularly hurrying, to have a look at the ice-choked river. He turns then and heads west, downriver, into the wilderness.

The kennel of Chat Chaaht ("older brother" in the Nez Perce language), a young dark gray male wolf, is opened next. He bounds out immediately, and follows the tracks of Moon Star Shadow through the snow.

Akiata, an almost-black female, is not so eager for what humans call freedom. Veterinarian Dave Hunter prods her from behind with a stick, but she will not budge. Her eyes are wide, almost circular. Her teeth are bared in a grotesque grin of terror. Finally Hunter gets a snare around her neck and hauls her out by main force. As soon as the snare is loosened, Akiata plunges through the ponderosa pines after the first two wolves.

The fourth, an eighty-two-pound dark gray female, bolts through the door of her box and charges upriver, then whirls around to follow the others.

"Thank God they're walking is all I can say," says Ed Bangs.

# An Arranged Marriage

JANUARY 20, 1995

From the Livingston, Montana, *Enterprise:*

> CHEYENNE, Wyo. (AP)—A week after wolves returned to Yellowstone National Park, a Wyoming House committee decided Thursday to put a $500 bounty on wolves that wander outside the park.
>
> The bill would also require that the state foot the bill for anyone charged with violating the Endangered Species Act for killing a wolf.
>
> Rep. Roger Huckfeldt, R-Torrington, the sponsor of HB13, said the bill probably violates federal law and encourages wolf-killing, but the House Agriculture Committee passed it anyway, 8–1. . . .

A second wolf bill is being introduced in the Wyoming legislature this morning, this one providing that whenever a wolf kills a big game animal outside the boundaries of Yellowstone National Park, the secretary of the interior is to be charged with poaching.

The Montana legislature, not to be outdone, has put forward a resolution urging that wolves be introduced in Central Park in New York City, the Presidio in San Francisco, and the Mall in Washington, D.C.

. . .

Seventeen more wolves are flown from Hinton to Missoula; eleven of them are offloaded there, to be trucked to Idaho and released. Sheriff Brett Barsalou of Lemhi County, however, has heard that there are armed men bent on stopping the wolf caravan somewhere up in the hills, and he has ordered the road blocked below where the self-styled militia is thought to be waiting.

The Fish and Wildlife Service decides to fly the wolves to Salmon, and thence to two remote landing strips far inside the wilderness. By a nasty coincidence, it was only last night that the lumber mill at Salmon laid off many of its workers, and the townfolk, blaming the layoffs vaguely on environmentalists, are in a collective rage. The bars are crammed. There are two hundred angry Salmonians at the airport, quite a few of them armed. The pilots refuse to fly.

The Fish and Wildlife Service team makes hurried arrangements for a helicopter, and the wolves are choppered deep into the wilderness of the Middle Fork of the Salmon River, well away from a mill town on the verge of riot.

Sheriff Barsalou seems to have shown some sharp political acumen here: to the wolf haters of his county he can be the man who stopped the wolf truck; to the federal authorities he can be the man who kept their wolves out of harm's way.

The plane flies on to Bozeman. From there the remaining six wolves come by truck to Yellowstone Park, with much more ease and much less fanfare than their predecessors experienced last week. Five of the wolves are packmates, and they go to the third enclosure, in the forest above the Lamar's tributary Soda Butte Creek. The pack comprises Twelve, a big burly male, one hundred twenty-two pounds' worth, black with a bluish cast, young, confident, probably the alpha despite one undescended testicle and an oddly splayed foot; two females, neither of whom seems to have clear alpha status: Eleven, a gray ninety-two-pound adult, and Fourteen, also gray, eighty-nine pounds, only a subadult but a sound candidate for young motherhood (you can tell by her dark, enlarged teats that she has already bred, presumably with Twelve); Fifteen, a seventy-five-pound black-and-silver male pup, who nearly died when a tranquilizer dart collapsed one of his lungs, but survived to serve as a Judas wolf;

and an elderly one-hundred-thirteen-pound male whose like even the experts have never seen: Wolf Number Thirteen's dense coat is a remarkable color, a strangely luminous silver that actually looks *blue*. A seasoned veteran like Thirteen will be a valuable uncle and teacher should there be pups this spring.

The sixth wolf is the finest specimen that Yellowstone has yet seen. At one hundred twenty-two pounds, Number Ten is exactly the same weight as Twelve, but Ten has lost a lot of weight since he was trapped, and he can be expected to regain it quickly. This dark gray wolf is big, but beyond his size and his imposing bearing there is a calm, a quiet, a confidence, something magisterial. His testicles are huge. He has bitten two jab sticks in half. Unlike any of the other captive wolves, he will stare a person straight in the eye and keep staring. Every wolf biologist who has had a look at Number Ten agrees: this is the very definition of an alpha male.

One of Ten's packmates, probably a son, has gone to Idaho. The rest escaped the traps and darts. Ten is here in Yellowstone because so splendid a wolf is the wolf most likely to persuade the lonely widow Number Nine that her dream mate has miraculously materialized in the Rose Creek pen. There is some chance that one or both of these wolves will be dead tonight. Wild wolves unknown to each other and confined in this small a space are a formula for violence. But the trapping conditions in Alberta have remained so poor, and the costs there have mounted so high, that the wolf team has made an anguished decision to give up the quest for another intact family group and shut the Hinton operation down. If they are to meet their quota of three pairs in Yellowstone, this, now, is all they can do.

The team is taking a big risk today, but there are also reasons to believe that this arranged marriage may just take. Foremost is Nine's continuing and emphatic state of estrus, which everyone is hoping will appeal to Ten's gentler instincts. Another is that his hours of travel will have Ten feeling bushed, disoriented, unaggressive, and generally grateful to be back among his kind. One more reason for hope is Dave Mech's finding that intraspecific (wolf-versus-wolf) mortal combat seems to reach a yearly low exactly now, at the height of the mating season. And then there is the simple magnificence of both Nine and Ten. They just seem right for each other.

Number Ten strides out of the kennel and goes straight to Number Nine. Young Number Seven edges cautiously away. Ten gives Nine a thorough up and down, a thorough sniffing. She is a pretty sensational specimen herself. He lays his head across the back of her neck.

This is not as romantic a gesture as it may look. In wolf language it means, I like you, yes, but I also outrank you. Nine bridles, snarls, and scoots out from underneath Ten's attempt at tough love.

Nine and Ten stiffen and stand tall, growling. They come together slowly, touch noses, sniff each other's rears, snarl, and separate. Two hours of nastiness pass, but they still have not really fought.

By the end of the day, Nine and Ten are curled up together, warily asleep.

# The New Congressional Ilk

JANUARY 27, 1995

From *The Washington Post:*

... Called [before the House Public Lands and Resources Committee] to defend his department's controversial program of reintroducing gray wolves into Yellowstone and a central Idaho wilderness, [Interior Secretary Bruce] Babbitt got a sobering glimpse into what his next two years may look like with Republicans in control of Congress. Acknowledging the new political pecking order, Babbitt said to the committee's pugnacious and pro-development chairman, Rep. Don Young (R-Alaska): "Mister Chairman, I have no doubt about who the alpha wolf is in this room."

Led by Reps. Helen Chenoweth (R-Idaho) and Barbara Cubin (R-Wyo.), conservative Republicans who now dominate the panel complained that the wolf reintroduction program violates states' rights, abuses the Constitution, drains millions of dollars from more deserving federal programs and was prematurely jammed down the throats of westerners. ...

Asserting that the U.S. Constitution and the laws of Idaho give her state dominion over wildlife, Chenoweth implied that Idahoans would be within their rights to shoot wolves. . . .

# Death in Idaho

JANUARY 30, 1995

From the Livingston, Montana, *Enterprise:*

> **CHEYENNE, Wyo. (AP)**—The American Farm Bureau Fed-
> eration and Mountain States Legal Foundation will drop
> efforts to block release of wolves from pens in Yellowstone
> National Park, but not their overall challenge of the wolf plan,
> a spokesman said Monday. . . .

Sheriff Brett Barsalou is on the phone to the U.S. Fish and Wildlife Service, and he is not happy. One of the reintroduced wolves has killed a
newborn calf. Oh, and somebody shot the wolf, we don't know who.

When Animal Damage Control agent Layne Bangerter and his team
arrive in Lemhi County, Idaho, to investigate the event, they meet both an
irate sheriff and the still more irate owner of the dead calf, seventy-four-
year-old Eugene Hussey. Hussey's first call, it seems, even before he
called the sheriff, was to a friend of his on the board of the Idaho Cattle
Association, who told him he had better be damned careful. Hussey then
called Robert Cope, a veterinarian in Salmon. Cope came the twenty-five
miles down to Hussey's ranch and did his own necropsy—yesterday. The
dead wolf wearing blue ear tags marked "U.S. Fish and Wildlife Service
B-13" had blood between its teeth. There were wolf tooth marks on the

calf's liver. Cope also retrieved black hair the color of the calf from the wolf's stomach. Hussey videotaped the whole process.

It turns out, however, that Cope's necropsy has destroyed the medical evidence that A.D.C. needs to come to its own conclusions. Also, the vet, the sheriff, and the videographic rancher have so trampled the scene of the crime that any tracks that might have told the true story have been obliterated.

It is now the Feds who are irate, but being well trained in this kind of thing, they remain polite, though perhaps somewhat stiffly so. The video-tape is going to have to substitute for a proper forensic analysis. Watching the V.C.R. closely, Bangerter sees big wolf bites on three of the calf's legs. A wolf-mouth-sized plug is torn out of its throat. Its belly is ripped open in classic wolf fashion. With Hussey and Barsalou breathing down his neck, Bangerter tells a clamoring press corps his preliminary conclusion that Wolf Number B-Thirteen did kill Eugene Hussey's heifer calf.

And who killed the wolf? Hussey says he didn't do it, and neither did anyone working for him. He just found her dead lying next to the calf.

If either the livestock owner or an agent of his did the killing, and reported it, and could convincingly claim that he saw B-Thirteen in the act of depredation (and who would there be to contradict that claim?), he would be protected under the experimental-population rule. But in the absence of any of those conditions, the killing is a violation of the Endangered Species Act, punishable by a fine of up to a hundred thousand dollars and as much as a year in prison. Because no one has admitted killing the wolf and cited the justifying conditions, this is now a federal crime.

In the weeks to come, Eugene Hussey will become a folk hero, not only in Idaho but wherever anti-government fanaticism is taking root—which in January of 1995 means much of rural America.

The Fish and Wildlife Service laboratory in Ashland, Oregon, will return its definitive finding regarding the death of Hussey's calf. The hair in Thirteen's stomach was from a calf all right, but not Hussey's. There was no dirt on Hussey's calf's hooves: it had never stood up. There was no milk in its stomach: it had never nursed. One of its lungs was barely inflated: it had taken one shallow breath in all its life. The mother cow had not licked the afterbirth off the calf's underside, the first thing she would do to a live newborn: she knew her baby was dead.

That finding will not deter Hussey from demanding four thousand dollars from the Defenders of Wildlife compensation fund, on the grounds that over the course of her lifetime the heifer would have given birth to ten calves of her own. Hank Fischer of Defenders will approve compensation for what would have been the market value of the heifer grown to selling size—at last year's better price, about five hundred dollars. Then the lab report will come in, and Fischer will have to stop payment on the check.

Three Fish and Wildlife Service law enforcement agents will come to Hussey's ranch with a search warrant to look for the bullet that killed Wolf B-Thirteen. Unbeknownst to Hussey, as *High Country News* will later make known to a national audience, one of the Feds will have a tape recorder running in his shirt pocket.

"Here. Take it. This is your copy, sir," says one of the agents as he wades across a stream to present the search warrant to Hussey.

Sheriff Barsalou has been notified but has not yet arrived. "I don't have to take a fucking thing," yells Hussey. "Only from the goddamn sheriff. Nobody's doing a fucking thing till he gets here."

Hussey starts heaving rocks at the men whom he calls "big federal turds."

"Don't hit me with rocks, Gene," says the agent.

"I can hit you on my fucking property, God damn you."

Sheriff Barsalou arrives, and things get worse. Finally, after barely averting a general brawl, the lawmen stage a strategic withdrawal.

In a later interview with the *Idaho Falls Post-Register*, Eugene Hussey will deny the validity of the tape recording. "There's things they're saying there that I know they didn't." Hussey will never be charged with anything.

Congresswoman Chenoweth, knowing a political bonanza when she sees one, and relishing her burgeoning reputation as the most rabid of the rabid Republican freshmen, will bring the Fish and Wildlife Service agents before her committee in Boise and berate them one by one. Two weeks later she will convene another hearing in Washington. She will claim that the autopsy of B-Thirteen cost half a million dollars. Under the rubric of "increasing evidence of a government-sponsored religion in America"—namely, environmentalism—Chenoweth will condemn the wolf project and conservation in general as "a violation of the establishment clause of the Constitution." She will assert: "This religion, a cloudy mixture of New Age mysticism, Native American folklore, and primitive Earth worship (Pantheism), is being promoted and enforced by the Clinton administration." Barsalou and Hussey will both testify to federal harassment. Hussey will pay his own fare to Washington, the first time he has ever been on an airplane.

An environmentalist lawsuit against the U.S. Forest Service, alleging inadequate attention to endangered salmon, will shut down every national forest in central Idaho: the Boise, the Challis, the Nez Perce, the Payette, the Salmon, the Sawtooth. There is little else in central Idaho besides national forest. The shutdown will mean that the principal employer of the region will have no jobs for anyone this spring. The mines will be closed, including a new one near the town of Challis that has been expected to provide two hundred jobs in an area so badly overcut that logging jobs have dried up. Cattle will not be turned out on national forest pastures.

The shepherds in Edo Tedesco's study are no longer reporting depredation losses. The pack is presumed wiped out, no one doubts how.

At Rose Creek, wolves Nine and Ten have been seen, as the Park Service spokeswoman delicately puts it, "engaged in mating behavior." They pace the perimeter of the pen in perfect step. They groom each other. They howl together in the starlight.

# *Menace*

A young wolf is found dead, run over, on the outskirts of the ancient city of Siena.

Political alarms are sounding in Helena, Boise, Cheyenne, Washington. John Varley, Yellowstone Park's highest-ranking and politically most astute scientist, is pushing wolf team leader Mike Phillips for an early release of the captive wolves. The anti-wolf forces in Congress are not settling down as expected. It will be a lot harder to stop this project once the wolves are out of the pens.

Phillips wants to keep them confined as long as possible. "If these wolves were to go north along the Yellowstone—which is the logical corridor to the north—and they traveled as far as some of those Idaho wolves have," says Phillips, "they'd be in Livingston."

An accelerated release may be the best of the options. Superintendent Mike Finley does not like what he is hearing on the grapevine. The Republicans in the House are trumpeting a bill that would rescind all federal rules (the specific instructions required to carry out federal laws) put into place since November 20, 1994. The reintroduction rule is dated November 18, 1994. On the other hand, it was not published in the Federal Register until November 22. Which date counts?

"All I know," sighs Phillips, "is you never hear the shot that gets you."

# YELLOWSTONE
## Freedom

# A Good Place

MARCH 21, 1995

It has been sixty years, thirty wolf generations, since the last wolf pups were poisoned in Yellowstone National Park, just there, across the Lamar. Thousands of people have dreamed of this day for decades. Thousands have dreaded it, fought it, fought over it, passionately desired it, patiently built the intricate structure atop which this moment glistens. Where are they this morning? I seem to be the only one here. The sun on this first day of spring is headache-bright on wide white meadows crosshatched with animal footprints. Snow-dust wind-wracked from the Douglas firs on the mountainsides swirls into snow-devils on the flat, dervishing down to the frozen river. Bison nest in pits in the snow. A few cud-chewing elk lie bedded just inside the forest edge. The south-facing slopes, melting bare, have been nibbled and trampled into barely vege-tated mud by the thousands of elk that winter in this valley.

A few first faint washes of green have appeared on the sunniest promi-nences. A thin cloud settles on the summit of a black mountain called the Thunderer. Mountain goats live up there, in inconceivable weather. Dozens of mountain bluebirds, still in their migration flocks, flutter criss-cross across the valley floor.

A pickup truck towing a snowmobile trailer labors past, shifting down for the long climb toward Cooke City, where, a thousand feet higher than here, it is still winter. Then the Lamar is still again.

. . .

At four forty-five in the afternoon, a crew of biologists, the one allowed reporter, and the obligatory videographer hike up over Crystal Bench and down to the pen containing the wolves henceforth to be known as the Crystal Creek pack.

In keeping with the interagency nature of this undertaking—one representative of the National Park Service and one of the U.S. Fish and Wildlife Service—project leader Mike Phillips and chief scientist Steve Fritts unlock the gate together.

The wolves flee to the farthest reach of the pen, pacing fretfully back and forth along the black trail they have churned up there. Twice a week for ten weeks, people have come to leave the elk, deer, and bison carcasses that have sustained the wolves through their incarceration, and every human visit has been marked by this anxiety and stymied flight. Familiarity has not tamed these wolves.

Working quickly, the men set up the electronic motion detectors that are to alert them by radio when the wolves pass through the gate and into the world. The videographer aligns and focuses the camera that is to run unattended for the next two hours to record for posterity the Crystal Creek pack's first free steps in Yellowstone.

Eight pounds of road-killed elk are left inside the pen, another thirty pounds ten yards outside. The wolves were last fed four days ago; their bellies are empty.

Gate open, gadgetry set, woods chummed, the people depart in a hurry, leaving the wolves to seek their liberty at leisure.

Back at the trailhead, cigars are distributed. Puffs of triumph rise stinking into the breeze and evanesce.

The wolves are here, and free. Yellowstone is changed. The world is changed.

As the sun descends, the Lamar awakens. Eleven bull elk, still splendidly antlered though soon to doff their crowns, appear on a ridgeline, then twenty-six, soon a hundred and more, all bulls still. A herd of cow elk and their calves move out of the trees and down to the roadside where sun-warmed asphalt and snowmelt have greened a fringe of grass.

Ravens, winter's old familiars, call *rock-rock* in the lodgepoles. Two

Brewer's blackbirds natter in a cottonwood top. A golden eagle walks along a snow-crusted hillside, rolling at the shoulders like a bar bully. A family of coyotes sets up a boisterous howl somewhere to the north, behind one of the few healthy aspen groves left in this elk-gnawed valley.

These aspens rise jungle-thick inside a high chain-link exclosure constructed many years ago to measure the effects of the absence of browsing. The effects have been dramatic: the aspens outside the fence are mostly lying down, dead, and those still standing are old, weak, losing their limbs. Any new shoot is clipped off by the thronging elk before it can put out more than a couple of leaves. The unprotected portion of the grove seems to be dying.

It is not. Beneath the soil, despite the massacre above it, the intertwined roots of the grove continue to thrive. Shoots appear every spring, and every spring are nibbled to the ground, and every spring more shoots appear.

An aspen grove is not made up of individual trees. The "trees" are actually all genetically identical sprouts of a single gigantic organism: they are clones. You can see this readily in fall, when one whole grove will turn exactly the same bright yellow at the same instant, while another nearby stays uniformly green and another has lost its leaves altogether. The Yellowstone Park botanist Don Despain describes aspen as an underground plant that makes occasional aboveground appearances.

Will wolf predation on these elk bring back the aspen the elk have suppressed? In time we will see.

There are elk everywhere. Some are in bad shape. Late-winter vegetable food tends to be scarce wherever herbivore populations are not drastically limited by humans. Most of these elk never leave the national park and therefore are not hunted. Some are already dead, lying crumpled upwind from a lee of drift. This is a good place to be a wolf.

But at midnight the Crystal Creek wolves have not left their pen.

# Consternation

The briefing room is stinking hot. Still cameras jostle for the just-right angle. Spotlights dip and swoop, blinding half the room. TV newswomen check their hair in compact mirrors. Unkempt print reporters scratch on their little pads. The wolf reintroduction is the biggest story Yellowstone has ever had.

Mike Phillips hunches warily at a taped-up cluster of microphones. He is a trim, compact, springy sort of guy, with a loud, ready laugh and a boyish falling-forward shock of blond hair. Phillips tends to look younger than his actual thirty-six, but this morning he is distinctly gray. He has been up much of the night, radio-tracking the nonmovements of the Crystal Creek wolves, who remain resolutely inside their pen.

Having seen the reintroduction of red wolves in North Carolina through its own sieges of hostility and misunderstanding, Phillips is a practiced spinmeister. He is also passionate about his work and about the unfamiliar realities of wolves, and his passion tends to emerge in an oddly argumentative tone, as though he is countering an accusation. "This is perfect, perfect," he insists. "We wanted them to come out on their own terms. We just have to be patient."

Phillips cites two possible explanations for the wolves' refusal of freedom. One is simple wariness of human scent. These wolves have come from what the wildlife biologists call a heavily exploited population. Wolves in Alberta are trapped, snared, chivvied, chased, and shot year-round. In fact, to keep a trapping license in Alberta you have to show that you have killed some certain *minimum* number of wolves annually, and there is no maximum limit. Human-caused wolf mortality in the Hinton region approaches 40 percent per year—right at if not exceeding the sustainable yield (the proportion of a population that can be lost annually without impairing its viability). From an Alberta wolf's point of view, anything that smells like people could be final trouble.

Since the gate of the pen is precisely the place they associate with human intrusion, it would be perfectly natural for these wolves to be very cautious about a change of circumstance there. The wolves' minders have been careful to stay as short a time as possible when they bring the carcasses, and the Lamar and Soda Butte valleys have been patrolled by rangers twenty-four hours a day to make absolutely certain that the wolves had no other human contact. The rare observations of the packs by anyone other than the soft-voiced biologists and security forces have been conducted from long distances and at heights well above the pens. It is essential that these animals' wildness be preserved. A wolf pack that will rip a nine-hundred-pound elk's throat out without flinching will run like hell at the first scent or sight of a sixty-pound child; if the child corners a wolf, the wolf will probably only cower. The ardent avoidance of people is essential to wolf survival.

Sometimes it would take the wolves an hour to calm down after a visit. The pacing-paths they have worn in all three pens all veer wide of the gates: the wolves avoided people-places even when no people were present.

The second possible explanation—which Phillips considers additive to the first and which he and his fellow biologist Doug Smith have been debating into the night and again this morning—is that the wolves may have no concept of an opened gate as something you can just walk through, any more than they had had a concept of chain-link fence. When they were first put in the pens, the wolves crashed into the fences, tried to dig under them, bloodied their muzzles trying to figure out just what this thing was that was keeping them in. Now, perhaps, they may not even know that they have been set free.

The fact of the matter is that the Crystal Creek pack has already begun to allay everybody's worst fear, that they would streak the thousand miles straight home to Canada. I say, "pack." That is what they were when they were hunting Petite Lake, but there is no guarantee that the Crystal Bench wolves will remain a social unit in their new world. Wolves react to stress in a wide variety of ways, but because their family life is the foundation of their nature, stress is often reflected in changes in pack structure: alphas deposed, subordinates kicked out, new wolves joining, fights, sometimes even murder. There is a reasonable chance that what we are all hopefully calling the Crystal Creek pack could atomize and scatter like a splash of water the minute they leave the pen.

Nobody really knows how much stress these wolves have been feeling. There has never been a wolf translocation this complex and this hard on the wolves, and in any case there is no technique known to measure stress reliably in wild animals. The invasiveness of any measuring device would, of course, be stressful in itself. Obviously, the chaos and terror of their travels were stressful. Being cooped up for ten weeks was probably no picnic either, even with the lavish food. But what were the effects of the stress? We cannot know. For all the intensity and plenitude of wolf study, wolfhood remains essentially impenetrable. Wolves are Other, and probably will always be.

After the first few frantic days in the pens, the wolves did seem to settle down. They ate, from the beginning, like wolves. They did not fight. The packs howled often, which wolves in distress do not do. Most significant, all three alpha pairs made serious efforts toward fulfilling their reproductive destiny.

Nevertheless there remains the possibility of a third explanation for the Crystal Creek wolves' not embracing their freedom. Maybe they are in some sort of stress-induced daze. Maybe their minds have been permanently screwed up.

Late in the afternoon, the gate of the Rose Creek pen is opened. Nine, Ten, and Nine's daughter Seven trot nervously back and forth at the rear of the pen, watching the biologists' every move.

Whatever stress he may have felt early on, Number Ten has put it well behind him. Unlike every other wolf in any of the pens, Ten would often continue gaily racing along his usual path even when people came inside.

When the people dragged the road-killed carcass to the regular feeding site near the center of the pen, Ten would actually dodge behind his visitors. As soon as they were gone, he would hop up on the doghouse just inside the gate and watch them as they hiked back down Rose Creek to the road. Surely this handsome guy will lead his family to freedom as soon as it is offered.

But no.

Nor, again tonight, does the Crystal Creek pack move.

# The Ur-site

On his radio show, which many a rancher makes sure to hear every lunchtime, the commentator Paul Harvey is making cracks about "welfare wolves." Why work for a living, is the idea, when the government is providing you with public housing and handout food?

And alas, as Paul Harvey and lunch go by, both the Roses and the Crystals are still inside their pens. There was a signal from the Rose Creek motion detector at six twenty-one this morning, but that particular sensor, unlike the cruder one at Crystal Bench, registers direction in or out, and this was an in—maybe a raven scavenging at the skimpy remains of roadkill left inside. Telemetry confirms that the wolves are still either in or near the pen.

They are bound to be getting hungry; it has been a week since their last square meal. That is not by any means an unacceptable interval for a wolf, but it ought to be enough to stir a certain urge to move.

Another possible explanation of their recalcitrance is pregnancy. The mean birth date for the mother wolves of northern Montana is April 21. With a gestation period of sixty-three days, our new Yellowstone wolves would be halfway there. As maternity approaches, most wolf packs begin to restrict their movements. The pregnant female travels hardly at all. Eventually the mother-to-be will dig or find a den and stay holed up there while the other pack members bring her food.

Whelping time is nicely coordinated with the period of maximum vulnerability of wolves' prey animals. In late April, in Yellowstone and Alberta, the weakest elk and deer are starving, and many already lie dead on the ground. Wolf dads, uncles, aunts, and cousins need not go far to find meat for mom and the kids.

"We still think it's more likely that they won't whelp at all than that they will," says Mike Phillips. "They've been through so much."

But there are also encouraging signs. Four, the alpha male of the Crystal Creek pack, was diligent in keeping the male pups away from his mate, Five. Sometimes Five would avert her tail to expose her genitalia so that Four could assess her hormonal status, and she was consistently showing blood under her tail. Both of the females in the Soda Butte pen have been seen in amorous circumstances. The alpha-female question has still not been settled in that pack, and it is possible, though not likely, that Eleven and Fourteen could both be pregnant. Nine and Ten have been total lovebirds in the Rose Creek pen.

Phillips continues to proclaim his perfect satisfaction with the process so far, but the park's managers are clearly getting nervous. Yellowstone's new superintendent, Mike Finley, has somewhat oddly chosen to be on vacation this week of the greatest photo op of his career. So has Wayne Brewster, deputy director of the Yellowstone Center for Resources, Phillips's direct supervisor. These absences bump any major decision simultaneously up and down the chain of command, meeting from both directions in the person of John Varley.

Although nominally director of the Yellowstone Center for Resources for the past two years, and for years before that the chief of scientific research in the park, Varley has been widely seen by close observers of the shadowy politics of Yellowstone as the power behind former superintendent Bob Barbee's throne, with a mandate much broader than mere science.

Barbee left the Yellowstone chiefship last year—squeezed out, many said—to be replaced by the younger and reputedly bolder Finley, who has gained a name for "turning around" problem parks. I don't know if you can say that Yosemite and Everglades are quite turned around—they have problems far beyond the reach of any chief executive officer—but Finley is regarded as having worked miracles in both. He is still finding his footing at Yellowstone, however, and must steady himself with a hand on the shoulder of Yellowstone veterans like his science vizier John Varley.

Nobody knows better than Varley that "mere science" tends to be somewhat less than omnipotent in the Machiavellian viper pits in which real-life park management decisions are made. When Barbee had to appear before some bloodthirsty committee of the Congress, usually in a position somewhere between embattlement and incipient auto-da-fé, Varley would be the quiet presence at his side, with a fat briefcase of statistics and the occasional classically Washingtonian brief whisper of guidance.

It is too early in the post-Barbee regime to know whether Varley will maintain his power base, but Finley's absence certainly suggests a high level of confidence. Yellowstone National Park is like Harvard, or the House of Lords, or some remote Amazon tribe, in that isolation and potency have endowed its culture with mysterious rituals, a dialect found nowhere else, and a sort of internal political weather all its own.

This is the world's first national park, after all, the *ur*-site of American conservation. Yellowstone Park is also the geographic, ecological, and spiritual center of the largest remaining essentially intact ecosystem in the temperate zones of the earth—the heart of an 18-million-acre complex of wildlands. There is a sense of august responsibility in Yellowstone's inner chambers. Some on the outside read this as pompous self-importance; on the inside it is simply considered consciousness of gravity.

It is recognized here that the single most powerful absence from the Greater Yellowstone Ecosystem—what demands the cautionary adverb in "essentially intact"—is the absence of the ecosystem's only missing component, the wolf. The wolf is potent not only symbolically; a recovered wolf population will have massive ecological impacts.

It is, therefore, gravely that John Varley approaches each decision point in the wolf project. This is certainly the most significant man-made event in the park in this century. (The fires of 1988 were, despite much ill-informed bombast to the contrary, essentially a natural phenomenon.)

If the wolf project starts to go wrong—especially if the wolves leave the protected lands of the national park and the adjacent national forest wilderness areas, and start killing livestock—then the chances are strong that the emerging anti-conservation forces in the national and regional political arenas will put a quick and perhaps permanent stop to wolf restoration. The crackpot anti-wolf bills of the state legislatures are beginning to give way to serious behind-the-scenes strategizing by the tribunes of the right wing in Washington, who see much political capital to be gained and little to be lost in villainizing the wolf. The ranchers, loggers, and miners will be busy hollering amen as Conrad Burns or Helen Chenoweth on the TV set at the end of the bar vows to choke off the waste of good tax dollars which is the wolf program. Meanwhile, Helen and Conrad's real work goes on offscreen, promoting the vertical integration of the meat industry which has brought cattle prices down to sixty cents a pound; or helping establish tariffs and depreciation schedules that make unbridled clear-cutting the only way to do well in the timber business, with the unavoidable side effects of killing forests and streams and grizzlies and salmon as well as putting loggers out of work when the trees run out; or making sure that the mining companies are not overregulated, burdened with paperwork, or otherwise inconvenienced.

The wolf has been an excellent fund-raising emblem for the enviros, too, to be sure, but that is not the wolf's only profitable use. The wolf makes an excellent sacrificial lamb.

Suppose the anti-wolf forces succeed, and the program ends where it stands now. These fourteen wolves are meant to be only the beginning of a minimum of three to five years of translocation of Canadian wolves to Yellowstone—fifteen or so more every year till the recovery goal is met. Let's assume that at least some of these first fourteen do settle down and breed here. If they are the only wolves we ever import, and no others arrive by natural means, then the genetic diversity of the future Yellowstone wolf population will be so low that its chances of long-term viability could be slim to none, for one of the principal effects of inbreeding is a declining reproductive rate. There are many other effects of small population size, none of them good.

In short, the wrong move now—harrying the wolves out of the pens, for example, and thereby setting off an exodus or damaging the packs' social structure—could mean that some of the wolves will kill livestock, the politicians will make the most of it, the reintroduction will be over, and there will be a very good chance that wolves may never be reestablished in Yellowstone.

Varley modestly (or cunningly) deprecates the extent of his responsibility. "You people outside of government never seem to get how we work," he complains. "You think it's all sort of military orders or something. I wish you could have heard us consulting far and wide on every last little detail of this thing. The pen design, the length of confinement, the timing, the trapping, the sites, everything—we always work by consensus. I don't 'make' a 'decision.' We arrive at conclusions together."

"You people outside of government" is a telling phrase. For all the years and reams of testimony and comment imposed on wolf recovery by the National Environmental Policy Act and the Endangered Species Act, the fact is that somewhere in a small, usually shabby, fluorescent-lit room, representatives of a certain arcane subculture—the dreaded *bureaucracy*—have formulated the options, sifted the public's opinions, and chosen a course of action.

This federal agency subculture is not free to enact its own will. Far from it. The managers of Yellowstone, and land managers throughout the agencies of government, are attuned to public sentiment, especially opposition, with a fineness that seems sometimes to border on obsessive-compulsive disorder. None of them is more finely attuned than John Varley.

He is a big man, with salt-and-pepper hair, prominent glasses, and, like Phillips, a passionate way of speaking that sounds defensive even when it isn't. His voice catches on a word sometimes, repeating it in searching staccato—*and-and-and-and*—sometimes the stammer of a person whose mind is going so fast his mouth cannot keep up, sometimes that of a government man who wants to be sure he does not say the wrong thing.

A fisheries biologist by training, Varley has gained a wide range of ecological knowledge in his supervisory position. Elk studies, coyote studies, geology, archaeology, acid rain, elk-gut parasites hopping rides on puffball spores, medical-miracle DNA extracted from the endemic algae-eating flies of Yellowstone's hot springs—you name it, Varley can reel off the findings.

He knows too that biology's facts sometimes rub the wrong way against politics' needful myths. There is one variety of grizzly bear, for example, that lives in policy statements and management guidelines, and another that shits in the woods, and Varley knows the difference. The policy bear conforms to expectations, follows the rules, and moves in an orderly fashion from threatened species to success story. The actual bear—a disagreeably demanding character, with zero sympathy for John Varley or any other sort of human—shows up uninvited at backcountry picnics, smashes through cabin doors, and, with considerable frequency, is denounced on the floors of various legislatures by dim-witted legislators with bad attitudes, bad haircuts, and real power. It has been among John Varley's tasks to reconcile the policy bear, the actual bear, and the flat-topped pols.

The policy bison and the actual bison represent a similar divergence of political need and biological reality, except that the poles are reversed. The actual bison, though predisposed toward goring tourists who crowd his space, is for the greater part a placid and gentle beast who just wants to go where he wants to go. Lately this has included a bit of private ranchland outside the park, some of it in the clutch of a highly aggressive religious cult known as the Church Universal and Triumphant, or C.U.T. (pronounced "cut" by its many non-admirers). The actual bison tends to see barbed-wire fence as something to be placidly walked through, but he is not the malicious vandal that the policy bison is.

The policy bison and the actual bison both carry a disease known as brucellosis, which causes spontaneous abortions in cows—I mean moo-cows, not bison cows. Brucellosis bothers actual bison even less than fences do—most Yellowstone bison carry the disease without getting sick—and cattle do not seem to catch it from them even when the two species are side by side. But in policy bison, brucellosis is an apocalyptic plague, leaping whole jurisdictions in a single bound and hell-bent on the destruction of the livestock industry and the richly romanticized way of life it supports.

Once again, whether for facing down C.U.T. lawyers, cement-headed senators, or importunate enviros, John Varley is the man whom Yellowstone Park turns to when the friction of political need against biological fact ignites trouble. He seems to have that special diplomatic skill of getting everybody to think that they have all arrived of their own accord, and simultaneously, at the right idea.

He has seen the irascible and the screwball and the prima-donna principals of Yellowstone research feud and breed and come and go. Many are gone; he, master of subtle consensus, is still here.

A consensus conclusion, then. The wolf team is going to cut a big hole in the Crystal Bench pen, ten feet wide by four feet high, in the back, where the wolves have spent nearly all their time—their comfort zone, Mike Phillips calls it. The gate at the front will be shut, the cameras and motion sensors moved. Fresh game meat will be left outside, twenty yards out, tied to a tree so the wolves cannot sneak out and drag it back in.

I find the team late that afternoon, sprawled on the ground in the lee of an elephant-sized boulder a couple of miles west of the Crystal Bench pen. A boisterous game of spades is in progress, punctuated with yowls of triumph, groans of defeat, barks of derision. Varley and the rest of the brass may be nursing incipient ulcers back at headquarters, but the biologist bivouac in the Lamar looks like What-me-worry City. Amidst scattered bags of pretzels and cans of Mountain Dew, a radio aerial, headset, and receiver lie close at hand.

The wolf team's gaiety is a little strained, and not unanimous: Steve Fritts leans back against the rock and peers upvalley toward Crystal Bench, his demeanor somber. "Everything these wolves are seeing," he muses, "it's all bound to be so unfamiliar to them. We humans foresee a nice neat sequence—capture, transportation, acclimation, release—and we assume they *must* want freedom. But the human idea is not the wolf idea"—he laughs, without mirth—"obviously. There's no way we can know what their experience is—of the pen, of the hole in the fence, of the world outside." The Crystal Creek wolves have not touched the meat left outside the gate.

Talk turns to possible improvements in the enclosure design. Maybe the pens next year should be smaller. Maybe there should be an automatic gate that is never approached by humans and so will not smell of them. Maybe the shape should be changed. These pens have no corners up which wolves might ladder themselves—so maybe the hole in the fence is not a distinct enough point to be perceived. Who knows?

The card game winds down. It's getting cold. The biologists repair to the big brown Chevy Suburban that the superintendent has lent them in his absence. Mike Phillips, in alpha position at the wheel, cranks the heater up. He is worrying now, too.

Phillips worries a lot. Today it is about a little-discussed but much-considered subject: potential conflicts among the packs. "These pens are very close together, in wolf terms," broods Phillips. "They're bound to meet up pretty soon. That's why we might as well go ahead and open Soda Butte. We don't want one of these packs to have the jump on the others—they might establish a territory and then defend it when other wolves show up."

In two hours hardly a car passes. Where are the curiosity seekers, the wolf haters, the wolf lovers?

I wonder how many of the hordes of tourists who will be here this summer will have even an inkling of the richness of this place and the passions behind the scenes. I wish they could see the "bureaucrats" in this station wagon. I wish they knew the fervor, the seriousness, the humaneness of these guys. I wish they knew the intelligence, the diligence, the sacrifice. I am quite sure that Fritts and Phillips and some of their colleagues could just as easily have been investment bankers or Wall Street lawyers and owned Porsches and custom-made suits and Rolex watches. But Annie Leibovitz is not likely to be taking their photographs for *Vanity Fair* anytime soon, and as soon as the wolf hoopla passes they will probably never be on television again. They do not have the look-at-me fixation that it often seems to take to be famous in our society—thank God.

I wish all those government haters out there could see Yellowstone as it is known by those whose lives are dedicated to trying to understand it. The scar on a tree trunk that dates a fire that swept down a ridgeline 324 years ago. The islands where pelicans will and will not nest. The mathematics of wildlife population variance. The chemistry of the soil. The hydraulics of geysers. Red squirrels caching whitebark pine nuts for grizzly bears to burglarize. Woodpeckers thriving on bark beetles, beetles thriving on forest fire. Such beauty, such intricacy.

A last check of the radio. There is still no movement.

.    .    .

For the third night in a row, in the conference room behind the superintendent's office at Mammoth Hot Springs, there is a sort of vigil, awaiting the return of the biologists and the results of the day. Pizza is ordered sent in. Reporters file their stories by modem. Phone calls home are made. Park staffers, conservation people, writers, filmmakers wander in and out. Mike Phillips drops by, back from the field with a shrug for a report. Doug Smith is still out in the Lamar with the radio, listening to the wolves do nothing.

Yawning sets in. Everybody goes home, or back to some motel.

The unhappy Pathfinder chatters, skips, and groans up five miles of washboard and ice to the cabin I have rented in a strange little cluster of houses, known collectively as Above the Rest, high on a mountainside overlooking the Roosevelt Arch at Yellowstone's north entrance. The cabin ceiling is so low that I, a scant five-nine, can touch it easily with the flat of my hand. Flying ants periodically hatch straight through the carpeting and swarm to the windows, sometimes stopping off to bite me on the back of the neck. On the other hand, you can see elk out the front window, and grizzly bears fresh from hibernation are working up and down the little stream just down the hill.

# *Out*

"Unit one, message oh-one," the radio squawks at 9:04 A.M. This is an automated signal from the motion detectors at the newly cut hole in the Crystal Bench pen. Whenever those sensors fire, they are then inactive for five seconds. Therefore this signal may mean one wolf, two, three, four, five, or six if they moved fast. It may also mean a windfall chute of snow from a tree.

"Unit one, message oh-one," it says again at 10:17, again at 10:24, 10:29, 10:30, 10:35. This is not snow. This is a pack of six wolves.

At a pullout on the Lamar road commanding a distant view of the pen, the biologists loaf the afternoon away, quasi-casually waiting for a sign of the Crystal Creek wolves exploring their new home (or setting out for their old). It is snowing and foggy, so the team cannot see much of anything, and a radio signal will tell you no more than that a wolf is moving and which way.

The team is back in what-me-worry mode, packing rock-hearted snowballs and hurling them across the canyon, competing for distance. The motion detectors have been going off from time to time all day, but telemetry shows the wolves to be still right at the pen. In fact they may well have gone back inside.

It is easy to imagine an explanatory scenario. You and your packmates finally get hungry enough to tiptoe out through the hole in the fence and gobble up the roped-down chunks of deer carcass left for you yesterday—two whole deer's worth, a major bellyful—but there are people out there. Even in this snow and at this distance, you can smell them. So you skedaddle back where you know you are safe, in the Paul Harvey Welfare Hotel.

But still. Why won't they go out and kill something, dammit, and act like wolves?

Actually, I suppose, this *is* acting like a wolf. If I ever needed a lesson in the essential shyness of this creature, here it is.

At four o'clock in the afternoon, with snow still falling heavily, the biologists start hiking up Rose Creek to cut a hole in that pen like the one at Crystal, and to leave a deer carcass tethered outside. They are only partway there when from behind and above them comes a long, low howl.

About a hundred yards away, silhouetted on the ridgeline in the swirling snow and mist, stands Number Ten, looking straight at them and howling without letup. This is definitely territorial behavior. This is *my* mountain, guys.

The men drop the deer carcass and high-tail it down to the road, exulting. Yesterday, the motion sensor signaled that something had gone *into* the pen. Apparently that sensor had been installed backward: what it was really trying to tell us was that Number Ten—the big gray mail-order bridegroom, the wolf we have always known to be the boldest—is free in Yellowstone.

# No News Good News?

While the biologists try to decide what to do next, the Soda Butte wolves remain locked up. Should they try something different? Should they just be patient, open the gate, and wait? After all, Ten left, right out the door. Surely it is just a matter of time. Surely this diffidence, this caution, is good—isn't it?

The ranger who patrols the valley road in the evenings reports that the Sodas are by far the most vocal of the three packs. Every night about seven, they have a great group howl. He believes they howl loudest in bright moonlight. If the moon goes behind a cloud, they fall silent. When the moon comes back out, they resume.

The Soda Butte wolves have been the least observed of the three packs, but when they have been seen, they seem the least bothered. Number Thirteen, for example, the old blue, is the only wolf known to have used one of the closed shelters provided within the pens, and the one he chose was just inside the gate, the last one you would have expected a people-fearing Canadian wolf to select. When Thirteen had his medical examination at Hinton, he was deemed, on the basis of tooth wear, to be much older than all the other wolves captured; maybe old age has promoted in him, as it so often does in humans, a quiet acceptance of life-altering disruption.

Another of the Soda Butte wolves, Fourteen, a gray female, will jump up on top of one of the doghouses to get a better look as people approach with food, and as soon as they are gone she will start digging busily beneath the gate. That will never get her anywhere, thanks to the underground chain-link barrier around the inner perimeter of the pen. Nevertheless, Fourteen's apparent enthusiasm for freedom, especially if she has been crowned alpha by her packmates, may foretell a braver exit for the Sodas than their neighbors downstream have been able to muster.

The wolf team sets up shop early in the morning at the roadside pullout with the view of the Crystal Bench pen. Today the blizzard is over and the air is clear, but even with their powerful telescope, it is hard to make out much at this distance—two miles.

After several hours, they spot five animals together, leaping, rolling, running in circles. "Canids" is the most specific description they allow themselves: typical scientists, they abhor saying anything more than they are sure of. The animals are playing in the snow near the pen. Coyotes? Doubtful. I can say it: wolves.

At Rose Creek, the hand-held antenna and receiver tuned to Number Ten's radio collar tell us that he is still outside the pen, and he has not moved far. The radio also tells us that Nine and Seven are still inside, although the motion sensors have been indicating movement in and out all day long—probably just Ten.

This much we do know: there have been five days of opportunity for the Crystals and four for the Roses, and nobody is on the way back to Canada.

# Dave Mech

The Crystal Bench pack has not budged. The motion detectors have stopped firing. Doug Smith thinks that the wolves have gorged themselves on the two deer carcasses, and are sleeping off a heavy meal—probably back inside the pen.

At Rose Creek, Number Ten continues to move back and forth through the gate, and Number Nine and Number Seven still refuse to venture out. Ten will roam around within a few hundred yards of the pen and then come back. From the ridges he has surely seen the great herds of elk on the valley floor. It sounds to me as though he has been trying to persuade Nine and Seven to show some nerve and join him in this paradise.

Everybody agrees that there is nothing to be gained by opening the Soda Butte pen until somebody figures out what is going on with the other two groups. Dave Mech has arrived; maybe he can think of something.

I have observed that wildlife biologists rather often resemble the animals they study. Grizzly bear biologists tend toward the irascible. The longtime head of the Yellowstone grizzly bear research team is the growling, get-out-of-my-way Dick Knight. Chuck Jonkel, a grizzly bear biologist at the University of Montana, is always in a scrape with somebody. Chris Servheen, the head of grizzly bear recovery for the Fish and Wildlife Service, seems to take a kind of combative glee in his never-ending wrangles with environmentalists. The twin brothers Frank and John Craighead have been fighting the Park Service ever since they were forced out of Yellowstone twenty-five years ago in a dispute over grizzly bears.

Wolves are subtler animals than bears. They prefer social status to raw power, your admiration more than your fear. Mike Phillips, God knows, is an alpha wolf, not by bullying but by strategy. Wolf biologist Bob Ream is a popular professor at the University of Montana, and also an influential state legislator. Ed Bangs claims to have arrived at his height of authority by not caring about anything—very cool. And then there is L. David Mech, the undisputed king of wolf research. John Varley calls him "the alpha of alphas."

As seems so often the case in leaders of real stature, Mech does not fit a simple-minded set of dominance criteria. His appearance is unprepossessing: he is drably dressed, bald, bearded, tall but a little stooped, quick-moving, tightly wound but also calm, with dark, penetrating eyes behind hooded lids. Sometimes he seems a little breathless, scattered, distracted.

The air of distraction is misleading, for it is actually Mech's intensity of concentration that is at the center of his genius. Like a wolf, he is a watcher and a listener. When he sees you, you know you have been *recognized*, and when he listens, you know you have been heard. Often, before he replies to a query, he will say, "That's a good question."

Mech's 1970 book, *The Wolf*, subtitled *The Ecology and Behavior of an Endangered Species,* remains the best single source of information on wolf biology. Luigi Boitani and Mech are co-editing a book that will bring together the last twenty-five years' worth of findings about wolves all over the world. Mech's technical publications far outnumber those of any other wolf researcher. When the first informal discussions of a Yellowstone reintroduction began percolating thirty years ago, it was Mech whom the Park Service called on to appraise the feasibility of the idea. His authority is unquestioned.

I have long been fascinated by the varieties of human success. What kinds of people really get things done in this world? How do they do it? What are the particular personal characteristics that make them effective? Are there essential qualities these alpha people all have in common, or are there only unique combinations with nothing more in common than their effectiveness?

In Mech I see a particular quality of simplicity. In him it seems that all irrelevancy has been pared away. He listens, he watches, he wonders. He thinks. He refines a welter of questions to a fundamental hypothesis. He finds a way to test it. If the answers are unclear, that seems to be fine with him. That just means another opportunity to design some good research, which seems to be his idea of fun.

# *Elk*

Telemetry indicates that the Rose Creek wolves remain in or near the Rose Creek pen.

The Crystal Creek wolves have been moving in and out of theirs, never going farther than a hundred yards or so. Somebody has heard them howling. Have the packs heard one another? What are they saying?

Dave Mech and Doug Smith think that the wolves' shyness is probably a legacy of Alberta, where anything with the smell of people on it could be deadly. And because they could not escape from the people who came to feed them in the pens, Mech says, maybe now, far from becoming habituated to humans, the Yellowstone wolves fear people and their scent all the more.

Mech suggests that a big, easily passable opening, twice as big as the hole at Crystal Bench, be cut in the Soda Butte pen, at the opposite end from the gate, and that the gate itself be left closed. Then, counsels Mech, just be patient. Don't worry. They'll leave in their own good time.

Late in the afternoon, Mech and the wolf team make just such a hole, six feet high, ten wide. They drag a dead deer and a half in from the road on a hand-pulled sled and tie the meat to a tree outside the hole. They hike up a hill from which they can keep watch until dark.

They see various members of the Soda Butte pack approach the opening repeatedly, but the wolves will come no closer than ten to fifteen feet. It has been more than a week since they were last fed, so these wolves are hungry. Finally, in the last fading light of dusk, two wolves, too dim to be identified, slink outside through Dave Mech's hole and feed avidly on the deer.

# The Wariness of Wolves

MARCH 28, 1995

As Mech, Phillips, Smith, and the rest of the team approach Crystal Bench, they hear a wolf howling, and not from the pen. One of the pups is out: he howls eight times in a row, hidden in the trees nearby.

The other five wolves are back inside, but there is what Mech describes as a superhighway of tracks in and out of the existing hole in the pen. The men have come to double the size of the hole, so that it will be as big as the one at Soda Butte, but clearly this opening is big enough already. They tie thirty pounds of fresh deer meat to a tree just outside. The videographer repositions his camera and loads it with fresh tape, which will be good for two hours.

On the way back to the road, Mech finds a winter-killed bull elk. There are at least two sets of wolf tracks in the snow, but the meat has not been touched. Mike Phillips confesses that he would not have left the deer meat at the pen if he had known about this elk, but by now it is too late. Despite Mech's confidence that doing nothing would be best—and despite everyone's knowledge that the increased human activity around the pens may actually be helping keep the wolves afraid to move—no one, typical restless do-something Americans as they are, has had the patience for that, not even Mech himself.

Ten is out prowling up and down the narrow Rose Creek drainage again, though he does not travel farther than the sage-covered ridgetops from which he can still see the pen. The restless biologists go in for a look. There is Nine, still inside, looking agitated. Ten is howling urgently somewhere nearby, out of sight. They do not see Seven—maybe she has ventured out with her stepdad. It is abundantly clear that neither Nine nor Ten is thrilled to have these visitors: she plunges frantically back and forth in the back of the pen, while he, still unseen, howls on and on, a low, baleful moan.

A dead elk lies crumpled in the snow about half a mile downcreek from the Rose Creek pen, surrounded by impatient ravens and surmounted by a feeding bald eagle. There are tracks of some sort to the carcass, but the biologists do not approach it. They want to get away as fast as possible, to alleviate the wolves' very evident anxiety. Hence it cannot be determined today whether the carcass is winter kill or predator kill, nor whether the tracks are wolf.

What are Nine and Ten so anxious about? Is it something to do with the people coming between them and the dead elk? Is it Seven's absence? Is it their separation from each other?

Another possibility: Could Nine already be so far advanced in pregnancy that she has decided to den inside the Rose Creek pen?

Mech is not very optimistic about the wolves' chances of breeding success this year. He recalls a group of four wild wolves he once held for three or four weeks in a pen at the height of the mating season: "There was lots of copulation," he says, "but no pups. On the other hand, this is a much more peaceful situation here, and these wolves have been confined longer than mine were. There seems to be a correlation between the level of harassment wolves have undergone and the length of the proestrous period.* That is, the more harassment, the shorter the time the female will be receptive.

"The suppression of breeding in the subordinate females, you know, in any wolf pack," he goes on, "seems to be primarily a social phenomenon. The dominant female will actively interfere with attempted breeding by any subordinate females in the pack. There's probably a biological component, too. The social suppression actually reduces production of

---

*The proestrous period, or proestrus, is the period immediately preceding estrus, or "heat," the time when a female mammal is most receptive to mating.

hormones in the subordinate females. We don't know very much about this yet—the biochemistry, I mean—but it's going to be an interesting question to explore."

Mech pauses a moment. "I don't want to generalize too much. There's so much variation among wolves, among packs, among populations. Sometimes subordinate wolves do breed successfully. Right here, in the Soda Butte pack, both the older female and the female pup have shown the whole gamut of signs of estrus. It's actually possible that both of them could be pregnant. The high level of nutrition they've had could contribute to a higher probability of breeding success.

"But then against that you've got to weigh the influence of stress. Which factor's going to dominate here? That's an interesting question. We're just going to have to wait and see."

The one thing we know for sure so far, Mech readily agrees, is that these wolves are at the super-cautious end of the wolf behavior spectrum. Mech thinks that the stress of their capture and travel may be a contributing factor. The unfamiliarity of their surroundings may also be repressing their natural curiosity. Yellowstone may be ecologically similar to their home in Alberta, but it looks—and smells, presumably—nothing like Alberta.

In any case, as soon as they finished the deer meat outside their pen last night, the Soda Butte pack apparently fled straight back inside, just like their peers at Crystal Bench.

A frigid silver mist on the Lamar turns pink as the sun drops below the horizon. There is a fresh veil of snow blown in from the southwest, and yesterday's sun-browned hillsides are pale tonight. Seven o'clock comes, and seven-thirty, but the Soda Butte wolves have elected not to comport with the patrol ranger's schedule or my hopes, and the valley is silent.

I seem to recall somebody saying something about howling by people being forbidden, so I am careful to look up- and downvalley for car lights, and I pray there is not some undercover ranger up in the woods with a night-vision scope and a parabolic microphone.

Then I let loose. At a wolf biology conference in Minnesota recently, I heard a large contingent of genuine experts having at it, and while I have yet to hear actual wolves howling, I have heard plenty of recordings. So I do have a certain notion of what I'm supposed to sound like.

Which little resembles the cracking, pitiful moan I actually produce. I try again. A little better, but in the Lamar's stillness and immensity the sound is too small, sort of stifled—the howl of the nebbish.

Then I think I hear a noise from over the ridge to the north. I try to be as still as stone. I strain to hear, and then, without effort, I do hear. There is no mistaking this. This is the sound of wolves—their voices rising, intertwining in crescendo, then a long sostenuto, a slow diminuendo, and now nothing, a vast, enveloping emptiness which itself seems the voice of a living thing.

I do not believe that this howling can be said to constitute an answer to mine, because I do not believe that I was loud enough for the Soda Butte pack to have heard me, and the wind, though light, is exactly wrong. Still, people say dogs' hearing is phenomenal. That of a wild wolf, who needs it more, is surely even better.

The Soda Butte wolves howl again. It is a long, dense, solemn sound, with none of the yipping exuberance of coyotes. This time I recognize the meaning of the granite-dense silence that follows it: it is the context of wolves. Silence in Yellowstone will mean no longer that there are no wolves to howl, but that they are not howling at the moment.

# Prey Image

Does Guinness have a world record for wolves doing nothing? I would like to nominate the Crystal Creek pack.

The Soda Buttes, on the other hand, have hit the ground magnificently. Not only individual wolves are individualists; every pack has its own personality. Is it too soon to conclude that the Crystals are going to be shy, the Sodas bold, the Roses romantics?

Bob Landis, an indefatigable filmmaker who is up before dawn every day to watch the Lamar come to life, saw one of the Sodas this morning crossing the road and then turning east. Now radio tracking confirms that the whole pack has moved east some four or five miles, crossing both the road and the creek along the way, and they are all five back together, on the west slope of the mountain called the Thunderer.

This puts them out of the broad and open part of the valley, and away from the concentrations of wintering elk. Up here, Soda Butte Creek runs along the bottom of a rugged, high-ramparted canyon. With the exception of a few long skinnyish meadows and one big snow-choked one, the surrounding landscape is either heavily forested—mostly with dense, mature spruce and fir, some of it burned into stick-jumble by the famous fires of 1988—or else too rocky and steep to support either trees or wolves.

The 1988 fires roared through here in long narrow channels of flame, creating a sinuous network of openings where baby trees are only now beginning to sprout beneath the skeletal remains of their forebears. These openings are part of an intricate mosaic of plant communities, in continuous flux through the centuries. Not only repeated fires but also insect infestation and disease keep these forests and meadows in constant renewal, with a wide diversity of ages, species composition, and cover density.

In some places in the spruce-fir forest, the shade is dark and constant, and moisture levels remain high all year. Here the vegetation is so thick and lush that both prey and predators can disappear and sleep in peace, and take shelter from bad weather.

In the recently burned patches, the shadowy woodland has been opened to the sun and the full power of winter storms. In these burns the intense winter sun and the savage winter nights have repeatedly melted and refrozen the surface of the snow, leaving a flesh-ripping crust on top of deep powder. Even under what remains of the canopy, the going is hard here, and animals of any sort are scarce in winter.

The only significant winter prey for wolves in upper Soda Butte Creek is moose. Moose are sparsely distributed in the best of circumstances, and these are not the best. Yellowstone's moose depend strongly on old-growth spruce-fir forest in winter, in part because the dense canopy catches much of the snow: getting around in these sheltered woods costs them fewer calories than traveling in deeper snow.

Owing to the heavy accumulation of fuels beneath the ancient trees—decades, even centuries, of dropped needles, dead branches, and fallen trees—the 1988 fires burned especially fiercely in the old-growth forest. Most of the younger forest was spared. Moose therefore have become much less abundant throughout Yellowstone since the fires.

The moose that have survived are the toughest and the healthiest, and such a moose does not have much to fear from wolves unless they manage to corner him, or he founders in deep snow. A healthy adult moose, weighing somewhere between six and fourteen hundred pounds, standing six or seven feet at the shoulder, strong-muscled, sharp-hooved, and quick to take the offensive, is a formidable adversary even for a pack of wolves.

That said, there will always be at least a few who are vulnerable, especially now at this gaunt shank end of winter—the oldest, the youngest, the sick, the starving—and the wolves can be counted on to find such moose in the course of surveying the Soda Butte valley.

Popular belief seems to hold that wolves kill only the weak, and there often seems a certain moral admiration attached to the belief. The fact is that a wolf pack will just as happily kill a healthy mother moose and her two strapping twins as they will some toothless old bag of bones. It is just that the bag of bones is easier to bring down, and a lot less dangerous. If that big healthy moose or one of her calves were entangled in a barbed-wire fence, for example, you would not see much wolf scruple.

Once wolves have worked up a mental map of their surroundings, they develop a network of travel routes that bring them into contact with as many potential prey animals as possible. They will visit and revisit the sites where prey is abundant, checking and rechecking the state of every animal they can find. After a while, they probably know their victims literally individually. They remember how old Bullwinkle looked last week, and they know if he is not looking quite so good today. When he looks even slightly under par, they will chase him a little, see how he does. If he falters, they will get serious.

If a well-aimed nip can open a major blood vessel, the wolves will patiently wait for their dinner to bleed to death. The clean and "humane" kill that some wolf lovers so happily believe in is mostly just a *quick* kill. A quick kill is possible only under certain circumstances. Those circumstances do not have a moral dimension.

There is another wolf characteristic which the sentimentalists like to believe in, and in this case they do so with justification: what the biologists call prey image. As young wolves grow up, their parents and their packmates teach them to hunt, and it seems that some iconic representation of the species they hunt is deeply imbedded in their consciousness thenceforward. The Alberta population from which these wolves were removed was chosen precisely because the wolf prey base there is principally elk, deer, and moose—the same animals they will find in Yellowstone, and in nearly the same proportions, meaning mostly elk.

There are no bison in their old homeland. What will the wolves think when they first encounter one in the Lamar? Or a herd of beef cows and calves out on summer mountain pasture north of the park? The accumulated evidence of wolf study suggests that they will be interested, even intrigued, but they will usually not strike, unless, for example, there are no elk, deer, or other familiar prey to be had. Early in this century, when unregulated commercial hunting had severely reduced the region's wild-game populations, the last of the Yellowstone wolves could sometimes find little other than cattle or sheep to eat. Now there is hardly an acre of land in the Greater Yellowstone Ecosystem that does not offer wild wolf prey.

Some wolves, nevertheless, like some people, will break the rules even when the risk is great and the reason obscure. The wolf reintroduction E.I.S. and all the biology behind it assume a certain level of depredation on livestock. But Yellowstone is not Alberta. There are lots of cattle and sheep not far away. In the twenty counties surrounding Yellowstone, the E.I.S. estimates that there are about 230,000 cattle and 60,000 sheep in midwinter; double that, for their young, in the summertime. These wolves, lacking inherited territories, may be likely to travel farther than more settled packs would. On the other hand, the abundance of wild prey here is so great, why would they even think of leaving?

As Dave Mech says, it's an interesting question, and we're just going to have to wait and see.

What all the experts think likeliest is that the wolves will stick with what is familiar. The main reason the Sodas have come into the heavily forested, deep-snow country of upper Soda Butte Creek may just be that it feels more like home than the intimidating openness of the valley bottoms below.

Their habitat in Alberta consisted almost entirely of boreal forest—boggy bottoms dominated by black spruce and bog birch, and upland forests of white spruce, aspen, and balsam fire. The only openings of significant size were clear-cuts, which these wolves tended to avoid in daylight hours. Before the wolves ever arrived from Canada, Mech was hazarding a hunch that they would not feel comfortable in the wide-open spaces of the main Lamar, despite the presence there of the prodigious herds of elk. Just as wolves have a deep-seated image of appropriate prey, they may also have one of appropriate habitat.

The biologists hike in to their vantage point overlooking the Soda Butte pen. There are no wolves in it. Tracking outward from the pen, the team finds that the Sodas found an elk carcass nearby and all walked up to it, but this meat too, like the winter-killed elk investigated by the Crystals, has not been touched. Wariness is a valuable characteristic in the world they will inhabit, and with wariness the founders of Yellowstone's lupine future are richly endowed. The legacy of Alberta's trappers to Yellowstone's wolves seems to be this: if you eat dead meat, you may be dead meat.

The Rose Creek pen, at last, is empty. Nobody knows where its inmates have gone. The ground-based antennas cannot pick up signals from any of the three wolves' radio collars. Visual tracking shows only that Ten, Nine, and Seven came down Rose Creek together toward the Buffalo Ranch, a cluster of rustic buildings that once served as the headquarters of the effort to save the last bison left alive in North America. The wolves stopped well short of the buildings, turned around, headed upcreek, and disappeared.

If Yellowstone is America's Serengeti, then the Lamar is Yellowstone's Serengeti. Find a promontory at dawn or dusk, and spread before you will be a landscape of Edenic beauty, the great herds moving slowly along the broad valley floor, the scattered groves of aspen, cottonwood, and spruce more perfectly placed than civilization's greatest gardeners could ever have done, the silence more awesome than the most terrible thunder. In winter the cold can be breathtaking—fifty below is by no means out of the question—and the snow is deep. Fifty-mile-an-hour winds are not uncommon, howling up from the Yellowstone canyon, scouring the windward hillsides of powder, laying bare the dry grasses and forbs that make this such superb winter range.

Long ago, the Lamar was the home of a particular race of bison different from their better-known cousins of the Great Plains. According to Mary Meagher's definitive *The Bison of Yellowstone National Park*, the mountain bison was "more hardy, fleet, and wary, and had darker, finer, curlier hair." The mountain bison was once distributed throughout the Rockies and their intermountain valleys, westward into Oregon and Washington, but as early as the eighteen-forties it was gone from most of its ancestral range. Meagher cites a review of the historical evidence, by Gene Christman, suggesting that the extirpation of the mountain bison began when the Indians acquired horses. White folks with guns no doubt accelerated the process.

The Lamar valley was the last place in the world where the mountain bison survived, and in the late nineteenth century even this remnant was being slaughtered—by miners from Cooke City, by professional poachers, by the crews building the big new hotels in the park.

All alone in so small a patch of suitable habitat, Yellowstone's last bison were afflicted by all the merciless ills of insularization: inbreeding depression (that is, lowered reproductive success as a result of lower genetic diversity in the population); random fluctuation of sex ratio and age distribution (so that in some years the number of fertile couplings is drastically reduced); absence of adjacent population from which immigrants might come to compensate for those reductions; absence of adjacent habitat which members of the Yellowstone population might colonize (actually, the habitat was there, it was just gun-infested); random variations in weather and food availability, which have far more severe effects on very small populations than on large ones. This dreadful list could go on, but you get the point. The Yellowstone mountain bison population was doomed to extinction. In 1902, only twenty-three animals were alive.

Sixty-five years later, Robert H. MacArthur and Edward O. Wilson's theory of island biogeography would show that isolated very small populations of any creature are similarly doomed. Understanding island biogeography is critical to conservation in our world of islandlike nature reserves, and toward such understanding, I think every conservation-minded person alive should read David Quammen's comprehensive, sobering, and very entertaining *The Song of the Dodo*.

Yellowstone's managers at the turn of the century knew that their bison were on the way out. Of the mountain bison's lowland kin too, only pitiful remnants survived, mostly in semi-domesticated private herds. With a fifteen-thousand-dollar dispensation from Congress to bolster the dwindling mountain bison herd in the Lamar, Yellowstone Park starting buying Plains bison in 1902, some from a privately owned herd in Texas, some from one in Montana.

At first the mountain bison and the Plains bison in the Lamar were kept separate; the Plains bison were even kept in a corral at night. The area was assiduously patrolled against poachers. Some of the broad valley floor was planted in timothy—a tall non-native grass then thought (erroneously) to be more productive than the short native bunch-grasses—and hay was harvested for winter fodder. Cowboys would round up the bison for vaccination and, ultimately, for culling. The Buffalo Ranch really was a buffalo ranch.

From about 1915 onward, the Plains and mountain buffalo were allowed to intermingle. Were they distinct subspecies? Probably so, even by modern taxonomy's ever stricter standards. In that heedless blending, therefore, something great was lost, both to American culture and to the continent's biological diversity. But think of what was gained, and be happy to gaze out across the Lamar with me, glorying in the sight of those hulking shag-rugged brutes. Were it not for Yellowstone, their kind might have vanished from the earth.

In some places you can still see traces of the hay farming and fences, and timothy has displaced quite a bit of native grass. The Buffalo Ranch compound itself is home to the Yellowstone Institute, where anyone from little kids on up can come to learn about the wonders of the ecosystem—geysers, volcanoes, flowers, waters, mammals. It was at the Institute, in the late nineteen-seventies, that I learned how critically endangered Yellowstone's grizzly bear population was. Until that week of hard-core biology I had been a dreamy fictioneer and poet, a connoisseur (so I deemed myself) of impressions, focused on my own mentation, ignorant of the infinitely beautiful fitting-together of ecology. From that fateful week onward, I knew that I needed be a student again, of nature, of what was known.

Walk out the door of the Institute classroom and you will see some of the best wolf habitat in the world. How many wolves will the Lamar sustain? That depends in great part on which prey they select. There are certainly plenty of elk to get started with. How long will it take for them to learn to kill bison? Better, let's get some already bison-wise wolves. Wood Buffalo National Park, on the far northern plains of Alberta and the Northwest Territories, is loaded with buffalo killers, and so are some of the wide grassy valleys of northern British Columbia. Starting off with wolves with the right prey image could certainly hasten the repopulation of Yellowstone's suitable wolf range. Mike Phillips worries about crowding and inter-pack strife, but the historical evidence, while admittedly sketchy, suggests that a number of wolf packs could coexist in the Lamar alone. God knows there's enough to eat.

Further tracking shows that on their way down Rose Creek, wolves

Ten, Nine, and Seven also visited the elk carcass that the wolf team had been wondering about yesterday. Like both the Sodas and the Crystals, the Rose Creek trio refused to touch what may seem to them to be trap bait. Was it the scent of humans wafting up from the Yellowstone Institute that turned the wolves around?

Then the wolf team discovers that the deer carcass they dropped in such a hurry last week—when they heard and saw Ten howling above them—has been quite thoroughly consumed, and by wolves.

# Effects: Plagued with Badgers

MARCH 30, 1995

To: Mike Phillips
FROM: Tom McNamee
RE: Sighting of Soda Butte wolves

Pam Gontz, of the Yellowstone Institute, and I observed five wolves from approximately 6:40 P.M. to 7:00.

The temperatures, distances, and other figures I cite are all approximate, since we had no measuring devices.

The weather was mild, the temperature approximately 35 to 40 degrees Fahrenheit, wind faint to nil, partly cloudy. Lighting conditions were fairly good, the sun just having set.

Pam spotted the wolves first, and spent the first several minutes getting rid of a known harasser of wildlife who was there with a video camera. He apparently remained unaware of the wolves' presence, and left.

The wolves were first seen lying curled up on the large meadow known as Round Prairie, just downstream from the Pebble Creek campground. The meadow was entirely covered with snow. The wolves were across Soda Butte Creek from us, approximately one-quarter to one-half mile away, at the far edge of the meadow, no more than twenty yards outside the lodgepole forest, perhaps one mile downstream from the bridge. Pam had a window-mounted spotting scope, and I had a pair of 8 × 35 Leitz binoculars. Throughout the period of our observation, the wolves seemed completely unaware of us, and never looked directly at us.

One black wolf was lying alone, and the other four—one black, two gray, and one "blue"—were lying together. Twice, the blue wolf rolled onto his back and wiggled on the snow with his legs waving in the air. From time to time, some of the four wolves would rise and stretch, sometimes touching noses with the others.

The black wolf lying apart remained lying down most of the time. After about fifteen minutes he rose, stretched, sat on his haunches, and lifted his head as though to howl. We heard nothing, however.

A pair of coyotes—one large, with a very dark back, the other medium-sized and quite blond—were moving around on the meadow about one-half mile downstream throughout the period of our observation. They worked their way gradually closer and closer to the wolves. It was not clear to us whether they were within the wolves' line of sight, but at one point one of the wolves rose, sat down, and seemed to be watching them.

After ten to fifteen minutes of little activity besides that described above, the wolves all rose and trotted around, touching noses. Their movements were leisurely, apparently relaxed.

By now the coyotes had come within about one-quarter mile of the wolves. We still could not tell if the wolves and they were visible to one another, but at a certain point the coyotes turned and ran fast downstream—that is, in the opposite direction from the way they had come.

The large black wolf joined the other four for a moment of nose-touching and then trotted downstream (more or less due west, I think) into the trees. One by one, the others joined him, and some were lost from sight. The forest at that location comes down a very steep slope from bare, nearly vertical rock and then extends per-haps twenty yards onto the essentially flat valley floor. The avail-able forested travel corridor, therefore, is relatively narrow, and the trees, which I recall as all lodgepole, are sparse. We could see the wolves from time to time, and I think they did not travel farther than a couple of hundred yards.

Within a few minutes they returned to the site where they had been resting. There was a brief bout of contact again, and then they headed upstream and again into lodgepole forest, again one at a time, each wolf separated from the next by fifty to sixty feet. We saw one wolf sitting at the foot of a tree, and another wolf approached it, and they touched noses. All the wolves then disappeared into the forest.

We waited another ten minutes or so, but we did not see the wolves again, or hear them.

Aerial telemetry begins today, in a leased Piper Super Cub. Mike Phillips and Doug Smith will alternate flying every day that weather allows. From the radio locations of the wolves they will gradually build range maps for each of the packs.

On the first flight, Smith finds the Soda Butte pack about four miles southeast of the pen, upstream and not far from where Pam Gontz and I saw them. The wolves are in plain sight on the snow, not doing anything much. I like this: it suggests that they are comfortable, calm, unintimidated by the broad, open valley and the automobiles that traverse it.

Later in the day, Phillips, Smith, Mech, and two field assistants hike in to the Soda Butte pen. The wolves have apparently been back inside. The biologists follow wolf tracks for about a half mile from the pen to a dead elk. It is unquestionably the work of wolves. The tracks are there, the blood, the rumen moved aside, the right-size tooth marks in the flesh. The Sodas ate no more than 10 percent of the carcass before they moved on. This is the first wolf kill in Yellowstone in more than sixty years.

The Rose Creek wolves also turned up on Phillips's flight, having traveled about fifteen miles north through some stupendously rugged country to the remote headwaters of the Buffalo Fork, a tributary of Slough Creek, which is a tributary of the Lamar. The Roses are deep inside the Absaroka-Beartooth Wilderness, many miles of snow ten feet deep and mountains ten thousand feet high from anywhere that ought to cause concern, but they are indubitably *outside the park*, just as all the wolf haters said they soon would be.

And in fact, the Billings *Gazette* runs a banner across the top of page one, 3 WOLVES SLIP OUT OF PARK—as if they've escaped from prison.

The snowbound fastness of the Buffalo Plateau does seem an odd place for the Rose Creek wolves' first foray, and it could be just a mistake, owed simply to their unfamiliarity with the countryside. On the other hand, this could be the first leg of the long walk home to Hinton. If that is what Nine, Ten, and Seven are determined to do, they are going to have a rough time. They are already at eight thousand feet, well above the winter range of any prey except a few scattered moose, and the going will get worse for a long way before it gets better.

If they continue to follow the Buffalo Fork drainage upstream, they will arrive at a brutally steep col known as Boulder Pass. If they get over that, through powder snow deep enough to swallow a wolf, they will find themselves in an old gold-mining district called Independence, which because of active mineral claims was excluded from wilderness designation when the Absaroka-Beartooth was carved out of the Gallatin National Forest. Being remote, high, and very snowy but still accessible to motor vehicles, Independence swarms with roaring snowmobiles all winter long.

There is nothing for wolves to eat in Independence, either. The snow is too deep for anything but the likes of snowshoe hares and bobcats, neither of which figures prominently in most wolves' diets. Passing quickly through Independence, or more likely skirting it, the Roses would start down the main fork of the Boulder River, a major tributary of the Yellowstone. Virtually the entire upper main Boulder valley, except for the openish bowl of Independence, is made up of steep, thickly forested mountain and canyon, clogged with snow and also, at this time of year, pretty much devoid of wolf prey.

I figure another twenty-five miles of that. Then, where the valley opens up and the uplands become less steep and more grassy, the wolves come at last to elk winter range. By then they will have passed the national forest boundary. They will be in ranch country, on private land.

Specifically, *our* ranch. This place is superlative ungulate winter range. From my front porch I look up southeast toward a grassy mountain that tops out at a single file of gnarled old limber pines along the long narrow crest, just shy of seven thousand feet. The treeless north-facing slope is broad and gentle, and it rarely stays covered with snow for long, for our winter storms are often followed by a chinook—a warm, gusty wind off the face of the mountains. Every year we have at least a few gusts of a hundred miles per hour, and fifty is common. The mountain is an uplifted many-layered sandwich of ancient lake bed, the grassy side being its top and the south side a violent break where a great sheaf of bedrock was pushed upward till it sheared off and a mountain sprang from a plain. This south side is rubble-strewn, steep, in many places sheer cliff, and it is covered with dense, dark Douglas-fir forest. So: on one side you have a windblown grassland—perfect grazing habitat—and on the other you have jumbled rock-and-tree country that rarely sees a human all winter—perfect cover. A half mile farther south lie aspen groves, high meadows, and more dense forest—still more forage and shelter. Beyond that comes the Gallatin National Forest, and only a mile or so inside it the Absaroka-Beartooth Wilderness begins.

Especially in winter, this is a very quiet place. Give an elk herd such quiet, food, cover, and isolation, and they will be entirely happy. That is why I can take my binocs down from their peg almost any day all winter long and look up from my front porch to the spine of Cow Mountain and see a hundred elk or so, mostly cows and last year's calves, some bedded and chewing their cud, some grazing slowly along in the swales.

On the lower slopes, amidst sagebrush, currant bushes, and shrubby cinquefoil, smaller pockets of grass are blasted free of snow, and here hundreds of mule deer find refuge. Still farther down, in the dense thickets of willow, alder, hawthorn, and bog birch that line the river, there are many white-tailed deer, and plenty of beavers to boot. It is a fine place for carnivores.

Our experience with one carnivore, the badger, illustrates how intricate are the surprises to be found in ecology, and how knotty sometimes are the dilemmas faced in ranching. Our most beloved horse was a quiet-spirited, elderly gentleman whose given name was Prince but whom we called Alpo because we had rescued him from a one-way trip to the cannery. Alpo was a paint, with a white face. White-faced horses often have eye problems, and Alpo did. When his eyes got foggy and gooey, we would paint around his pink eyelids with a bright purple medicine. This made him look like a clown, and we loved him all the more.

When we let the horses into the pasture at sundown, they thunder through the corral gate in a swirling cloud of dust, tossing their heads, biting, kicking, dodging, bumping, celebrating their freedom and imminent dinner. One afternoon, galloping gamely along with his juniors, Alpo caught his foot in a badger hole and broke his leg.

Our ranch manager put a bullet in Alpo's head. With tears streaming down his face, he wrapped a heavy chain around Alpo, hooked it to the tractor, and dragged him a mile or so to the top of a ridge. As the chokecherries ripened over the next few weeks, so did Alpo's corpse. The black bears came down out of the mountains as they do every year at berrying time, and followed their noses to the great reeking bonus. The coyotes found him too, and the ravens and magpies, and the golden eagles. Thus Alpo was recycled into the ecosystem that had sustained him.

Our next-favorite horse was a big, strong, dutiful gray. Ghost stood just under sixteen hands, but you could put a twelve-year-old greenhorn on him with confidence. The next summer, Ghost also broke his leg in a badger hole.

Why, all of a sudden, were we plagued with badgers? The proximal reason was an irruption of their principal prey in these parts, the Richardson's ground squirrel, called gopher hereabouts. But what caused that? Was it simply a cyclical event? Many rodent populations do undergo extreme fluctuations. That may have been part of it, but there also turned out to be a human component.

In a small pasture, horses will severely overgraze certain patches of grass while leaving others untouched. The close-cropped patches make ideal ground squirrel habitat. Papa gopher can stand at the entrance to the family burrow and spot a predator coming from a long way off. Each father stands sentry on his doorstep. Comes a coyote out of the brush or a hawk out of the sky or a bobcat fading through tall yellow grass, up goes a sharp whistle and everybody dives down the holes.

Ground squirrels tend to choose very hard, dense dirt in which to make their homes, so most predators cannot easily dig them out. But the badger was designed to eat ground squirrels: Ms. Badger simply claws her way in, sending dust, clods, and rocks flying. When she finds a hole she particularly likes, she remodels it to her liking and sets up housekeeping.

Overgrazing had created perfect conditions for a ground squirrel explosion, which was naturally exploited by their chief predators, badgers—more of whom, being better fed, were surviving than previously. Hence more big badger holes, hence more dead horses. It was our own damned fault.

We invited some local boys to come on over with their twenty-twos. Nearly every dawn or dusk, we would hear the echoing *pop-pop-pop* of kiddie fusillade. Then I realized something. Who stands at the gopher house threshold? Papa. Mom and the kids are down in the hole. By singling out the dads, you increase the available forage for their families, but you have not hurt the system of mutual defense, because enough males to stand guard duty will always survive. With more to eat, more baby gophers survive to breeding age. Worse yet, better nutrition means larger litters. Most of the males are surplus, because one male can easily sire a number of families. As every fish and game department knows, removing some large percentage of the males actually increases the size of the population.

Which in turn increases badger food, and thereby badger numbers. And you will never be able to shoot out a badger population, simply because they stay so well hidden. The only thing you can do is set traps or dangerous poisons, and this we declined to do.

The only way to stem the tide, then, was to nail the mother gophers. But how were you supposed to get at them? We hired a consultant. He sold us scary-looking canisters of poison gas, which he assured us would be harmless to dogs, cats, and us. Pull pin, toss down hole, plug hole with dirt, and good night, gophers. But the gas canisters failed about half the time. About half the other half, the gopher would scoot off into some side burrow and pop up for air ten feet away.

Finally we started rotating our horse grazing into bigger pastures. The old pasture is resting now, the grass is tall, and the ground squirrel population has plummeted. Most of our badgers have left, or starved.

The ecological consequences of wolf predation here will surely be just as complex. If wolves reduce the numbers of ungulates, we will see widespread changes in vegetation. Elk and deer die in late winter in considerable numbers, and their carcasses, like Alpo's, are recycled into coyote et al. If wolves are taking the dying elk before they die, for example, isn't the resultant reduction in carrion likely to reduce coyote numbers? Besides, wolves are known to kill coyotes. If coyotes are reduced, might there not be more of their prey, such as ground squirrels—meaning perhaps more foxes, more raptors, and oh, Lord, more badgers?

Wolf reintroduction responsible for an increase in broken horse legs? And the dead horses then improving bear nutrition and thereby increasing bear litter size and cub survival? At that extent of remove from direct effects, it is impossible to make accurate predictions, but such and so far-reaching are the branchings and twinings of natural forces.

As far as we are concerned, wolves are welcome at the ranch. I would dearly love to win the five thousand bucks that Defenders of Wildlife is putting up for the first private land owner to host denning wolves. I'm not so sure, though, how hospitable my neighbors will feel. No sooner is the news out that the Rose Creek wolves are out of the park than busy gab comes racing up the Boulder valley, up the West Boulder, up the East Boulder, back to Big Timber, Livingston, Springdale, Greycliff, Wilsall, Clyde Park, and points north: here they come, we told you so. Better haul that dusty old rifle down from the rack in the pickup and clean her up good.

# And About Time, Too

The Crystal Creek wolves are out of the pen.

Well, all but one. Mom, Dad, and three of the lads have moved four or five miles due south, over the top of Specimen Ridge and into the Yellowstone Grand Canyon country, a nice lonesome place to be a wolf pack. They do not seem to have killed anything yet, but there are plenty of wobbly winter's-end elk around.

Number Two, the black-and-silver pup, is still hunkered down in the pen. The biologists hike in yet again, to enlarge the existing hole in the fence and cut another. They accomplish the first half of the mission, and while they are working on the second, young Two strolls out the original hole and heads south, apparently on his family's trail.

From the Super Cub, Phillips spots the Sodas within forty yards of what looks to be a bison kill.

The Roses have settled in on the Buffalo Fork, having moved only half a mile since yesterday.

Park e-mail: "ALL WOLVES ARE OUT OF THE PENS."

# A Theft

Mike Phillips flies over the Sodas' kill again, and there is a big old grizzly bear on it, thrashing around in the deep snow, trying to wrestle the carcass back into the trees. Phillips sees the wolves, too, only thirty or forty yards away, watching. Despite their numerical advantage, the Sodas are evidently unwilling to dispute the bear's arrogation of their property.

At several of the E.I.S. hearings, wolf opponents put forward the argument that in restoring the threatened species *Canis lupus* we would be endangering another, *Ursus arctos horribilis*, by reducing the supply of carrion and prey. Winter-killed and winter-weakened ungulates provide much of the nutrition available to Yellowstone grizzlies fresh out of hibernation in the spring, when most plant food is yet to appear. Even as late as June, no berries have ripened, and few roots and corms have stored their energy for the winter to come. The great spawning runs of cutthroat trout begin only toward the end of June. But the elk give birth in June, and grizzly bears prey extensively on the calves.

Also, by June nearly all of the weak, the sick, and the starving have been culled from the elk population. The survivors are the strong, the well fed, the fit—the elk least vulnerable to attack by predators. In June, therefore, wolves too will turn to the calves. The anti-wolfers' hypothesis was that because wolves in general are more effective predators than bears, the wolf would profit at the bear's expense.

The biologists tend toward the contrary hypothesis: they think the remains of wolf kills will probably benefit both grizzly and black bears. There are, they contend, far more herbivores here than are needed to feed so few carnivores. Admittedly this kill on Amphitheater Creek is only one instance, but it certainly does seem that the Soda Butte wolves have done old Ephraim a major favor.

In Ephraim's honor, Mike Phillips, Mark Johnson, and Doug Smith elect to postpone snowshoeing in to analyze this particular kill.

Nine, Ten, and Seven are still holed up in the frozen wasteland of the Buffalo Fork. Whether they have gotten around to killing anything yet, or eating at all, is not known, but there is no sign of it.

Pup Two seems to have lost what little nerve he has shown. Now that the intruding biologists have quit making a ruckus at Crystal Bench, he has given up the pursuit of his family and returned to the pen.

The rest of the Crystals, still on the south side of Specimen Ridge, continue to uphold the family tradition—doing nothing, going nowhere.

# So Far, So Good

After each telemetry flight, the wolf team sends specific wolf locations to Jim Halfpenny, a freelance wildlife biologist headquartered in Gardiner, Montana. One block uphill from the motel-and-souvenir strip that is Gardiner's main street lies a narrow gravel lane of close-packed little bungalows, locally known as Dogshit Alley. Halfpenny's dwelling here is a shadowy warren of precariously stacked boxes of files, slides, maps, diskettes, God knows what-all. Halfpenny himself, with his long, lank black hair, dark penetrating eyes, and big bushy beard, looks like something just arrived via time machine from a Civil War field tent.

Halfpenny enters the wolf team's radio-location data into a spreadsheet program called Quattro Pro, which I always thought was for stuff like making financial projections but which in Halfpenny's hands produces maps of wolf home ranges. As more data arrive, the maps grow in complexity and precision.

As I study them I realize that what Mike Phillips calls "northeast" or "south" may only roughly resemble the bearings on Jim Halfpenny's maps. Today's report says, "Soda Butte—drifted to the north. Were last seen on the east slope of Mt. Hornaday (3–4 miles to the northeast of their acclimation site)." The map shows the east slope of Mount Hornaday to be very slightly east of *due north* of the Soda Butte pen. In a way it is comforting to know that somebody with the impervious self-confidence radiated by Mike Phillips can occasionally err.

The Crystals are off their duffs at last. They have come back over Specimen Ridge and returned to the Lamar valley. Are they looking for Two? If so, he will be easy to find. He is still at (or in) the Crystal Bench pen.

But the Crystal pack travels on past the pen and upstream. Above its confluence with Soda Butte Creek, the Lamar rises into the winter silence of the backcountry, hidden from the sight and deaf to the noise of the road to Cooke City. The Crystal Bench wolves push upstream through deep snow. They settle in on a high ridgetop between two of the upper Lamar's tributaries, Cache Creek and Calfee Creek, by now eight thousand some-odd feet above sea level.

The Crystal wolves have approached at least three winter-killed elk, but they have touched none of them. It is possible that they have made a kill or scavenged a carcass that has not been discovered, but chances are, given the snow cover, that any significant feeding site would have been noticed on one of the overflights. It is also possible that the Crystals' caution—or stress—remains so extreme that they are just not ready to dare killing or feeding yet.

The Rose Creek wolves have hardly budged from their redoubt in the upper reaches of the Buffalo Fork. Could it mean anything that they seem to be resting at almost exactly the same elevation as the Crystals at Calfee Creek?

The movements of all these animals could hardly be more pleasing to the biologists and park managers. Yellowstone's new wolves are all being very careful. They are not streaming north; they are all still within the physiographic limits of the river drainage in which they were released. They are *here*.

# *Territory*

Mike Phillips is worrying again, this time about intraspecific aggression: war within the species, between the Yellowstone packs. All sorts of combat combinations are possible among the wolves wandering this new world. The packs are not very far apart, and unrelated groups of wolves often regard one another somewhat less than cordially. If a resident pack with an established territory can kill a trespassing wolf, they (usually) will.

Here, we cannot yet speak of resident packs or territoriality. In the short time they have been out running around, all these wolves seem just to be exploring, trying to figure out where they are. The repetitive and systematic scent-marking and boundary patrols that characterize territory maintenance have not been seen. If territoriality is defined as defense of a home range against conspecifics, and there are no other wolves nearby to do the trespassing, can there be said to be a territory at all?

This is not a simple question. For starters, our very definition of territoriality may be wrong. Wolves may start feeling possessive soon after they have begun to occupy a new home range and well before they have settled down to the business of marking the boundaries. Colonizing— when wolves disperse naturally from existing territories to unoccupied but not far-distant land—may be quite different from the artificial, long-distance, and non-voluntary move that our Yellowstone wolves have undergone. There are no precedents for what is going on here. Nobody has ever transplanted three packs of wild wolves to a completely unfamiliar place far from their homes.

Of the three original groups, the Soda Butte pack is so far the one whose behavior seems closest to territorial. They have been moving rapidly up and down Soda Butte Creek, making kill after kill, eating a little of each, then moving on, but never very far. Their movements suggest that they are finding plenty of nutrition within the bounds of this little valley. Because prey availability is probably a prime determinant of territory size, it may be that the Sodas' eventual territory will not have to be very big. That in turn could mean that a good many packs could fit into the Northern Range. As for now, is the Soda Butte pack prepared to defend its creek and valley if other wolves blunder by? Would any of the packs consider the propinquity of one of the others an offense this early in their own residency?

Phillips worries that these questions may be coming to a test. Sometime between last night and this morning, the Rose Creek alpha pair has come down out of the Buffalo Fork and back into the park. This is a relief—you can read it in the shallowing of the crease between Phillips's eyebrows—but it puts the Roses within possible fighting range of other wolves. Also puts me out of the running for Hank Fischer's five thousand bucks.

Nine and Ten have split off from Seven, or she has from them. The pair has moved eastward, upstream, along the Lamar, away from the road and into the valley of Cache Creek, a twenty-three-mile trip in the dark. They are now within howling distance, and probably smelling distance, of the Crystals, who remain on the ridge between Calfee and Cache Creeks. Any confrontation between these packs would be a very uneven match—two wolves against five.

As for Seven herself, she is moving closer and closer to the pen at Crystal Bench, where Two, the solo pup, has been whiling away day after day doing absolutely nothing. But as Seven approaches, Two chooses the same moment to leave the pen. He has traveled only about two miles, but he is gone. Might he and Seven make a match? Whatever my romantic hopes for them, I have to admit that their first meeting could fall somewhat short of love at first sight.

The Sodas are not far from either the Crystals or the Roses. They have killed another elk near their pen, and they remain in mid-valley of Soda Butte Creek, on the south slope of Druid Peak—a grand total of seven miles from the other two packs, a leisurely one-hour trot.

The pen spacing was always a little uncomfortable for Doug Smith. "We knew they were bound to meet up," he says. "They've undoubtedly heard one another howling. So interpack aggression has always been a possibility. There's nothing we can do now but watch and see what happens."

My guess is that in the absence of established territories, the wolves will not risk mortal combat. After all, isn't war nearly always about real estate? If they do meet, there could be some bluffing, some aggressive display, but especially given the disparity of pack size between the five remaining Crystals and the Rose Creek duo, I am trusting that discretion will prove the better part of any valor shown. Trusting indeed—hoping is more like it, on the basis of sheer sentiment.

On the other hand, I am also wishing for some behavior that could be read as territorial, for territoriality and the bearing of pups are closely associated. Alpha female wolves with established territories tend to locate their dens in the very center of them. As the birth date approaches and the mother-to-be holes up, her packmates' defense of the territorial perimeter rises in intensity. The wolves sniff their way diligently around the edges, freshening their own scent marks and checking for those of others, especially other canids. When they come upon a yellow spot in the snow and it tells them a coyote was here, or a fox, or another wolf, they will pee all over it, obliterating the signature. What all can they read in a scent mark? Species, certainly. But does it also tell them sex, age, status, mood, personality? It is possible. We, toolmakers and talkers, cannot imagine what it is like to live in a world in which so much communication is done through the sense of smell.

Protection of the vulnerable newborns and their nursing mother is a basic function of the pack. Laying down a territorial boundary and allowing no foe to cross it obviously helps to insure maximal pup survival. As long as the subordinate members of the pack are closely related—and they almost always are aunts, uncles, cousins, or siblings to the pups—helping the pups is good for everybody. The principle known in evolutionary biology as inclusive fitness tells us that when those non-reproducing wolves promote the welfare of their relatives, they also promote the passing on of at least some of their own genes.

How, then, can we explain the fact that packs sometimes take in completely unrelated newcomers and treat them like homefolks? This remains a mystery. It may be that there are certain circumstances in which a pack feels it needs another body or two. Or maybe they sometimes just like somebody—especially if that somebody seems to represent a potential complement. Certainly we see something like the same thing in humans—seeking in the loved one the pluses to sum out one's own minuses, and so forth. So if pack formation in some way emulates pair formation, then the occasional induction of a well-qualified nonrelative could make perfectly good and ordinary genetic sense. Of course, so can murdering the competition.

After the pups are weaned, usually about the end of May, their pack-mates will be bringing them premasticated prey meat, which they regurgitate in front of the pups or sometimes right down their little gullets. (Have you ever noticed how weanling puppies nibble and nuzzle at their moms' lips?)

Through the spring and summer, when the pups are growing fast and have so much to learn, the pack's life focuses on their protection and education. As soon as the pups are old enough to leave the den, their mother will usually take them somewhere else—one at a time, by the scruff of the neck—to what is called a home site or rendezvous site, and the rest of the pack ups and follows. From time to time, she will call for a move to another home site. The main purpose must be to keep the pups a moving target, but there is probably also an education in geography going on. Several times a day, the whole family will gather at the rendezvous site for a festive bout of howling. If any pack members have wandered off, the music from home will call them back.

As the pups grow bigger, the demands on the hunters do too, and nutritional stress can cause social stress. The bigger the pack grows, the less there is per share at any given kill. Hence as the young mature or as pack size grows, antagonism in the family increases. As household antagonism increases, so then does dispersal of subordinates. The social bond in larger packs seems to be weaker than in small ones—another encourager of dispersal from crowded homes. Larger packs also tend to behave more aggressively toward non-members, limiting the chances of would-be adoptees and thereby keeping pack size down. The experiments of the German biologist Erik Zimen with captive wolves have shown that intra-pack strife increases as hunger rises; consequently, big packs should be more common where food is more abundant, and when food is short, pack size should fall. Conversely, when food is abundant, litters are bigger and a higher proportion of the young are likely to survive.

The system is socially nifty, but for an individual wolf forced out it must be devastating. Social anxiety is probably a gnawing constant in the lives of all but the securest of wolves. And unless sudden death gets them first, even those prideful alphas' day of reckoning and rustication will come. A beloved uncle like Thirteen develops arthritis or gout, and he's out the door.

Where the principal prey animals are big and abundant, then, wolf packs can be quite large, ranging occasionally up to twenty members or so. There does seem to be a ceiling, however, at about that number. Because the pups of the year represent the best investment of the alpha pair's energy, the lowest-ranking non-pup members will be first to be forced out of the pack as food supply dwindles or the pack grows excessively big. And as the size and social structure of the pack vary, so will the boundaries of their territory.

The more unpredictably the territorial boundaries vary, the more likely becomes strife between packs. Imagine a newly colonized piece of wolf range with very abundant prey—like the Lamar. With plenty to eat, the packs grow rapidly larger, and new packs form every year, until their territories blanket—maybe I should say quilt—all the available habitat. Food remains abundant, but space grows short. Dispersers are hounded to outlying and inferior habitat or are killed for trespassing on other packs' territories. Aggressive, expanding packs steal land from their weaker neighbors.

Much, obviously, is missing from this picture—most significantly, the human influence on wolf distribution. That is to say, guns, traps, poison, eighteen-wheelers. Oh, and Animal Damage Control.

.　.　.

Night in the upper Lamar. The Soda Butte wolves are howling. The Crystal Creek wolves are howling. The Rose Creek wolves are howling. The packs are announcing themselves to one another. They do not meet, they do not fight.

# Spring in the Lamar

April 4, 1995

Fluffy wind, fluffy clouds, wisps of white cirrus above them: all of a sudden it is blazing spring in the Lamar. Snowmelt races down pale creases in the sage-gray hills, pooling in bison-churned mud on the flat. Overnight there are swaths of green so green it looks fake. Half blinded by conjunctivitis (a persistent problem for wild sheep in Yellowstone) six rheumy-eyed bighorns stumble along a bench above the road, kicking occasional rocks over the cliff below, one of which, as I lollygag at the junction of Soda Butte Creek and the Lamar River, damn near brains me. Spring's first butterfly flutters by.

The hunting conditions could hardly be better for wolves: green, steep sun-warmed highlands to lure elk out of the somnolent forest, deep crumbly snow on the wide valley floor to chase elk into.

The Soda Butte pack has withdrawn from the crowded ridges of the upper Lamar and returned to the vicinity of their pen. On the trail to Trout Lake, they have shown again today how easy to catch and bring down some of these pitiful elk can be. There is hardly a sign of struggle in the snow. The broad smear of blood extends perhaps twenty yards, ending at the twisted carcass of a yearling bull. Again the Sodas have eaten only some of the carcass before moving on—no more than a quarter.

Do wolves kill for pleasure, as the wolf haters bray? We cannot know if pleasure is what they feel, but we can plainly see that if the opportunity presents itself, wolves will sometimes kill more than they need.

As green growth appears, elk must undergo a transformation of their digestive chemistry: their winter diet of desiccated vegetable matter is rapidly supplanted in spring by fresh green plants, and a whole new set of digestive enzymes must come into play. The cost of that changeover drives many of them into irremediable energy debt. The resulting weakness and lowered immunity often lead to a ghastly ulcerative disease known as necrotic stomatitis, which destroys its victim's digestive ability—effectively starving the elk to death. Just when it looks to the sympathetic human eye as though the grazers' nutritional fortune is taking a turn for the better, they wizen and wobble and stumble and fall. Wolves can kill such elk with hardly any risk to themselves. They need eat no more than their favorite morsels, for there is plenty more just around the corner.

In mid-valley an emaciated old bull lies on his side with his nose skidded into the mud, heaving his last few breaths in heavy mud-bubbles. Come night and morning, his substance will enter that of coyote, raven, magpie, grizzly, and the legions of microscopic diners on the dead. The Sodas gaze down from the forest at the valley edge, sated to the groaning point.

At the instant life leaves him, the elk's form seems to flatten, to shrink. Gravity is sinking him already toward the center of the earth. His flesh lies looser and thinner over the harp of his ribs. Air and moisture have new jobs to do, elsewhere. His great gold shape becomes a shape of the land.

Seven is still on her own, and has revisited the Rose Creek pen. Timid Two has not yet had the nerve to strike up an acquaintance, though he does remain nearby—and has traveled another two miles. Go, Two!

The Crystal Creek five and the Rose Creek pair remain only a hump of rock apart—the former near the mouth of Calfee Creek, the latter on the south slope of Mount Norris—and Doug Smith wears an untroubled smile. Smith has seen how quickly things can go bad when wolf numbers are low. As Dave Mech's research assistant, studying the wolves of Isle Royale National Park, in Lake Superior, he was witness to a catastrophic outbreak of disease and social disintegration that led nearly to the collapse of that world-famous wolf population. It was another classic example of the island effect: Isle Royale is separated from the nearest mainland, northeastern Minnesota, by twenty miles of frigid water. Northeastern Minnesota was the last great redoubt of the wolf in the lower forty-eight United States, and it continues to sustain a large and thriving wolf population. Minnesota could easily supply Isle Royale with dispersers if an ice bridge formed between the island and the mainland—which is precisely how the existing wolf population was founded, in 1949—but Lake Superior, though it never gets anywhere near warm, freezes only rarely, even in the depth of North America's meanest winters.

Wolf inbreeding on Isle Royale is extreme. Not only have the wolves been genetically isolated for almost fifty years, the entire population seems to have descended from a single female. Another effect of inbreeding can be lowered immunity to disease, as the repertoire of antibodies in the population declines over time. Canine parvovirus appeared on the island in the early nineteen-eighties, probably carried by an illegally brought pet dog, and the wolves of Isle Royale had never been exposed to the virus, or at least this variety of it. Larger wolf populations can adapt to parvo over time, and can carry it without getting sick, but on Isle Royale it wiped out or severely reduced several pup crops in a row, and the population plummeted. Perhaps because of all that stress, the social structure of the affected packs went to hell too.

Occasional drastic disruption of pack structures is an inevitable fact of wolf life, and in large populations the ample supply of possible new combinations allows wolf society to build new structures rapidly. But in small populations, disruption can lead fast to disaster. Inter-pack warfare, if it involves, for example, the killing or disabling of an alpha wolf, can cause a pack to disintegrate. In the new and strange landscape of Yellowstone, no matter how good the food supply may be, the loss of social stability, and of the food-getting prowess it enables, could stymie the successful rearing of a new generation. With only three packs, Yellowstone cannot afford that.

Isle Royale has given us not only the world's best-known wolves but also some of its best wolf science and some of its best wolf scientists. Durward Allen began the wolf study there in 1957, well before the invention of the radio collar, and his work culminated in the classic book *Wolves of*

*Minong*, which reviews over twenty years of Isle Royale study. Allen's first and best-known student was Dave Mech, whose doctoral dissertation was "The Ecology of the Timber Wolf in Isle Royale National Park." Rolf Peterson was Allen's last student; Peterson has been in charge of the project for the last twenty-two years. Doug Smith in turn is Rolf Peterson's protégé. Isle Royale's wolves are not its only dynasty.

Smith's interest in wolves began when he was twelve years old. When he hit fifteen, he wrote to Mech asking to help. Mech replied with a form letter. Smith persisted: his last six weeks of high school were spent on a wolf project. Summers during college, he worked for Rolf Peterson on Isle Royale. His senior thesis at the University of Idaho was on wolf pack leadership. He went on to a master's on Isle Royale's beaver population, with Peterson as his major professor. When Mike Phillips hired Smith away from the University of Nevada, Smith lacked only a little more work for his doctorate—but when you get a call asking you to be the chief biologist on the Yellowstone wolf reintroduction project, well, the beaver Ph.D., can wait.

Spring comes only fitfully to the Lamar. Snow tonight trumps this morning's bluebird and butterfly. Beneath the snow, however, grass is seeking the sun, flower buds are forming, worms are working the soil. These revisitations of winter are only delays.

This is the time of year when prey is most vulnerable, and being a wolf is easiest. It will be somewhat harder come summer—feeding a growing family, chasing and killing better-fed and therefore more vigorous prey, defending territory against the young wolves forced out of other packs with the arrival of new pups—but not very hard. Nothing compared to being an elk, who has to be out there hour after hour, chewing, chewing, watching his back every second. Being a wolf, as long as you are spared human persecution, is really a pretty easy job all year long, and nowhere more so than in the abundance of Yellowstone. Once a week, maybe, you have to go to work. The rest of the time, you sleep, you play, you mess with your buddies, you sing.

They are singing tonight in the snow.

# Mike Phillips

The weather is bad, and flying inadvisable. Mike Phillips blithely ignores the nearly ceaseless ringing of his phone, letting his message tape fill up. Like Mech, Phillips is a man who can *concentrate*—another get-it-done guy. His ruling manner is intensity. I note his big biceps, how he grips the arms of his chair as he talks. I wonder how sharp those elbows may be. To land the job as head of the red wolf reintroduction program in North Carolina, he worked according to a carefully constructed plan for eighteen months. He was still a graduate student. It was the first full-time job he had ever had.

"It was time to introduce myself to the real-world players," Phillips says, "and by God, we got it done." He downplays the redneck rage that still afflicts that program. "Sure, we made mistakes. But what we did there is what we're doing here: adaptive management. You learn, you flex. I mean, we're doing something that has never been done before. We don't know what's going to work and what isn't. We make educated guesses." He shrugs. "We learn."

The wolf project is quartered in a little house between a Park Service dorm and a trailer court, some miles and well uphill from park headquarters at Mammoth Hot Springs. The physical distance perfectly expresses the psychological distance. Phillips does not look comfortable in a National Park Service uniform. But he is a Park Service employee, and down the hill he does have a supervisor, Wayne Brewster, assistant director of the Yellowstone Center for Resources. Brewster is John Varley's lieutenant and is generally thought of as the master strategist who moved this project step by step through an ultra-cautious bureaucracy.

Brewster's demeanor is stern; he smiles rarely, hiding his wicked sense of humor. Back when he was an endangered species biologist for the Fish and Wildlife Service, he wore a gigantic handlebar mustache and drove a mean-hombre motorcycle, but the mustache has now assumed the trim dignity commensurate with his position at the nation's flagship national park, and he drives a Subaru. (He does, however, keep a red Thunderbird in reserve for special occasions.) Brewster looks right at home in the green uniform. His pants are perfectly creased, and his shoes are shined.

Phillips's phone rings yet again. This time he picks it up, for it is Brewster. I can hear only Phillips, of course, and I don't know what they are talking about, so I concentrate on mood, inflection, body language. Phillips's voice slows and grows deeper. His diction and syntax are formal, almost memolike. He is disagreeing with Brewster about something, very politely. He radiates tension. When he puts down the phone, his body unclenches, in a long silent exhalation. He looks at me with a tentative thin smile. We understand each other. Mike Phillips is going to get his way again.

Brewster and Phillips work together toward an entirely mutual goal, and they do so with punctilious civility, but Phillips was obviously born not to knuckle under to a boss, especially one as bosslike as Brewster. Brewster expects his subordinate to be subordinate, while Phillips sometimes skates close to the edge of insubordination. Two alpha males in one territory about sums it up.

# In the Field

The snow is too gunky to ski on, so the wolf team snowshoes up Amphitheater Creek to investigate the bison kill. When snow conditions are like this, you end up collecting great clotted gobs of it on top of your snowshoes, and soon your shoes can weigh ten pounds apiece. As Mike Phillips, Doug Smith, and Mark Johnson struggle up the last steep bank to their truck, they are drenched with sweat and panting so hard they can hardly talk.

Phillips is a little abashed. There was prominent press coverage last weekend about the first bison killed by Yellowstone wolves. Well, the bison turned out not to be a bison. Nor a moose. From the air, Phillips's pilot had reasoned that any carcass that a big grizzly bear had to work so hard to move could only have been one of those two, more likely the former. But it was only an elk, a calf at that. And now we know the real reason the grizzly had to wrestle and thrash around so furiously to move it—this rotten snow.

The team is in a hurry, late for a rendezvous down the road with the Mexican wolf recovery team. That is Mexican wolf, not Mexican team. These are Americans, soon to be reintroducing the thin and rangy Sonoran subspecies of the gray wolf to the American Southwest.

The U.S. Fish and Wildlife Service considers that race of wolf to be extinct in the wild, in both Mexico and the United States. The writer and wildlife authority Doug Peacock, however, believes that there are still a few wild ones out there, on private ranchland in the Mexican state of Sonora. If that is so, the capture of even one wild Mexican wolf would be an immense genetic gift to the recovery of the subspecies. There are only a few in captivity, and their genetic diversity is very limited, so the Mexican wolf team's margin of error is going to be extremely narrow: if the release of the captive Mexican wolves into the wild should go poorly—specifically, if early mortality is high—inbreeding among the surviving wolves could doom the subspecies. The reintroduction of the Mexican wolf does not have the luxury of the Yellowstone project's all-but-infinite supply of Canadian wolves; the Mexican wolf release must work the first time out.

The Mexican team and the Yellowstone team hike in together to visit the Soda Butte pen. The visitors are interested in every detail. How much chewing on the wire did the wolves do, and how much injury was there as a result?

Some, and some, replies Johnson.

How much helicopter time was needed to get the materials in?

All of one day, even using a gigantic freight helicopter. It was *very* expensive.

Did the wolves use their shelters?

Only one, Thirteen, the blue. He used the doghouse right next to the gate.

Did the pens really have to be a whole acre in size?

Phillips thinks they could be a lot smaller next year. You could use the salvaged materials then to make a fourth pen.

Any thoughts on the wolves' reluctance to leave?

For next year, they are thinking of putting in a second door, which no human ever approaches and which can be opened by remote control. That way, the exit could be kept free of human scent.

Did anything ever get zapped by the electric wire around the perimeter?

Nobody knows for sure, but the evidence speaks for itself: neither blundering bison nor ravening bear chose to invade. A fence that keeps out such notorious gate-crashers as those is a serious fence. A red fox did manage to get into the Soda Butte pen somehow, in February, and the wolves ate him like a bonbon.

Next on the agenda is another Soda Butte kill, another yearling elk. One party hikes in from the southwest, led by longtime Yellowstone biologist and educator Norm Bishop. Bishop has devoted most of his life for the past ten years to promoting the wolf reintroduction, even under strong pressure to find something else to do, in the Reagan-Watt dark ages. He has focused particularly on schoolchildren, to the dismay of many a ranch family. Bishop is a marathon runner; he pushes his body to the limit—also his luck. Like other long-timers of the Yellowstone Park elite, Norm Bishop is a survivor. He also knows his wind and his snow-drift formation patterns, and his group, on the way to the wolf kill, strolls across windswept open ground. We others follow Mike Phillips. Phillips did his graduate work in Alaska, and northern Alaska at that, so you would think he could read snow conditions. Maybe he just likes the exercise. On the Phillips route the drifted snow is nearly waist-deep, crusted over just enough so that right when you think it is going to hold you, you crash through and fall on your face. In places, crawling is the only way to make headway. Fine drizzle is falling from a raw, low sky. The snow is wet, the wind is wet, and the people are wet. Phillips is in his element— the field. He is also in such alpha physical condition that despite his small stature he plows through the snow like a moose, hardly breathing hard.

The dead elk lies on its side with its head tucked under one front leg. The rib meat and most of one haunch have been eaten away, but not much else. All four limbs are still connected and still covered with hide. Doug Smith cuts off the head and scalps it. Antler pedicels bulge from the skull, in the early stage of development; it is a yearling bull, born last June, an adolescent. Smith whams the thigh bone with a rock. Split open, the femur reveals a sorry mess of depleted marrow. Marrow is the last fat to be consumed in a starving animal, and this elk was well into his. Healthy marrow is pale pink and has the consistency of peanut butter. This stuff is sallow red, thin, gelatinous. If the wolves had not killed this young elk, he would have died on his own within days.

This reintroduction of a top predator is a magnificent scientific opportunity, but the National Park Service apparently does not even have the money to measure such bare-bones basics as the effect of wolf predation on the elk population. Yellowstone's elk are counted only twice a year, by the crudest of methods—seat-of-the-pants guesstimating from an airplane.

The wolf's return will be felt throughout the ecosystem, as its effects cascade down through the trophic levels. We need measurement and serious study *now*. Most of all, we need the before-and-after numbers: abundance of elk, coyote, sheep, willow, ground squirrel, bluebunch wheatgrass; species distribution, movement patterns, energy consumption, growth rates. With information like that, we could look into some of the most challenging questions in ecology, and there would be plenty of time for unhurried study as long as we had the pre-wolf numbers. Controlled experiments on the impact of top predators on whole ecosystems have been possible only in very limited conditions—a closed box in a lab, say, or Isle Royale, neither of which has anywhere near the ecological complexity of Yellowstone. If only enough baseline work had been done beforehand, this could enable experiments of unprecedented scope and richness. But much of the baseline data is crude, patchy, and uncoordinated. Much more simply does not exist. We do not know how many elk were wintering in the Lamar before the wolves came, and we will not know how many there are in the first years of wolf predation, not to mention the changes in the elk population's age structure, sex ratio, geographic distribution, and feeding regimes. Nor will the effects of those changes on many other species be known. Most important, we will not be able to measure large-scale ecosystem effects.

The budget for research in Yellowstone has shriveled—thanks in large part to politicians who have disliked its results—to the point where the work of the park botanist, Don Despain, depends on handouts and volunteers for data collection. What will be the aspen response to the return of the wolf? We will be lucky to find out. Streambank willows are now scarce along the bare mud margins of the Lamar, a fact popularly attributed to there being "too many" herbivores. Will willows burgeon now? Would a willow and aspen resurgence repopulate the river and its tributaries with beaver? Beavers are almost never seen in the Lamar, though they once were abundant. If beavers recovered to large numbers, how would the availability of that new prey item change wolf behavior, distribution, energetics? How would a proliferation of willow, aspen, and cottonwood affect stream flow, stream-bed physiography, and the spawning of cutthroat trout? If there were changes in trout abundance, how would that affect the grizzly bear population? If cutthroat spawned in greater numbers and sustained more bears, how would the increased abundance of bears affect the amounts of carrion and live prey available to wolves? Might coyote numbers be reduced by the increased competition of both bears and wolves? Would a coyote reduction benefit foxes? Somebody ought to be weighing sample patches of forbs. Somebody ought to be monitoring moose survivorship. Somebody ought to be putting it all together in grand syntheses of systematics, biomass restratification, energy flows.

Where was the National Science Foundation when this project was gearing up? Where were Harvard, Yale, Stanford, the University of California, all the other great bastions of ecology? Why isn't Yellowstone swarming with systematists, gopher gazers, soil chemists, bug counters, geneticists, epidemiologists, woodpecker watchers, grizzly bear gurus?

# Cooke City

The Sodas go to have a look at Cooke City, Montana.

Cooke City matters to wolves. All the places where people live amid wolves matter to wolves, because it is humankind that is the primary determinant of wolf life, because it is humankind that is the primary instrument of wolf death. Even in the remotest wilderness of Alaska, the majority of wolf deaths are human-caused. To grow old, to grow weak, to act as the wise adviser to her juniors in the pack, perhaps only to trail the pack that has left her behind, scavenging at the scattered remains of their kills—these are privileges almost universally denied to a wolf on a planet dominated by technological human societies. Old Blue Thirteen is a rarity in more than his color.

Wolves have evolved under intense human pressure, however, and they are well adapted to survive the sort of hunting and trapping of which humankind, in most of its history, has been capable. Wolves have lots of babies; the average litter size is about five, and can range up to ten and sometimes even more, and most packs produce a litter every year. Wolves can breed at the age of two. A wolf population can afford to lose substantial numbers of its young; indeed it must lose them if there is to be enough food to go around. Where wolves are properly managed, most of the wolves that people kill would have died anyway, by other means.

Alas, there are many places around the world where *Canis lupus* populations are hanging by a thread, and it is fraying fast.

Gray wolves once occupied virtually the entire Northern Hemisphere. Nearly all of their ancestral habitat has been changed by humans, often drastically, yet wolves have managed to survive in an amazing number of places—thriving in some, in others disappearing. Their status in any given place does not correlate very closely with the degree of official protection. As in Tuscany, what seems to matter most are social attitudes. It seems that more people consider wolves dangerous than know otherwise. Why are so many people afraid of them?

There is a rich literature of wolf attacks on people in Europe and Asia, and Dave Mech and others believe that there may be some basis in fact for at least a few of the accounts. On the other hand, an eyewitness to a recent alleged wolf attack on a child in India reported that the wolf was wearing a leather jacket and a motorcycle helmet.

Mech comes down decisively: "There is no basis for the belief that healthy, wild wolves in North America are of any danger to human beings." This is pretty amazing when you think how easy it would be. A pair of wolves like Nine and Ten could have Granny and Grandpa dismembered under the picnic table in five minutes.

Wolves never lose their essential gentleness toward people, but only where wolves have had no experience of humans do they lose their shyness. On Ellesmere Island, in Canada's historically unpeopled northern Arctic, Dave Mech visits the magnificent white wolves every summer, and, after an initial brief period of hesitation, they have simply accepted his presence. He lies in the midst of them as they tutor their pups outside the den. The wolves take down an ailing musk ox in classically businesslike fashion and begin to feed. All the while, Mech watches, takes pictures, takes notes. The wolves do not touch him, or bring him food. He has never once been threatened by an Ellesmere wolf. Nor have the Ellesmere wolves ever been threatened by a human being.

They are probably the only wolves in the world of whom this can be said. As the human capacity for killing wolves has risen with the rise of industrial technology, people have killed wolves at a level of mortality far past that for which evolution has fitted wolf society. Despite the

United States' extensive systems of nature reserves, and our prodigious abundance of ungulate prey, Americans have been the most effective wolf killers of all. The nearly total extirpation of the wolf from the lower forty-eight United States has not been a matter of habitat destruction. It is the result of killing, killing alone.

Despite their total victory, many Americans continue to hate and fear the wolf. I cannot claim to understand this hatred—it seems to me as dark and inaccessible as racism, or child abuse—but I have seen it in American eyes and heard it in American speech, and it is chilling, and real.

Fear and hatred thrive on ignorance, and ignorance thrives on isolation. Cooke City, Montana, is one of the most isolated towns in this nation outside of Alaska. You can get to it in summer via U.S. Highway 212 out of Red Lodge, over the lake-spangled alpine expanse of the Beartooth Plateau, but even then you must traverse a pass almost eleven thousand feet above sea level, where serious snow is eminently possible on any summer day. In winter—which means pretty much everything from Labor Day to Memorial Day—the only way to Cooke City is through Yellowstone Park, along the narrow, winding, potholed, and usually icy road from Mammoth Hot Springs through the Lamar valley and up Soda Butte Creek—fifty-two harrowing miles from the nearest town, Gardiner, Montana. Gardiner's population is about nine hundred. Cooke City's, in winter, is a tenth of that.

The best word to describe Cooke City's appearance is godforsaken. In fact there is no church in town; the house of worship sits halfway between Cooke and its equally bedraggled little sister, Silver Gate. Much male fashion in Cooke City epitomizes that special absolute-end-of-the-road look: filthy torn clothes, greasy cap advertising a machinery company, long stringy hair, long bushy beard, unfriendly eyes. Suspicion and resentment of the National Park Service, on which the town depends for everything from snowplowing to garbage removal, are the most frequent topics of conversation in the dark and dingy bars, which do strong business all year.

You would think it a quiet place, but all winter long Cooke City is engulfed in din; it is a snowmobiler's mecca. Many of the recreationists enhance the joyful noise by removing the mufflers from their machines. Belt-heads, as they term themselves, teem along the one paved street in multicolored, heavily padded snowmobiling suits. Snowmobiles in various stages of disrepair and disassembly, in fact, are among the most prominent ornaments of the townscape year-round.

Cooke was founded as a mining town, and some of the tributaries of upper Soda Butte Creek still run bright orange with nineteenth-century toxic waste. Oddly enough, the fishless dead zone above the town protects the pure-strain Yellowstone cutthroat trout of lower Soda Butte Creek and the Lamar River from invasion by Eastern brook trout, which were introduced into the headwaters years ago and rapidly drove out the natives.

Here in April of 1995, Cooke City is seething with fury over the prospect of a gold mine on a scale the city's fathers could not have imagined. A company called Crown Butte Mines has been formed for the purpose of extracting about a billion dollars' worth of gold, silver, and copper by ripping the top off ten-thousand-foot-high Henderson Mountain, which rises just north of Cooke City and less than three miles from the northeast corner of Yellowstone National Park. The mountain feeds the headwaters of three of Greater Yellowstone's watersheds: the Clark's Fork of the Yellowstone, the Stillwater River, and Soda Butte Creek—hence including Soda Butte's downstream recipient, the Lamar River, and the Lamar's downstream recipient, the hallowed Yellowstone River. The Yellowstone is the longest free-flowing river in the United States, one of the few essentially undegraded wild river systems left in the world, one of the world's greatest trout fisheries, and a thing of beauty beyond comparison.

Crown Butte Mines is situated within a corporate labyrinth, presumably to assure that the folks who put up the eighty million dollars in startup capital would not be liable when things went wrong. Crown Butte Mines, Inc., was, until the fateful summer of 1996, a subsidiary of the Canadian company Crown Butte Resources, Ltd., of which 60 percent was owned by Hemlo Gold Mines, Inc.; then Hemlo bought the rest of Crown Butte Mines. Crown Butte Resources and Hemlo are both former subsidiaries of Noranda Minerals, Inc., of Toronto, which retains 44 percent of Hemlo. There is a second Noranda Minerals, this one not an Inc. but a Corp., headquartered in Delaware, a subsidiary of Noranda Finance, Inc., of Delaware, which in turn is a subsidiary of Noranda, Inc., as well as the parent company of Noranda Exploration, Inc., Noranda Minerals, Inc., is also a subsidiary of Noranda, Inc., which is jointly owned by Brascan, Ltd., and Hees International Bancorp, Ltd., both of which are controlled by the well-known Bronfman family.

To contain the six million tons of poisonous mine tailings, Crown Butte is planning to build an impoundment a third of a mile wide, four fifths of a mile long, and one hundred feet deep, obliterating a fifty-six-acre wetland, destroying important grizzly habitat, and situated some nine thousand feet above sea level in subalpine forest that gets about fifty feet of snow per average year—in a seismically active valley.

In the interest of fairness, I should point out that Crown Butte is promising to treat any poisonous water that leaches from the tailings and to protect the downstream watersheds from the consequences of avalanche, landslide, earthquake, flood, arsenic, lead, or human error—in perpetuity.

When a coalition of environmental groups led by the Greater Yellowstone Coalition sued Noranda in 1993 for violating the Clean Water Act, Noranda denied that it had any direct link to Crown Butte Mines and therefore could not be held liable for future damage. They lost anyway, luckily.

Noranda has poisoned backwoods lakes, defoliated forests, and killed even the humus in the soil at its mine in Quebec, where the local children now show high levels of lead in their blood. It has incurred millions in pollution fines—two million dollars' worth for offenses in the United States alone, including toxic waste discharge from a paper mill in Maine, hazardous waste in California, and air pollution in Missouri. The company has been repeatedly fined in Canada, reports *U.S. News & World Report* in its issue of March 13, 1995, for "toxic spills and discharges, insufficient record keeping, hazardous waste storage deficiencies, toxic air emissions, exceeding of permit levels, accidents due to negligence, pollution of coastal and fishery waters, failure to install cleanup and antipollution equipment, and failure to notify authorities of pollution events." It has spilled toxic mine waste into Babine Lake in British Columbia, the headwaters of the Babine River's huge sockeye salmon run. It has leaked cadmium, lead, zinc, copper, and arsenic from its Utah smelter into the groundwater.

There are over half a million abandoned mines in the American West, which have produced some seventy billion tons of tailings. Twelve thousand miles of waterways downstream from them lie stone dead. Under the Mining Law of 1872, the fixer's dream that still governs all mining in the United States, mineral claims on federal land are still being sold for between $2.50 and $5 an acre. In May of 1994, in Nevada, an 1,800-acre claim on a gold mine worth somewhere between $8 billion and $10 billion was sold by the U.S. Department of the Interior to another multilayered Canadian mining company for $9,000. For the forty-five acres of the Gallatin National Forest that Crown Butte needs to acquire, the company is going to pay $225. Under the 1872 law, the government is not allowed to refuse to sell. In recompense to the American people, mining companies pay a royalty of zero.

It is typical of Cooke City that the mine has brought about a nasty little civil war. The anti-mine faction is bigger, but not by as much as you might think, so there is plenty of ground for Cooke's leading indoor sport: argument. All winter long, Cooke City stews and gossips and bickers. Meanwhile, the countryside obliviously abounds in moose, elk, and bears both black and grizzly. Most of the forest is old-growth spruce-fir, interspersed with springs and wetlands. It is a great place for wolves.

In the summer of 1996, Cooke City will find out that all through the previous year, the Greater Yellowstone Coalition's executive director, Mike Clark, will have been engaged in secret negotiations with the U.S. government and Noranda. Not even Clark's own staff will know what is going on. But the president of the United States will. At his weekly lunches with Vice President Al Gore, Bill Clinton will get the latest on Noranda.

The vice president, the attorney general, the secretaries of both agriculture and the interior, the chief of the Council on Environmental Quality will all be involved. Doug Honnold and his Sierra Club Legal Defense Club colleagues will show that the litigation over the Noranda mine could go on for many, many years, and cost everybody millions. The company's C.E.O., Ian Bayer, will see lawsuits and legal expenses stretching well into the twenty-first century. In no small part owing to Mike Clark's diplomatic skills—and his vivid depiction of endless future miseries—Noranda will make a deal.

On August 12, 1996, President Clinton will stand on a makeshift platform on a meadow above Soda Butte Creek. Clark and Bayer will sit behind him. Sue Glidden, proprietor of the Cooke City general store and a leader of the local opposition to the mine, will introduce the president. Wearing a WOLFSTOCK '95 cap, Clinton will announce that in return for $65 million in federal assets still to be chosen, Noranda has agreed to give up the Cooke City mine. Twenty-two million of the payment to Noranda will have to be spent on cleaning up the existing pollution caused by earlier mining.

Cooke City will immediately resume its bickering. The biggest threat to Yellowstone in the twentieth century, beaten! The biggest boon to Cooke City in the twentieth century, lost! And so forth. And yet Sue Glidden, her husband, Ralph, and a handful of other local activists will have shown that Cooke City is not as isolated as it may have thought itself. Truth, fairness, the love of nature, and concern for future generations will have penetrated to its heart.

The Crystal Creek wolves remain at Calfee Creek. Number Two has set out after them, but he has just now reached Specimen Ridge, which they left five days ago. Seven is still in the Lamar. Nine and Ten seem to have vaporized.

# *Carnivore*

APRIL 8, 1995

The Soda Butte pack has come home. They have killed an elk within sight of their pen. Some people may picture wolves pursuing their prey in a breathtaking headlong chase, like cheetahs hauling down gazelles at forty miles an hour. In fact—and especially here and now, when so many Yellowstone elk are so vulnerable—the process is slow, deliberate, orderly.

Bob Landis has gotten some remarkable film footage of events leading up to this kill. The wolves approach a big bull elk. He draws himself up tall, a portrait of outraged dignity. He stares at the wolves. They sniff the ground and look at one another. They move in closer, quiet, each step a decision. The elk lifts a front leg, as though to remind them how powerfully he can strike out. He puffs out his chest and raises his head high. He stands his ground. The wolves quit.

This is almost always the way. Wolves do not waste time charging up hill and down dale in pursuit of prey in good shape. First of all, they probably would not catch them. Second, if they did, they could easily get hurt. So the basic program is to keep moving around your territory, testing, testing, testing. You identify an elk who is still standing her ground, but not looking so hot. In a few days, you check her again. Barry Lopez writes that vulnerable prey animals "apparently announce their poor condition to the wolf in the subtleties of a stance, a peculiarity of gait, a rankness of breath, or more obvious signs of physical incapacity, such as wounds, massive loss of hair, or visible infection. Wolves are alert to such nuances." If the elk is at all vulnerable, stiff with arthritis for example, the wolves will know it immediately, and she will know that they know, and she may simply yield. Or she makes a break for cover. Flight also being a sign of possible vulnerability, the wolves give chase. If she falters, they kill her. If she doesn't, she gets away. When the chase has failed, the wolves nevertheless have increased their understanding of her condition, her body language, her personality. They pocket that knowledge and wait.

They cannot afford rash mistakes. Landis also has film of a coyote that has just killed an elk calf, which the mother is still defending. As the coyote approaches, she flails her sharp front hooves in a blur. No wolf, much less coyote, could survive that tornado of blows.

The Soda Butte wolves move up a steep brushy ridge where a small group of bull elk is outlined against a red evening sky. The fierce black summit of Baronette Peak jabs the clouds behind the elk. As the wolves come near, the elk bunch up, nearly touching, shoulder to shoulder, shifting nervously back and forth, never falling out of formation, never going more than a few dozen yards. The wolves close in, very slowly. One wolf lunges forward to nip at the Achilles tendon of an elk, and the elk kicks back viciously. The attacker dodges, then withdraws. The wolves circle, looking murderous. In fraternal solidarity, the elk stand their ground. The wolves give up.

Somewhere out of sight, they find their victim, dine, and depart.

The Crystal Creek pack seems to be moving less and less. Could the alpha female be denning at Calfee Creek? It would be a good place to raise a wolf family. Upstream stretch many miles of steep backcountry that rarely knows a human footstep. Up any of these drainages—Calfee, Cache, the main Lamar—the land grows wilder, steeper, more remote. Most of the elk that now graze the valley floor and the grassy benches adjacent will move up these streams as summer comes on and the massed herds of winter gradually break into groups sized just right for each branch of each watershed they ascend. In the peak green of August, they will spread across the trickling headwaters of Calfee, Cache, and the

Lamar, above timberline, in the sublime alpine pastures of some of North America's least-bothered wilderness. Summer here, though brief, is rich. Grizzly bears crowd together in the talus to gobble down estivating cutworm moths. Bighorn sheep and the fattening elk find an abundance of forage and the isolation they crave, in Hoodoo Basin, Bootjack Gap, Hurricane Mesa, the serried arêtes of the high Absaroka. Fine wolf country.

Two is back at the damned pen again! I suppose I shouldn't complain. His timidity may serve him well in the future. Seven has moved well up into the Buffalo Fork, perhaps on the stale scent of her mother and stepfather—whom, thanks to bad weather and a consequently abbreviated flight, Mike Phillips has again not found.

# *Still Alive*

On our way to lunch in Gardiner, John Varley and I hear a small plane throttling back near the airport, and on a hunch we go in search of Doug Smith. The rumor earlier this morning was that Smith had found Nine, but Ten was not with her. It has now been seven days since Nine and Ten were last located together.

Smith has been airborne for an awfully long time. I don't like the feel of this. Nor the stench that suddenly permeates the Pathfinder despite its closed windows. Below the grass-and-gravel single strip of Gardiner International Airport and past the bear-proof garbage Dumpsters, the municipal sewage-treatment pond boils brown. On a strip of concrete beach beside it are gathered several dozen big black squawking ravens.

"What the hell are they doing?" I inquire as a raven dips his beak in the seething ordure.

"Guess," replies Varley.

"Naw!"

"Oh, yes," says Yellowstone's top scientist. "They just seem to love human shit."

Yet another anthropogenic influence on the ecosystem.

Smith steps down from the Super Cub in his orange fireproof flight suit, against which his complexion is distinctly green. The weather has not been kind. He tells us that the Crystals have split up, although probably only temporarily. The parents have taken off on their own and left the kids behind. Smith has radio-located the alphas right across from the Buffalo Ranch, while pups Three, Six, and Eight have stayed behind at Calfee Creek with an elk kill, this pack's first.

Just as Two's parents were coming toward the pen, Two left it. He has moseyed over to the tawny, broad-shouldered grasslands where Hell-roaring Creek debouches into the Yellowstone—a paradise of an ungulate winter range—and there, all by himself, young Two has brought down an elk! Smith saw him from the air, at the center of a big round blotch of blood-red snow, standing on his dinner.

The Soda Buttes continue to explore the nooks and crannies of a relatively small area, basically up and down Soda Butte Creek. This morning they have moved high into the mountains near the park's eastern border, on the southern flank of a big lonesome peak called the Needle. Come summer, there will be elk aplenty here.

Seven is still on her own and still close to home, in upper Rose Creek.

And Nine and Ten have turned up safe and sound. Smith saw them trotting along Bull Creek, above the high, marshy flat known as Frenchy's Meadows.

The snow cover is receding fast, followed apace by advancing green. Grass begins to grow when the soil temperature reaches about fifty degrees Fahrenheit, so it must be spring, though my bones tell me different. As darkness falls the wind rises, blowing grit and grainy snow into abrasive clouds. The elk take their places out across the shadow-stippled valley floor. One pack of yowling coyotes excites a quadraphonic chorus of coyote replies, one from each point of the compass. The Environmental Impact Statement predicted a big increase in Yellowstone tourism directly attributable to wolves—most of it, naturally, focused on the Lamar—but tonight, once again there is nobody here.

It is god-awful cold, but there are little moths flapping around, and there is birdsong in the trees. Four weeks after the first pen gate was opened, all fourteen new Yellowstone wolves are still alive, and still here.

April 12, 1995

The weather closes in again. Snow and whirlwind blur the grass, the road, the sky into one sourceless, shadowless white light.

# *Aroma as Meaning*

APRIL 13, 1995

The Crystal alphas have rejoined the three youngsters who stayed behind at Calfee Creek, and all are dining there on the pups' precocious elk kill. It is a big bull, sporting a big rack, and they have torn him to pieces. Unlike the Sodas, whose m.o. seems to be kill, snack, and run, the Crystals are consuming this carcass down to the last bone. In a way, this fits with the pack's cautious personality. Why risk injury by killing more than you can eat?

The same question might well be addressed to the Soda Butte wolves. I wonder how they would answer. Because it's fun? Because it's so easy?

They would be answering with their mouths full. The Sodas have made yet another kill, hard by the Pebble Creek campground, in the heart of the Soda Butte valley, which is really beginning to seem to be their territory.

How will we know that the day has come when we can say, "Yes, this is their territory"? Will we actually be able to draw lines on a map? Well, territories do change over time and with the seasons, but the short answer to the latter question is yes. By repeatedly locating the wolves, month after month, year after year, the biologists will develop a map. The wolves themselves, of course, will long since have known exactly where their territory's boundaries are.

The principal means wolves have of denoting the extent of a territory is by scent marking. The alpha male usually takes the lead with a short lifted-leg squirt of richly aromatic urine, which seems to convey a great deal of information. Sometimes the alpha female will also perform the lifted-leg scent mark, though as in dogs the general rule is that males lift their legs and females squat. Territory boundaries and trail junctions get the most scent-marking attention. Dave Mech has found that in winter, wolves do one raised-leg urination for about every nine hundred feet they travel, and that these messages can remain "readable" for two weeks. Hence a wolf is on average never more than four hundred and fifty feet from an olfactory signpost.

Scent marking probably also communicates sexual information, particularly the readiness of females. As her proestrous period advances, an alpha female will squat to leave a message, sometimes including blood, which the alpha male will sniff and then reply to, crisscrossing it with pee-talk of his own.

Feces also convey information. All canids have scent glands inside their anuses; this is why Fido and Fifi, on meeting, perform that embarrassing sniffing ritual. Alpha males present themselves butt-foremost most often, tails raised high, while the lowest in the hierarchy tend to keep their tails tucked down tight when approached.

There are more scent glands on the back above the tail, on either side of the face, and between the toes. No one knows what messages they may send, or even how they work.

Wolves, like dogs, seem unable to resist rolling in stinky stuff. Maybe they carry that information back to their packmates, but why? "What to the human nose just smells like 'the woods,' " writes Barry Lopez, "may for the wolf be hundreds of discrete bits of information." We cannot imagine the range and subtlety of the wolf's olfactory knowledge, but the main message seems usually to be "This is mine." My mate, my kill, my territory.

Scent marking defines boundaries both for the wolves in the pack and for their neighbors. In fully occupied wolf habitat, these boundaries will usually overlap by a half mile or so, in a sort of no-wolf's-land. One pack encountering signs of another will usually leave an aromatic memo of their own and then quickly vacate the overlap zone. Except when prey is extremely scarce, trespassing on other wolves' territories is quite rare, for good reason. One study, also by Mech, showed that more than 90 percent of wolves killed by other wolves were killed within two miles of a territory edge (sometimes inside, sometimes outside the boundary).

Wolf packs are in constant flux, in part because of the yearly addition of pups. Expulsion from the pack is frequent, especially for aging non-breeders. Sometimes an expelled adult wolf will be able to find a mate and found a pack; he or she may be able to join another pack, though this is rare. Most often, in what must be an emotionally devastating experience for this most social of animals, the expelled one must become a loner.

Lone wolves in areas saturated by pack territories often eke out their meager livings entirely within the small zones where territories overlap. Because packs visit no-wolf's-land infrequently—fearing for their lives—a lone wolf is safer here than trespassing within a territory. In many wolf habitats, prey animals tend to cluster along territory boundaries, also presumably because they know that wolf packs will be encountered there less often than in the hearts of the territories.

Wolves tend to travel habitual, well-worn paths throughout their territory, often along remarkably straight bearings. Do the multiple scent marks at each trail junction provide directions, reminders? "Black second daughter, come to the rendezvous site this instant—love, Mom"? If wolves can identify one another individually from the scent of their tracks and can also determine how long ago those tracks were made, then they can know pretty precisely who is where.

Wolves' ability to follow a compass direction is amazing. Even when they have to deviate widely to get around an obstacle such as a cliff, they will return to their original heading and maintain it within five to fifteen degrees. Some sort of innate magnetic compass may well be at work when transplanted wolves try to go home. The hope here has been that their urge to go home will be offset by the abundance of prey in Yellowstone, by the difficulty of crossing the steep and icebound mountains that block a direct route to the north, and, if they ever did get over the mountains, by the human-dominated landscape they would encounter on the prairies of central Montana. On the other hand, central Montana still does have a lot of empty space, and wolves can move fast when they want to. If they decide to go home, they can.

Indications of territoriality will come slowly and will be hard to read. Wolves do not patrol their boundaries with military regularity. On average, they complete a circuit of the edge about once every three weeks. Howling, because under many conditions it cannot be heard from very far away, is not necessarily a proclamation of land possession, although a good group howl, when it is heard, must surely proclaim to neighboring wolves that the pack is at home.

What seems most clearly to define territory for a wolf pack is what the biologist Roger Peters calls a cognitive map. These mental maps develop over long periods of territory maintenance and are probably handed down through the generations. Peters's studies have shown, for example, that in the early days of a new territory, wolves tend to follow a few habitual paths between "nodes" of significance, and only later do they start taking shortcuts, which are clear proof of the pack's knowledge of their travelways' geometry. Eventually the shortcuts also attain status as full-time pathways. In time, the pack has a comprehensive mental image of its territory. Their movements are purposeful, never random. When they go somewhere, they are not wandering. They are going back where they know hunting is good, or where the boundary needs touching up, or where Mom can den without fear of disturbance. And they are both reading and distributing information every step along the way.

# Cause of Death: Wolf

Number Two seems to have finished with his kill near Hellroaring Creek, so Mike Phillips, Doug Smith, and Norm Bishop hike in to "work the carcass." As we expected, this yearling elk was in miserable shape when he died. The biologists labor through the carnage with impressive sangfroid. They have seen, and smelled, plenty of mutilated corpses in their day. They come to a wolf kill not with the horror or squeamishness you or I might feel but with curiosity, calm, and admiration. A wolf kill does have a sort of magnificence. Wolves are so good at what they do.

---

### KILL AUTOPSY FORM

Yearly Kill No. __95-7__ Autopsy No. __6__ Date Examined __4/13/95__

Species __Cervus elaphus__ Species ID __hide-carcass__

Location __1 mi. NE Hellroaring patrol cabin__

UTM[1] __54559/498249__ Elevation __6720__ ~~meters~~ __feet__

Terrain __ridge__ Cover __semi-open Doug fir__

---

1. Universal Transverse Mercator coordinates. These figures denote a precise location.

Sex: M/(F)(if male Cond. Antlers): 1) pedicel   2) velvet   3) polished

Age: 1) calf   2) sub-adult   3) adult   4) old adult

   Teeth wear class _____cementum age __no skull found__

Bone Marrow:  1 (solid)  2 (semisolid)  3 (gelatinous)

Arthritis: vertebrae - yes /(no):

   If yes list type vert.$^2$ _____ & # vert. of each _____

   pelvis - arth.$^3$ yes/no: which acetabulum - right/left/both

   severity - slight/moderate/severe (if diff. specify which)

   femur ball examined?_____arth. yes/no

Jaw Necrosis: uppers - slightly/moderate/severe

   lowers - slight/moderate/severe         __not checked__

Utilization:

   1) carcass completely consumed = little hide or hair; legs/verte-
      brae disarticulated; no soft tissue

   2) carcass mod. consumed = hide or hair present on leg bones,
      skull; legs and vert. gen. articulated; some soft tissue
      remaining

   3) carcass lightly consumed = all hide or hair left on leg bones;
      legs, vert. intact; soft tissue remaining

Bones Found: skull __no__  vert. col.$^4$ (%) __100__   no. scapulae$^5$ _2_
   no. mandibles _no_ pelvis _✓_
   no. leg bones: Fe$^6$ _2_ Hum$^7$ _2_
                  Tib$^8$ _2_ R&U$^9$ _2_
                  Mt$^{10}$ _2_ Mc$^{11}$ _2_

| | | | |
|---|---|---|---|
| 2. | Vertebrae. | 7. | Humerus (upper foreleg). |
| 3. | Arthritis. | 8. | Tibia (lower hind leg). |
| 4. | Vertebral column. | 9. | Radius and ulna (lower foreleg). |
| 5. | Shoulder blades. | 10. | Metatarsus (hind foot). |
| 6. | Femur (thigh bone). | 11. | Metacarpus (forefoot). |

Bones collected: skull  pelvis  vertebrae

teeth UR/UL/LR/LL[12] incisors

marrow bone (Fe or Hum best; winter only)

other _____ MT _____

Date of death _4/11/95_____  Cause of Death _wolf #2_____

Cause of Death Explanation ___wolf killed; wolf #2 observed on___

____kill, blood and drag mark seen on ground and tree_____

Wolves Present (identify) __#2_____ Wolf Pack __lone wolf_

Snow depth (fresh kills only) __none____

Other remarks (bear sign, coyotes etc.) _no sign of other predators_

____at kill; skull missing_____

_____

Examined by: _DS, MP, NB_____

_____
12.  Upper right, upper left, lower right, lower left.

# Renée Askins

From the day Renée Askins started the Wolf Fund, it had only one goal: the return of the wolf to Yellowstone. When that was accomplished, she said, she would shut the organization down.

Tonight its demise is to be celebrated, at the Chico Hot Springs Lodge, not far north of Yellowstone Park. The government-agency folks from Helena and Yellowstone will be there, and the conservationists, the donors, the volunteers, the Wolf Fund staff, the local tree huggers and armchair propagandists, the many who can claim their little piece of the credit. I think a great deal of it is Askins's.

She has been planning this victory party for a long time—who ever thought that the return of the wolf would take this long?—and she has said to her (all-female) staff that her idea of appropriate attire for herself on this festival occasion is a very short miniskirt, fishnet hose, and stiletto heels.

I will always remember the moment I first laid eyes on Renée Askins, in the summer of 1985. She was helping run the "Wolves and Humans" exhibit at the Grant Village Museum in Yellowstone Park. As a seasonal park employee, she was required to wear a National Park Service uniform. Buxomly buttoned into that stiff polyester Smoky-the-Bear drag, complete with clip-on tie, she projected a sort of smoky, young-Marlene-Dietrich-ish dangerousness. She spoke softly, and close up, her voice intimate, breathy, seriously female. Soul-searching China-blue eyes completed the picture.

Over the next decade, I watched as the foxy young ranger grew into one of America's most effective conservationists. Askins has always had her facts straight, always spoken plainly and vividly. She has known what will and what won't pass muster in the political arena. She has been realistic about the opposition, and sympathetic. And if she chooses, she can usually twist a man around her finger with the force of sheer charm. She has done it to me more than once, and I have always been happy to submit.

She is a woman with a woman's gifts, and the moxie to make use of them. When she began to be noticed, the prevailing political orthodoxy of the day held sex differences and their effects to be the creation of the "male power structure," fictions put to the use of oppression. Hard-edged, square-cornered feminist dogma had no room for charm. But Askins's feminism existed on a higher level. First of all, anyone who knows wolves knows that attraction, power, status, and decision making are complexly interactive in wolf society. Anyone who knows wolves has also observed plenty of resemblance between their behavior and our own. Watching Askins do her stuff was watching biology at work. Hers was a feminism not of victimhood and repression, but of strength and freedom. Its roots were not in theoretical ideology but in nature.

Askins was not beloved by some of the other conservationists working for Yellowstone wolf reintroduction—mainly, I think, owing to envy. She was the one the reporters would call first. She was the one with articles about her in *Life* magazine and *Bazaar*, and a piece of her own in *Harper's*. She was the one the networks would put on a plane to New York, the one the American Museum of Natural History invited to lecture. When multi-group strategy meetings were held, Askins dominated them, not so much intentionally, I think, as by force of personality. When policy people in Washington wanted advice, they asked her. When the press called or the cameras rolled, she was always ready with a trenchant quote and that hundred-watt smile. Alpha female.

As the prospect of actual success in the long campaign for wolf reintroduction drew nearer, honest differences began to push certain conservation groups further and further apart—experimental–non-essential versus full protection was the big dispute—and the ideological schisms led to personal fallings-out. People allied in their commitment and of one mind in 99 percent of their values were no longer speaking. By 1993, the rift had grown particularly wide between the Wolf Fund and the Greater Yellowstone Coalition, my institutional home. The G.Y.C. staff opposed the wolf reintroduction if it was to take place under the experimental-population rule, which permits killing wolves under certain circumstances; the Wolf Fund and Defenders of Wildlife could not believe that their fellow conservationists would allow this chance to pass by for the sake of an ecologically insignificant legalism. Though no longer on the Coalition's board of directors, I maintained close relationships with the senior staff and many of the board members, so I was a logical bridge. With a plea to the board to overrule the staff's adamant position, I tried to renew the alliance. I failed.

But I had a book to write, and Askins had her own work to do, and we both forged ahead. She was confident that her political acumen and her singleness of purpose would get the job done. Which of course they did. And so, this afternoon, Askins is headed for the Lamar valley with two Suburban-loads of now-former members of her board for a hike in what is now wolf habitat. Naturally, being well informed in the ways of wolves, and with yesterday's flight report from Mike Phillips showing all of the wolves well back in the backcountry, nobody is expecting to see wolves. They just want to see where they live.

As the cars bear down on the Lamar Narrows, the coyote researcher Bob Crabtree is standing at the roadside gesturing wildly at them to pull over. The Wolf Funders follow Crabtree up to a vantage point on the hillside, and there below, in full sight, on the floor of the open valley, lolling with swollen bellies around an elk they have just killed, are the reunited Crystal Creek wolves—including laggard young Two.

Askins sees these wolves, I think, as her metaphysical kindred. For almost everybody else involved in the restoration of the wolf to Yellowstone, wolves are an "issue," and their importance is ecological and social-historically symbolic. The ecologist's central image is of wolf *populations*—bounded and functional entities, amenable to quantitative analysis, and interesting to study. The conservationist also focuses on the population, seeing wolf reintroduction as a triumph in a zone of history with few triumphs to its name. Askins certainly recognizes those factors, but I believe she also sees these wolves as individual possessors of souls. Her presence in the struggle for the wolf's return has been strategic, certainly; it is also personal, and spiritual. For the biologists and most of the partisans, the numbering of the wolves is sufficient identification. Askins gives them names.

Renée Askins was born in 1959 in a small town in northwestern Michigan. She grew up in a house without a television set. The little girl and her mother and her mother's best friend, a wildlife biologist, would drive in a black Volkswagen bug to meadows in the state forest and count deer. For a religion course at Kalamazoo College, Askins wrote a paper on the role of wolves in religious traditions, and then for her junior-year thesis, in biology, she spent a semester studying a captive pack of wolves at Purdue University, in Indiana, assessing the relative contributions of various pack members to the survival of the pups.

"The day before I got to Indiana," she says, "the alpha female was killed by the pack." Three other females in the pack were also pregnant. In wolf packs in the wild, subordinate females do sometimes manage to breed, but they rarely bear young, so this was a very unnatural situation. Social strife was inevitable. In Askins's captive pack, two of the pregnant young females bore litters of three and four pups, and the lowest-ranking one had only two, of whom one was promptly killed by its packmates. The other was certainly doomed unless somebody intervened. Askins took custody of that lowly survivor on the first day of its life, and bottle-fed it through infancy. She named the pup Natasha.

John Weaver, at that time (1979) the endangered species biologist for the Bridger-Teton National Forest, had already been thinking toward a Yellowstone wolf reintroduction. It was Weaver who had pored over the disordered records of half a century's purported wolf sightings in Yellowstone to determine whether there might remain a remnant population. After that review as well as extensive searching on the ground, Weaver concluded that there were no wolves resident anywhere in Greater Yellowstone. He believed that there should be.

This was not the politically correct position for a Forest Service employee, but Weaver worked quietly. He was widely well liked, even by what Forest Service insiders call the Timber Beasts. Through the long years when not much seemed to be happening on the wolf front, John Weaver and Dave Mech kept the flame alive.

Weaver came to Indiana to consult with Askins's supervisor, the renowned wolf biologist Erich Klinghammer. Weaver's descriptions of Yellowstone and the opportunities for wolf restoration there lit a fire in the college junior. Askins had grown disillusioned with the whole idea of captive wolves. She had discovered that a great deal of what was typical of the Purdue wolves—like their excessive reproductive rate and excessive violence—was not typical of wild ones. She also hated what captivity did to their spirit. Even her cherished Natasha retained a shy wildness, and Askins could no longer bear to keep her. Then Weaver's Bridger-Teton colleague Timm Kaminski visited later in the year and suggested that Askins come and work with them after she graduated.

She spent her senior year at a backcountry agriculture school in Sierra Leone, writing long, longing letters to Weaver and Kaminski. She got no reply. "I was shattered," she remembers. "I was so hurt. I supposed they thought I was just some punk kid." She decided to take up law.

At the end of the summer of 1981, after her graduation, Askins loaded her possessions into her Mustang for her move to Vermont, where she was going to work till she had amassed enough money for law school. Late that night, the phone rang. It was Kaminski: "Weaver and I were just wondering why we hadn't heard from you." Her letters from Africa had never arrived.

They could not offer her an actual job, he said, but they did want her to come. She waitressed in Vermont for two months, raising the money to get herself west. Askins presented herself in Jackson, Wyoming, accompanied by her eighty-three-year-old granny. She waitressed some more, and she hung around Weaver trying to help with his paper for the wolf recovery plan, on wolf ecology and behavior. She went to every possible wolf-related event, and put together a slide-and-tape program promoting the return of the wolf to Yellowstone. Unpaid, she hauled her screen and projector hither and yon across the region, learning how far the great idea still had to go.

Finally, money started trickling in. The U.S. Fish and Wildife Service contracted with Askins for a second slide presentation on wolves. The Teton Science School in Jackson Hole hired her to run its seminar on "humanities and the environment."

By early 1984, Askins was trying to help bring the "Wolves and Humans" exhibit to Yellowstone in an atmosphere of mounting political trouble. Under pressure from the savagely anti-conservation Reagan White House, the Fish and Wildlife Service suspended her slide program. The National Park Service withdrew its promise to provide space for the museum show. Intensively lobbied by Defenders of Wildlife and Askins, the Park Service then reversed itself yet again, and in 1985 the show went on. "My first great lesson in perseverance," she recalls.

She was accepted for graduate study at the Yale School of Forestry, but a vision was beginning to glimmer in her mind, and she asked Yale for a deferral. She began studying the people who really got things done in the world, and asking how they did it. A businessman and philanthropist in Minnesota named Wallace Dayton (another Greater Yellowstone Coalition board member) cited the success of the Peregrine Fund, which had reintroduced the peregrine falcon to habitats ranging from desert cliffs to the Brooklyn Bridge. He liked the idea of an organization with a single goal. So did Askins.

A pattern begins to emerge. A young person finds her passion, and changes course to follow it. She struggles in related fields, gradually homing in on a path. She witnesses and analyzes success stories in her field. She does not act impulsively, but ponders and considers and consults. She finds out who is known to be the best and seeks them out as mentors: Mech, Dayton, the writer Peter Matthiessen, the conservation godmother Mardie Murie (who is also the widow of the legendary wolf researcher Adolph Murie). She listens. When she speaks, she is well informed. She is sweet. She is optimistic. She is charisma itself. Powerful people want to help her.

The vision takes shape, not only of wolf restoration but also of the strategic means to it. Again she seeks out the big shots. She asks them how they would feel about a single-purpose organization called the Wolf Fund. Oh, and would they please consider serving on its board of advisers? "I wanted a brilliant board," she says. "Not necessarily experts but so bright that they could see the undertaking as a problem-solving exercise."

Her appeals were very successful. The Wolf Fund's board of advisers included Matthiessen, Murie, Mech, the conservation philanthropist Yvon Chouinard, the actor Harrison Ford, George Lamb of the Rockefeller Foundation, the geologist David Love, the wildlife biologist George Schaller, the movie star Robert Redford, and the mogul Ted Turner.

The Wolf Fund came into being under the wing of the Craighead Wildlife Research Institute (the creation of the biologists Frank and John Craighead, the story of whose epic battle with the Park Service over Yellowstone's most famous denizens—till now—is told in my book *The Grizzly Bear*). Through the spring of 1986, Askins raised money for the Wolf Fund, and in the fall she enrolled at Yale; she would run the Wolf Fund from her house in Connecticut. She knew that communication would be the key to the Wolf Fund's success; in addition to science and organizational behavior, therefore, she studied writing. Non-academically, she also studied human behavior. She remembers: "I began to focus on problem solving—grassroots acceptance, access to particular legislators, the ag opposition. The great point, I saw, was simply that *people move things*. The Wolf Fund's intent was to make the decision makers care."

How?

"Simplify, simplify. Every morning when I walked into the office, I would look at the roster of tasks and ask, 'How will this, this, this help put wolves on the ground in Yellowstone?' "

She also mastered a deep political truth, which I have never heard her put in these words but which is well expressed (by my father-in-law) as "It takes a thousand attaboys to cancel one aw-shit."

In 1988, with grad school behind her, Askins teamed up with Hank Fischer of Defenders of Wildlife, Tom France of the National Wildlife Federation, and Michael Bean of the Environmental Defense Fund to hatch a highly unconventional strategy. You will recall that Senator James McClure, Republican of Idaho, recognized the natural return of the wolf to Idaho and eventually Yellowstone as inevitable. Fischer had a hunch that McClure might find them a chink in the hitherto solid brick wall of Republican opposition.

Well over 90 percent of Yellowstone National Park lies within the state of Wyoming, and both of Wyoming's senators, Malcolm Wallop and Alan Simpson, were rigidly aligned with the livestock industry. Askins, Fischer, and their colleagues wanted only an Environmental Impact Statement—not a decision to bring wolves in, just a study. No wolf E.I.S. was going to be undertaken without the Senate's imprimatur, and it is an unwritten but ironclad rule of that body that you do not do *anything*, ever, that the local delegation unanimously opposes. If McClure could get Simpson and Wallop to accept his view that preemptive action to seize control of wolf management would benefit the livestock industry more than resolute opposition to wolves would, they just might agree to the E.I.S.

Here was the beginning of the schism that would in time divide the conservation community into hostile camps. Rumors of the meetings with McClure grew into allegations of treason—collaboration with the enemy. And here is what differentiates Askins's ultimate success from the excuse-riddled defeats of the warriors pure in heart: she knew that when people moved things, they usually did so by making deals. This is an impure-hearted world.

Picture the choice of forms of success: *A*, you browbeat some asshole politician by mail and denounce him on TV until he is shamed into doing what you demand—fat chance—versus *B*, you find what he needs and trade him some quiet untelevised help in return for some reasonable approximation of what you have politely asked him for. Is this so hard to understand? Apparently it is. How often do our moralistic saviors throw away their scant political capital on scenario *A*!

So the wolves are here, and Renée Askins and her now-former directors are on the road to Chico for one very happy funeral.

# Drainage Ditch

Why do I care? How much does the return of the wolf to Yellowstone really matter? In terms of global biodiversity, even just in terms of endangered species conservation, it is of marginal importance, given the vast numbers of the same species elsewhere. I begin almost to believe what conservation's enemies have always thrown in our faces: that we are in it, really, just for ourselves, just for esthetics, just for irrational love. Edward O. Wilson's elegantly written book *Biophilia* asserts that the love of nature is part of our evolved biological being. But there is a sadness, too, in our love, the sadness of what we have known in our lives.

When my family moved to Whitehaven, Tennessee, in 1954, it was an unincorporated hamlet of a few thousand people, and just beginning to serve as a suburb of Memphis, several miles to the north. We were surrounded by country.

To the south lay the Mississippi Delta, destination of the early-morning busloads of black children turned out of their schools each spring to chop cotton and each fall to pick it while we white children stayed at our desks. The Delta was my daddy's ancestral home, and his kin all still lived there. When we drove down to see them, Highway 61 would plunge from the wide bright cottonfields into dark bayou bottoms, and the windshield would be so spattered with bugs that we had to stop to scrape them off. Dead deer and snakes and owls and opossums lay sprawled on the bridge sides. Ospreys nested in the cypress tops, and there were alligators in the mud.

To the east of my home rose the scrub-and-clay uplands of Fayette County, Tennessee's poorest county, pig country, Klan country, buzzard country. West was the river, too huge and too strong to be quite real to a boy of seven.

What was real was closer to home. A big Hereford bull lived across the road, a chaser of children. Down our side of Oakwood Drive there was a row of seven new houses, and beyond its dead end a deep forest began, with swamps and lakes and mysteries in it. Spring nights, the frog chorus there sang loud. In an abandoned barn pulled half down by honeysuckle vines, mud daubers built their terrible castles, tube on tube of wasp-brick. Because I was allergic, my mama said, one sting could kill me. I grew to dread all insects—June bugs, yellowjackets, bumblebees, dragonflies— alike.

The hedge, the lawn, the big hollow sweetgum in the front yard, the maples and dogwoods and pines, even the scruffy bushes that screened our garbage cans were wildlife habitat. Hundreds of songbirds squabbled at my mother's feeders. A family of rabbits every spring, shuffling quails and burbling doves, and countless reptiles and amphibians all thrived around our house. At lightning-bug time, my friends and I had toadfrog-catching contests. You could catch three dozen of those warty, poison-peeing monsters in an hour, some of them fat as a softball. Terrariums, their glass walls slimed with the leavings of mudpuppies, skinks, snails, and prize toads, were my pride. I also tried to keep box tortoises and various snakes, but they always escaped, often inside the house.

Behind our house was a sharecropper's shack, with a friendly old retired workhorse. Later, when the shack had given way to the grounds of a grandiose white-columned pseudo-mansion, there came a fancier horse, who would eat my father's Chesterfield cigarettes from my hand. At the bottom of the pasture, a little creek had its source.

I cannot remember when I first began to follow that creek downstream. It flowed slowly and opaquely along the bottom of a deep winding gouge cut through layers of the wind-deposited silt called loess. Loess is a very fine and viscid stuff, and it makes one hell of a mud. Where the water backed up, the muck could be waist-deep on a boy.

Miraculously, there were at least a dozen boys within a year of my age all living on one sparsely settled square-quarter-mile quadrangle of roads (and only one girl). I was small, and bad at sports—nearly always last to be chosen for a team—but in the swamp I often led our expeditions, and was usually first to test the footing. My mother always said I was the muddiest boy of all when we came trudging home at suppertime.

Above a pool perhaps a mile downstream, we would swing on grapevines and do cannonballs into water the color of coffee with cream, where the bottom was a bottomless ooze. Snakes swam there, including the dread cottonmouth. Kingfishers laughed in the willows and tall tulip-trees. Catfish took hooked bits of hot dog we dangled from cane poles on lines bobbered with porcupine quills. Once, a gang of us blundered on a hobo camp so freshly abandoned that a half can of beans was still warm on the coals.

As we grew older, I often went into the swamp by myself. I was a melancholy boy, sometimes lonely even among my friends. My solitary wanderings began, I think, as flights, from games in which I could not excel, from an uncomprehended restlessness, from the sweat and tumble and perplexity of social boyhood; but before long my long after-school afternoons alone in the woods had grown into pilgrimages, my weekends and summers rhapsodic quests: I felt that I was seeking something, and sometimes, I know, I found it, though I still could not tell you what it was.

Beyond the tangled muscadine and honeysuckle jungles, beyond the canebrakes in which whole chattering flocks of birds could hide, beyond the old overgrown fields snarled with blackberries and cocklebur, there came an even, easy, open floor of dead leaves and low, soft plants, pillared with trees of awesome girth and height. The canopy was far above, punctured only intermittently by the sun. I believe that this forest had never been logged, although, like some of these others, that memory may be colored by desire. I remember the air as very humid, very hot, very still. I remember the buzzing of wasps in that air, and, in response, the beating of my fretful heart.

My little creek (did it have a name? I never wondered) fed a larger one that fed Nonconnah Creek, which in turn fed the Mississippi River. Nonconnah was occasionally so audacious as to flood its own flood plain, and the Army Corps of Engineers dealt severely with such impertinence.

Their chosen instrument of correction was the dragline, a great toothed scoop on a crane. It could rip out a ton of root-riddled earth in one bite. The messy, inefficient eccentricities of Nonconnah Creek—the oxbows, the riffles and pools, the braided channels, the islanded swamps, the tupelo bottoms—were chastened into an orderly, straight-running ditch. The rate of flow was thus increased, and flooding prevented, and development of previously unusable land made possible. That thousands of such acts of discipline would bring on anarchy downstream was not particularly a worry, for quelling the Mississippi's rebellion farther south would mean more contracts for the contractors, one of whom was the father of one of my neighborhood pals. Racing ever faster, full of the sediment that the old flood bottoms and swamps used to retain, the Mississippi today wants to crash through its banks down near Natchez and pour into the Atchafalaya basin—and leave New Orleans sitting on a mudflat. To prevent this will require one of the most expensive public-works projects in the history of the United States.

The dragline first came when the old one-lane wooden bridge at Mill Branch Road was to be replaced. Growling and grunting, it chewed out the bridge pool and left on the bank two alps of mud. They were the only steep hills we ever had, and they made a splendid place for dirt-clod fights—just the kind of thing my friends loved and I hated. In that deeper water the fishing improved, but where once a boy could sit all day undisturbed but by an occasional truckload of cotton banging over the planks toward the gin, now there was constant traffic: workers and materials for the tract-house subdivisions springing up to the south. I took my cane pole farther now, to the lakes.

My prey was mostly smaller here than the catfish of the creek, but better eating—bream, and crappies, and once in a while a largemouth bass. No matter how early I might come or how late stay, the best fishing spots always seemed to be occupied by an elderly black man or woman with little to say to a white child. I wonder now, did they fear that I might be the landowner's son? And who did own that land? The thought never crossed my mind. They would nod, and keep on fishing, catching ten fish to my one. For them, of course, it was not sport.

There was a place on the creek we called the rapids—it was just a gravelly riffle, really—and there, one day, my best friend, Bobby Towery, and

I came upon the most stupendous animal we had ever met outside the zoo. I knew at once, from my avid reading in field guides, that this was the mighty *alligator snapping turtle*—you could tell by the three mountainous keels on his carapace—the largest species of freshwater turtle in the world, sometimes surpassing two hundred pounds. He was very far from his home, which was supposed to be the Mississippi River.

Snappers are swimmers, not walkers, and this one seemed to have run aground. A gingerly probe with a stick elicited only a slight drawing-in of his huge plated head. We agreed that there was only one thing to be done: we had to capture the turtle. With my trusty Boy Scout hatchet we cut down a small tree and laid the trunk, about two inches thick, across the gravel shallows to block him from escaping into the opaque pool below. While Towery stood guard, I ran home for my green coaster wagon. When I got back, the turtle had not moved a muscle.

We had the idea that if we could get him to bite the pole he would not let go, and then we might haul him to land. How to get him into the wagon we would worry about later. But even with some pretty rowdy poking at his great hooked beak, the snapper could not be tempted to do more than flinch.

We sat on the bank and considered waiting him out. How hideous, how beautiful, how fierce, how still he was! How primitive, how ancient. What was time to a creature like this? Two boys could never outwait such a turtle.

We decided we would try to flip him onto his back. And then what? We'd see. At least he would be immobilized. Prying and pushing and sweating and slipping—and terrified that one slip would tumble us in on top of him—we got our pole beneath him, and the alligator snapping turtle came to life. He whirled—I know, turtles aren't supposed to whirl, but this one did—and bit our two-inch pole in half, and clawed his way into deep water and was gone.

Corpses of frogs, fish, snakes, and crawdads were ranged along my bedroom bookshelves in jars of denatured alcohol. Then my wild bachelor uncle from the Delta, to my mother's horror, gave me a BB gun. No songbird was safe. The first shot usually only knocked it senseless from its perch, and I would seek it out in the brush to administer the coup de grâce to the brain. I made no pretense of collecting them; I left my victims where they lay. My favorite target was the mockingbird, the Tennessee state bird, illegal to kill. What could have possessed me? Remembering this makes my throat clench with shame.

The pursuit of Eagle Scouthood led me to gentler concerns. To take casts of animal tracks for my nature merit badge, I traveled deeper into the old forest than I had ever gone. There were mysteries at every step. Why did the mother raccoon and her family stop here? What made the heron take flight? Fox prints at the edge of the water: did the fox swim, or leap? Hence, slowly, my rage to possess wild creatures was displaced by empathy.

In a little pasture far back in the woods I found a dead calf. The head was twisted half around, the eyes staring into the sky. The skin was peeled back from the rib cage, which was crawling with flies. One leg had been eaten down to the bone. The day was hot, but the flesh had not yet begun to stink, so the kill must have been very recent, and the predator nearby. Crows called. A sharp hind edge of cloud-shade swept across the grass, and in the sudden brightness there was a clarity that I had never seen before, as if a veil had been lifted from the face of the world.

I looked for tracks, found one, and took its cast. It was big, three inches across. My field guide said, unbelievably, cougar! Mountain lion! *Panther.*

Not until years later, when the cast was long lost, did I realize what a find that may have been. *Felis concolor* is extinct now in the Mississippi valley. Indeed the cougar may be gone everywhere east of the Rockies, except for the minuscule and dwindling population of the Florida panther subspecies. Could this have been one of the last eastern cougars? Or was it, as a wildlife biologist suggested to me recently, the hybrid of a calf-killing dog and a boy's eager imagination?

The old-growth forest was cut down, and not even for lumber: the great trees were bulldozed into piles and burned. Most of the topsoil washed away, and the red clay beneath it required laborious cultivation to sustain the newly unrolled swaths of zoysia and Bermuda grass sod. Saplings were planted, and wired upright. The lakes were drained, and the black people moved out. The last hobo known to have visited White-haven was found dead beneath a hedge. We got a shopping center, and an interstate highway. Fluoridation of our drinking water was fought, thought to be a Communist plot to curb the birth rate. I had my first summer job as a carpenter's helper, putting up drywall in new houses.

Improved pesticides came onto the market, and it was possible now to drive through the Delta bottoms with no more than an occasional sweep of the windshield wipers. My wild uncle, who kept bongos and a conga drum in his den closet, got married. The ospreys disappeared from the cypresstop nests, the alligators from the bayous. The only lake left was appropriated by tough teenagers as a beer-drinking hideout; they raped a girl there. Quails no longer shuffled in the leaves on the lawn.

What had been done to Nonconnah Creek was done now to its tributaries. New sewers leaked into the stagnant trench that was all that remained of my creek's headwaters. Our grapevine-draped swimming hole and the alligator snapping turtle's riffle lasted longer, but we could get there on bicycles now, on smooth blacktop. Often I didn't make it that far, having stopped off to chew gum and laugh in Mary Scott Moyers's or Joellen Krayer's yard and lost track of time. When the last of my creek was ditched out, I believe I did not notice.

Twenty years later, home one Christmas from New York, I saw a dragline working in the parking lot of the cabana apartments that stand where my old creek went under the old wooden bridge. I was astonished to see that there was still some life in what the people there now called the drainage ditch: each time the great machine took a bite, the muddy water boiled with creatures forced downstream before it. The V-shaped ditch was being made into a box-shaped one. A chain-link fence was being built along both sides, to keep children safely out. The walls and floor of the drainage ditch were being lined with concrete.

# Singing

The snow cover has slipped off the Lamar like a coroner's sheet. The valley floor looks raw, unseemly. Dead grass lies flattened, mycelium-laced, profoundly ungreen. New birds have arrived, however—a Swainson's hawk, a sudden descent of kestrels. Spring's first ground squirrel stands alert at the roadside, poised to dart beneath your wheels—the first of many of that nerve-wracked species' suicides. A dead spruce grouse lies intact on the center line of the Soda Butte road, in breeding plumage. There is no traffic, only the crawling, wolf-seeking Pathfinder.

Upstream, where the forest closes in, the snow lingers, melted just enough to yield a winter's-worth of bison cocoa-flops atop the crust. Mist veils the spires of the Thunderer and Baronette Peak. Then sun spills through and turns the snow silver. Wolf Fifteen, a black pup with an odd silver saddle, has dawdled behind his Soda Butte packmates. Perhaps he is feeling lonely, for he stops to let fly a lonely-sounding *woof-woof-woof-woooo, woof-woof-woof-wh-hoooo*. Almost instantly the others turn and come bounding back to him. They touch noses and swirl around, and now, bumping jovially against one another, they move inside the forest margin, where they have themselves a walloping family howl. One voice rises from a low baritone note; another cuts in, higher. Coyotes answer from the woods behind. A third wolf and a fourth add their notes to the chord, higher and thinner—these must be the pups—and now the fifth, deep and low. The howling stops abruptly, and an echo returns from the cliffs across the valley.

Howling can bring separated wolves together, even across long distances. Sometimes it seems to say no more than "Here I am." Wolves of the same pack know one another by voice. They may read well beyond identity, into intention, need, pain, desire. Where territories share common boundaries, neighbors too interpret messages—not only the basic "Stay away" but also perhaps greetings, the pack's size, location, constitution, even hunting plans.

There are howling dialects. Erik Zimen, in his book *The Wolf: A Species in Danger*, describes a jaunt in the Minnesota woods with Dave Mech. Mech homes in on an already known rendezvous site and howls, and immediately an adult and five pups answer. "I climbed a tree to get a better view," writes Zimen, "and kept howling in my 'European wolf dialect' while the cubs responded in 'American.' The howling of American wolves is in fact different from that of their European counterparts. I maintained that the howling of European wolves was more protracted and melodious, while that of the American wolves, perhaps because of stronger emphasis on the initial syllables, seemed rather louder. So far as the melodiousness of the howling was concerned, Dave and his colleagues naturally did not agree with me."

A group howl often signals a change in activities. After the members of a pack wake up from a snooze, they will often gather for a song, especially if they are about to go out hunting. Sometimes even a denned-up alpha female will squeeze out from the dark to join in. After the howl, in summer, the hunters file along behind the alpha male, and the mother returns to her brood. A lone wolf trailing along behind a pack will often howl in a sad, soft moan—from a healthy distance. If a member of the pack should go to meet the stranger, the pack wolf may not be particularly friendly, but the loner, apparently wishing to ingratiate himself, will go rapidly through his whole repertoire of friendly, humble, plaintive behaviors, smiling, groveling, showing his belly, trying to lick the haughty pack ambassador's muzzle. If the loner should fail in his appeal for pack membership, he still will howl on his travels, and may thereby

find other loners, a female perhaps. If the space and the prey are sufficient, the new pair may found a pack of their own.

The pack is a social universe, and in constant flux. Pack members
near or adjacent in the social hierarchy often fight, sometimes inflict-
ing serious wounds—and then the victor may spend hours licking the
loser's wounds. Touching, grooming, sniffing, licking, nuzzling, batting,
mounting, soft-biting, "standing above" (where one wolf lays its chin
across another's back, indicating submission on the part of the one
below), barking, whimpering, snarling, growling, cowering, strutting,
snapping, presenting the throat or belly or genitals, shouldering someone
aside, stepping aside so that someone may pass—the pack members
never cease interacting.

The birth of pups often throws the social order into paroxysms of
rearrangement. Decisions have to be made about who can stay and who
can go. The pups soon establish a hierarchy among themselves, although
it is fluid and often revised. The pups must also learn their elders' social
status and act toward each accordingly.

Dominance is never total. Of two wolves of roughly the same size and
age, one may get first dibs on food while the other is allowed more
freedom of movement in social affairs. One wolf may learn gestures and
postures of superiority from an alpha wolf and use them to gain
dominion over a less perceptive wolf who until then has outranked the
good observer. The highest-ranking wolves can almost always be identified by their vertically held tails, waving like flags of honor. The middle
ranks carry the tail from half angled up to straight out toward the rear.
Submission and low status advertise themselves with a hanging tail or
one tucked all the way between the hind legs, often accompanied by a
drooping head—the classic hangdog look. A sister on whom her two
brothers are always ganging up may rise rapidly in status if one of her
persecutors leaves the pack or is killed. Illness and injury often exact a
social cost of their own, however solicitously the victim's packmates may
be treating his affliction. Sometimes a pack member may be nobly self-
sacrificing for the welfare of the group, and the next moment she may be
angrily self-serving. All these behaviors, of course, have developed over
millennia of natural selection, and the choice between one self-sacrifice

and another self-serving act must, at least on average, serve the genetic self-interest of the actor. The nature of altruism in social animals is still poorly understood, but it is the subject of much fascinating study. Nowhere, I think, except in our own species, is the nature of group behavior more complex than in wolf society, with its ever-shifting mysteries.

# The Cardwell Wolf

April 18, 1995

In the summer of 1994, near the tiny hamlet of Cardwell, Montana, the Animal Damage Control unit of the United States Department of Agriculture set a leghold trap to try to catch a family of coyotes that had been preying on calves. When the A.D.C. agent went in to check his trap, he found a wolf in it. He promptly called the U.S. Fish and Wildlife Service office in Helena and spoke to Joe Fontaine, the Montana wolf project leader.

To understand how big a deal it was for a wolf to turn up in the middle of Montana in 1994, we must go back to 1982, when the Endangered Species Act was up for reauthorization. At that time there was near panic in the areas proposed for recovery of the red wolf, in Tennessee and North Carolina. Farmers there, like the ranchers of Greater Yellowstone, had never actually had to deal with wolves, and they envisioned a beast of incalculable destructiveness. The most hotheaded openly proclaimed that they intended to destroy the destroyers, law or no law. Congress, under the quiet guidance of the wolf biologist community and some congressional staffers who feared a wholesale toss-out of the Endangered Species Act, decided to see whether making the law less strict might buy the farmers' cooperation, or at least their grudging assent.

The Endangered Species Act forbids the "taking"—meaning, generally, killing—of any member of any species designated as *endangered*.

"Endangered" is the strictest category under the act, reserved for those species in imminent danger of extinction, which the red wolf certainly was. That is to say, it was if you accept that the red wolf is a separate species, *Canis rufus*. Noting that there is a prodigious range of appearance, size, and habits within *Canis lupus* worldwide, and also on the basis of the minuscule differences in bone measurements and tooth patterns that undergird the obscure art of taxonomy, a growing number of biologists consider the red wolf to be in fact *Canis lupus rufus*, a mere subspecies.

In any case, endangered subspecies qualify for protection equal to that of full-fledged species, and not a single red wolf was left alive in the wild. A few wolf-coyote hybrids had recently been captured, and these were euthanized. (Hybrids generally occur only when a wolf cannot find another wolf—as would be the case in very sparsely occupied habitat, such as the Texas and Louisiana woodlands where the last red wolves had lingered, dwindled, and disappeared.)

The only pure-blooded red wolves left in the world were in a captive-breeding facility, and they were losing their wild qualities rapidly. Those qualities, and the knowledge and skills passed down from elders to the young through practice and example, were essential to the species' ability to survive in the wild. It was imperative that the captive wolves be released as soon as possible.

But what good was that going to do if the farmers were going to shoot, poison, and trap the wolves into oblivion? They had the Endangered Species Act's beautiful purity by the shortest of its hairs. "Laws can never be enforced unless fear supports them," wrote Sophocles, and there was little fear in the wolf hills of Tennessee and North Carolina.

This was where the new idea would come in, in the amendment known as Section 10(j). Under it, a reintroduced population of an endangered species could be managed as though the species had been "downlisted" to *threatened*, the next-lower category of endangeredness, as long as such a change could be considered to enhance the species' prospects for recovery. The reintroduced animals (or plants, I suppose, though I don't think anybody really had plants in mind) would then be known as an "experimental-nonessential population."

Members of a "threatened" species can be taken under certain circumstances—for example, if they are directly imperiling your property, your cow Bossie; *endangered* species are protected almost absolutely. Under Section 10(j), an experimental-nonessential population of reintroduced red wolves could be—that favorite euphemism of wildlife managers—controlled. Usually meaning shot.

The underlying assumption was grounded in the paradox to which Carter Niemeyer testified in Cheyenne. The legislators and their advisers believed that hatred of the wolf was so intense that full legal protection would be likely to result in more illegal killing of wolves on the part of the wolf haters, whereas if the Feds cut the farmers some slack and actually offered to kill the wolves that killed livestock, maybe there would be less hatred and less of the ignoble rural tradition that goes under the rubric of "shoot, shovel, and shut up." And if the reintroduction went haywire somehow, another provision of the rules was that you could go out and round up your whole experimental-nonessential population and terminate the experiment.

As we have seen, the wolf's reproductive rate is so high that a certain amount of what is known as background mortality does not hinder the species' recovery. People kill somewhere between 25 and 40 percent of the wolf population in Alberta that gave us our Yellowstone wolves, and yet that population is not declining. Human-caused mortality can reach 30 percent and sometimes more, and still a wolf population can grow. On the other hand, when mortality crosses a threshold somewhere between 40 and 50 percent, the population will begin to decline. Eventually it will fall to zero with a sudden, unforeseen crash.

The National Environmental Policy Act of 1969 (NEPA), the law that introduced Environmental Impact Statements to the world, stipulates that a wide range of options must be considered for any federal action expected to have a significant effect on the environment. Usually these options range from one extreme to the opposite. In the Draft E.I.S. for the Yellowstone and Idaho proposals, the span was from "no wolf" to "reintroduction of nonexperimental population." (One of my favorite anti-wolf groups was an outfit in Cody, Wyoming, called the No Wolf Option Committee, an incomprehensible name till you know the E.I.S. jargon.) A reintroduced *nonexperimental* population would be classified as "endangered," the highest level of protection. "Reintroduction of experimental population" hovered in between, which as you can imagine is right where the Feds like to plant their own choice.

Designation of the red wolf reintroduction as experimental had been working well in the Southeast, and so when it came time for Ed Bangs and his colleagues to select what in NEPA-ese is called the "preferred alternative," the experimental-population option, to no one's surprise, was the one they picked.

But you cannot use 10(j) if there is an existing population either in or adjacent to your designated experimental area—and in recent years there had been more and more reports of wolf sightings in central Idaho and Greater Yellowstone, some of them highly reliable.

One incident was more concrete than a report. In September of 1992, a hunter named Jerry Kysar shot and killed a male wolf in a big meadow just south of Yellowstone called Fox Park. Reporting the kill as the law required, Kysar claimed that he had thought this *ninety-two-pound* and *black* canid was a coyote—but because he had turned himself in and said he was sorry, the United States Attorney for Wyoming let him get away with it. (You may recall a distinctly nonremorseful Kysar from the 1993 anti-wolf rally at Cody, reciting his doggerel of self-praise and waving the black wolf's pelt over his head.) It took nearly a year to conclude the DNA testing, but Kysar's dead wolf was eventually identified as a long-distance disperser from the famous pack of the Ninemile valley northwest of Missoula, Montana, the subject of Rick Bass's book *The Ninemile Wolves.* They in turn were descendants of the earliest wolves to have resettled in Montana, the Magic Pack, who continue to thrive in the valley of the North Fork of the Flathead River, along the western boundary of Glacier National Park.

After the killing at Fox Park, the Feds redoubled their efforts to see if there were wolves in Greater Yellowstone. Biologists trudged through the snow and flew across the landscape all winter, and they found none. Kysar's black wolf was a lone wanderer, not a member of a population. In the course of the E.I.S., Steve Fritts had consulted most of the major wolf biologists in the world to see what they considered to be the smallest possible number of wolves that could be deemed "a population." The consensus was two breeding pairs—which of course would usually mean two packs.

If there had been even one pack of wolves in Greater Yellowstone that winter, and as long as the seekers put in enough observation effort, the wolves would surely have been found. Wolves tend to be highly visible, especially when seen from the air on snow-covered land. In the snow there will be a great sort of starburst of tracks leading to and from a kill. The wolves themselves often sleep out on the open snow or on frozen lakes.

Many people who have lived all their lives with mountain lions, bobcats, wolverines, and fishers living right next door may never have seen even one. But if wolves are living near you and you keep your eyes open and your ears pricked up, sooner or later you are going to hear them howling, and see their tracks, and see the wolves themselves.

Nevertheless, some people, notably a passionately vocal couple from Wyoming named Jim and Cat Urbigkit (pronounced "ER-be-kite"), continued to insist that there were wolves out there somewhere in the Yellowstone ecosystem. And many of the environmentalists who would settle for nothing less than full protection for all wolves saw a way to enforce their position, for if there were wolves there already, the translocation of Canadian animals to Yellowstone and Idaho would be legally no longer a reintroduction but an "augmentation"—a designation under which no experimental-nonessential flexibility would be allowed. Hence it became advantageous for these wolf advocates to believe in the Urbigkits' phantom population, and they did so.

According to the rules for the wolf reintroduction, any finding that a wolf population was present in Greater Yellowstone or central Idaho would bring the reintroduction to an instant halt—precisely what the Urbigkits wanted. What astonished me was that a number of enviros—holding out for full protection of all wolves, in the category of "endangered"—also seemed not to mind if the experimental reintroduction crashed and burned. The absence of scientific confirmation of any presence of breeding wolves, in either Yellowstone or Idaho, did not deter them in the least.

A more delicate question was whether wolves would recolonize Idaho and Yellowstone on their own in the future—that is, whether the reintroduction should be put off for a while longer, to see if natural immigration would do the job. Wolf range in northern Montana was clearly expanding southward.

The problem with natural recovery was that those northern Montana wolves—fully endangered and therefore fully protected—would be doing their range expansion across several hundred miles of ranch country, perhaps raising hell along the way. The illegal but nonetheless likely reaction could then put a quick stop to the flow of immigration, and Yellowstone and central Idaho might not by then have gotten enough wolves to found a population. In any case, the Fish and Wildlife Service had concluded that the Endangered Species Act, which calls for *action*, mandated the reintroduction.

The Wyoming Farm Bureau Federation's witnesses in Cheyenne last Christmastime claimed not to mind if wolves reestablished themselves in Wyoming on their own. Maybe this was just a disingenuous trial tactic to forestall the reintroduction, but at least some ranchers I know who detest the wolf translocation proclaim that natural wolf recovery would be fine with them.

At the far reach of the other wing, the Sierra Club Legal Defense Fund, generally known in the green community as S.C.L.D.F. (pronounced "skull-duff"), was making noises about suing the secretary of the interior over the plan to restore wolves to central Idaho and Greater Yellowstone, on the grounds of existing wolf populations in both.

Within two days after the Cheyenne decision that set both the Idaho and Yellowstone reintroductions in motion, however, S.C.L.D.F. decided that the reports of existing wolves in Greater Yellowstone were not sufficiently convincing for the group to sue the government over that part of the project. This decision may have been aided by the intense pressure that S.C.L.D.F. was under from conservation groups supporting the experimental-nonessential plan. But on that same day, a coalition of groups represented by S.C.L.D.F. did file suit against the U.S. Fish and Wildlife Service over the Idaho plan, calling it "a scientifically misguided and legally unjustified attempt to mollify those opposed to the presence of wolves in the region."

Dave Mech, among the mildest-mannered people I have ever known, fired off a letter to Victor M. Sher, the president of S.C.L.D.F. "The repopulation of the contiguous forty-eight states by wolves will stand as one of the most important conservation achievements of the twentieth century," Mech wrote. "Society will have come full circle and corrected its grievous overreaction to its main mammalian competitor. . . .

"[At the trial in Cheyenne,] the Farm Bureau made no pretense of understanding the science involved with wolf management, and their case was based solely on their fears as livestock operators. While I testified that their fears are unjustified, I can understand why they have them. I find it far more difficult to understand how conservation groups can so willfully disregard the best science. I simply do not understand your motivation for trying to stop what otherwise will be a national success story."

The true-believer environmentalists' demand for full protection, and therefore no reintroduction, then engendered a very odd conjoining of interests. In the spring of 1995, with the wolves already on the ground but the lawsuits dragging on, U.S. Tenth District Court Judge William F. Downes *combined* the Farm Bureau and S.C.L.D.F. cases! The mortal enemies were now co-plaintiffs. To those of us who found absurd the very idea of environmentalist opposition to wolf reintroduction, this was grimly funny.

S.C.L.D.F.'s was essentially not a biological but a legal argument: if there were wolves already in Yellowstone and central Idaho, then they were ipso facto endangered wolves, and you cannot have reintroduced wolves treated as less than endangered in the same place. That is, you might think you were legally shooting an *experimental* wolf who was chewing on your newborn lamb when in fact, if you were shooting a native wolf—one that was not reintroduced—you were shooting an *endangered* wolf and thereby breaking the law, and how were you supposed to know which is which?

On the other hand, I figured, and so did the Feds, What if you just declared all wolves in the experimental zone to be experimental, even if a couple of them had arrived there naturally? You would still get recovery. But that argument held no water for the Sierra Club Legal Defense Fund: the law was the law.

It seemed to me that underlying the legalism was a gut aversion to seeing any wolves shot, especially by government agents or ranchers. To many in the conservation community, the Endangered Species Act must be pure and absolute, and any fudging—which, at bottom, the whole experimental-population idea is—amounts to crime.

This inflexibility is precisely what fuels the rage of the Endangered Species Act's legion enemies. As the wolf reintroduction was nearing, so too was the time for reauthorization of the E.S.A., and in the newly elected Congress, sentiment was growing to disembowel the Act, which for the right wing has long been the perfect emblem of federal meddling. The moderate enviros argued themselves into exhaustion trying to get the hard-liners to lighten up on this one. Can't you see, they said again and again, that you're playing into the opposition's hands?

This was the battle that Renée Askins and I tried to avert. My greatest concern was with my dear Greater Yellowstone Coalition, which was caught in the middle and leaning the wrong way.

My interest in G.Y.C. dated to 1985, when the young organization's first executive director, Bob Anderson, and I got to be friends. Anderson talked his directors into electing me to the board sight unseen. Then, at my first board meeting, in May of 1986, they fired him.

What followed may not have been total chaos, but it was close enough. The annual meeting, only a couple of weeks after Anderson's firing, was a barely contained insurrection. Anderson was a conservation hero, one of the West's true visionaries. At its headquarters in Bozeman, Montana, G.Y.C. was down to an office manager and one professional staff member, a tireless, tough, and polymathic activist named Louisa Willcox. G.Y.C.'s membership was small, shrinking, and disaffected. Its records were a mess. Nobody was sure whether Anderson was going to sue the board for unjustified dismissal.

Willcox and a squad of volunteers rolled up their sleeves. It took six long, unpleasantly suspenseful months before G.Y.C. was back on course, and a high-paid, high-powered Arizona lawyer named Ed Lewis took a whopping pay cut, moved his family from the land of twelve-month summer to the land of six-month winter, and took the helm.

The seven national forests that make up about 75 percent of the Greater Yellowstone Ecosystem were drafting master plans at that time, and these plans were shaping up as a massive betrayal of the National Forest Management Act, which had mandated their creation. The grizzly bear population was continuing to slip toward extinction. Oil and gas development, new timber sales, new mines, recreational complexes, and dense networks of roads threatened to break the ecosystem into isolated fragments. The lack of coordination throughout the management agencies was abysmal.

Bob Anderson's great achievement for G.Y.C. had been a round of congressional hearings focusing on these very crises, in the fall of 1985, but when Ed Lewis took office at the end of 1986 there was as yet little public evidence of what Anderson had set in motion. All that time, however, the Congressional Research Service had been quietly verifying the accusations that G.Y.C. had leveled at the federal land-management agencies. When the C.R.S. report finally came out, the federal government's stewardship of the largest remaining essentially intact ecosystem in the temperate zones of the earth looked very bad indeed. Employees of the National Park Service and U.S. Forest Service had actually been forbidden to utter the term "Greater Yellowstone Ecosystem."

The C.R.S. report was our breakthrough. Suddenly, at the national level, the Greater Yellowstone Coalition was a force to be reckoned with. In contrast to the bubble-gum–and–bobby-pins style in which the constituent pieces of Greater Yellowstone had for decades been held tenuously together, the Coalition's simple but revolutionary idea of *ecosystem thinking* was so obviously useful and so powerfully integrative that even the most ossified of the agencies, gradually and sometimes grudgingly, began to see its advantages.

The famous Yellowstone forest fires of 1988 respected jurisdictional boundaries no more than grizzly bears did, and I think it was the fires that finally made it undeniable that this truly was one ecosystem and ought to be managed as such. I had become president of the Coalition that spring, and some of our best friends were enraged at our position that wildfire is a natural and inevitable event in a semi-arid forest system. In time, however, anger gave way to understanding. By the time I came to my presidential term limit in 1990, the words "Greater Yellowstone Ecosystem" were being spoken in the agencies without fear of reprisal. Yellowstone was turning green again, and Congress was appropriating serious money to study reintroduction of the wolf.

A little giddy on the good news, I believed that the Greater Yellowstone Coalition was at the forefront of a worldwide awakening, an awakening to the connectedness of the planet and all who dwell on it. Two hundred years ago there had been a similar worldwide awakening, to the universality of human rights. The operant principle was individual independence. The new awakening would be to the unity of the planetary ecosystem, with the operant principle of global *inter*dependence.

I saw those historical moments as analogous, and the second as the completion of the first. Individual independence and social interdependence, ultimately, were indispensable to each other. They were halves of the human whole. G.Y.C. was relatively small, mainly local, and firmly grassroots (the nice word for parochial) in its outlook, but I believed we were part, perhaps even a leader, of a historic wave of change.

And then—well, I'm not quite sure what happened. All I know is that I was swept up in a wave of cynicism. I served out my last two years on the board in a hell of divorce, disillusionment, and pessimism. Wilderness, I saw now, was just what the anti-wilderness cadres had always said: a plaything of the educated and the rich. Wolf reintroduction had nothing to do with the recovery of endangered species; it was sentimental swashbuckling, the conservation equivalent of the nauseating wolf calendars and T-shirts that were becoming so popular. The wolf opponents were right: there were plenty of wolves, and the same damn species, too, in Alaska, Canada, Russia. The puritanical, pony-tailed, Birkenstocked, vegetarian, recycling idealists of the environmental movement were, if not pawns, then fools, or if not just a new stripe of cultural hegemonist, then villains.

It was just then that the proposal for a wolf reintroduction under Section 10(j) was circulating, and in that proposal I saw a beautiful synthesis of pessimism and optimism. The pessimistic assumption was that some people were going to kill wolves no matter what. The optimistic assumption was that this was okay, because the wolf population was going to prosper anyway. Conservation was almost always saying no: stop this timber sale, end that abuse, promulgate new rules against such and such. Wolf reintroduction was saying yes.

I could no longer believe that wilderness was some sacred state of earth-being, for as I was coming to a better understanding of ecology, and as I came to know the wolf, I saw that biotic diversity is not necessarily better protected in officially designated wilderness, and that wilderness alone as we know it in the United States is often a rock-and-ice world of low species richness. Those places were fine—places of transcendent beauty in fact, soul-feeding places—but if it was conservation of nature we were after, we were going to have to look also to the valleys full of farms and ranches, the wetlands behind some shopping mall, the remnants of lowland rivers that have somehow escaped the ministrations of the U.S. Army Corps of Engineers.

For wilderness to fulfill our philosophical requirements of it, we must allow its ecosystems to work on a very large scale. The prairies below the mountains must burn from time to time. The air above must not breathe poison into the soil. The faraway ozone must survive to temper the sun's ultraviolet light. The system itself must be guarded against the island effect that ordains extinctions. Can we meet those demands? Not in this world. Not with *Homo sapiens americanus* at the wheel.

But the wolf! He was just as romantic, just as mysterious, just as wild as the grizzly bear—but the wolf could nap next door to Tuscan farmhouses, howl in the night near Aunt Winnie's cabin, walk through herds of cattle on the way to kill a white-tailed deer in the willows below the corrals.

The wolf could reconnect us to the natural world along the tiny creek near home. In the world of the grizzly bear, you see lonely miles of unpeopled mountainscape, miles of pristine trout-spawning streams, immensities and grandeurs and solitude. In the world of the wolf you see a line of rusty pickup trucks rammed into the riverbank for cowboy riprap, you see hamburger stands, fences, people, particularities—you see a world you already know, not quite a sacred place, just a real one.

Let us grant that we who love the wolf, the bear, and the wilderness are a privileged élite. Let us grant that the costly conservation of the wolf and the bear takes bread out of hungry babies' mouths. Let us grant that the gray wolf is not in any biologically significant sense an endangered species, and that the cost of its reintroduction will be borne less by us than by good people who do not want the wolf next door. Grant even that we are starry-eyed fools of a sort, pursuing a mythical fulfillment that will never be ours.

Let us also proclaim that the return of the wolf to Yellowstone is an act of the greatest of all human capabilities: out of the inner darkness where loss mingles and ultimately merges with love, the creation of beauty. Cathedrals and Holbeins and operas also snatch bread from needy lips.

The attempt embodied in the sanctification of wilderness, in the setting aside of Yellowstone National Park, and in restoration of the wolf is to protect some of creation's greatest beauty, most ancient beauty, beauty that our bones remember. As we walk in such beauty we travel back in time, to the time before cathedrals and portraits and divas, when the landscape was as nature gave it to us. This—come down to the creekside—is how it smelled ten thousand years ago. There—on the ridge—that elk is exactly like the one our forebears saw for a hundred thousand years. They too feared the grizzly bear and laughed at the antics of her cubs. They heard the same wolves howling that we hear tonight, under this same moon.

But they did not see the transcontinental jet airplane razoring a slice across the moon's face. Yes, okay, this wolf reintroduction is an act of imagination, a kind of make-believe. Isn't God, too? Isn't sacredness itself?

Can we say that Yellowstone is a sacred place? I am uncomfortable with the term, but I know that many people do consider it to be. If so, does not the wolf make it more sacred?

These dreamy ruminations of a recovering pessimist crashed head-on into political reality. We expected vigorous opposition from the likes of the Wyoming Farm Bureau. But from our allies, our friends? The Sierra Club Legal Defense Fund, the Sierra Club, the National Audubon Society? They were all co-plaintiffs now, arrayed against Defenders of Wildlife, the Wolf Fund, the National Wildlife Federation. Couldn't they see that division among the wolf advocates could spell doom for the whole program, even for the Endangered Species Act?

The Greater Yellowstone Coalition was undecided whether to join the suit or not. The heart and soul of G.Y.C. was the same Louisa Willcox who had been the heroine of our 1986 nadir. She was now famous in the world of conservation as the most knowledgeable, the hardest-working, the most ferocious environmentalist in the West. She was also recently married to Douglas Honnold, the S.C.L.D.F. attorney who was leading the charge against the experimental-population plan.

In the early fall of 1993, Honnold and Willcox were trying hard to per-suade G.Y.C. to join in the lawsuit. After some considerable hemming and hawing about whether I ought to get near this tarbaby, I called Renée Askins and asked her how things stood.

"Louisa won't speak to me," she said.

"What about Ed?" I asked (G.Y.C. executive director Ed Lewis).

"Ed agrees with Louisa. I really think they're lining up with Skullduff."

For years I had been the most vocal wolf advocate on the Greater Yellowstone Coalition's board of directors. When there was a hearing in Washington, I would write some red-hot testimony and hop on the Metroliner in my best gray Paul Stuart suit and black cap-toed shoes. When Senator Simpson snarled, I smiled and tried to parry. When the other conservation groups were sending paid staff to strategy sessions, I, unpaid, showed up too. All through this time, I was engaged in a long-running sales pitch to my fellow board members, many of whom thought that so controversial a campaign could not possibly be worth the political cost. I believed that the wolf issue would soon come to dominate the nation's perception of Yellowstone.

In September of 1993, I made an impassioned and rather long-winded pitch to the coalition's board of directors to support the pre-ferred alternative of the final E.I.S. and *get the wolf on the ground*. The experimental-nonessential designation, I said, was justified at every pos-sible level—the biological, the social, the legal, the political, the strategic, the philosophical.

At the biological level, I contended, the individual animal would have no idea whether it was in an experimental population or a fully protected one. I talked about wolves' high reproductive rate and their ability to sus-tain substantial mortality even in an expanding population. What did the ecosystem care whether a certain number of wolves were killed by humans or by other means?

This was a great opportunity for our social concerns as well. Couldn't the control provisions in the plan be a starting point toward better rap-port with the ranching community? Wolves did sometimes kill livestock and must sometimes be controlled. Could we expect a rancher who saw a wolf at the throat of a calf not to shoot?

Regarding the legal aspects of 10(j), there were admittedly disagreements, but these were highly technical. In any case, a number of respected conservation lawyers, including Michael Bean of the Environmental Defense Fund, Tom France of the National Wildlife Federation, and the Interior Department's solicitor, who all knew every word of the Endangered Species Act, had found this plan to be in perfect accord with it.

In the political realm, a successful reintroduction would demonstrate that the E.S.A. could flex and did work—a strong point in its favor at a time when the Act itself was endangered.

As for strategy, the goal of conservationists for the past twenty years had been *wolves on the ground* and thriving through the future, and this plan would have that result. Nearly every wolf biologist in the country agreed that it would. What conceivable strategic advantage could there be in opposing those scientists?

My philosophical case was that the Greater Yellowstone Ecosystem must be seen as including a certain amount of human activity. It was a simple fact, and one of far-reaching ecological consequence. Active intervention in certain cases was inevitable, especially around the blurry "edges" of the ecosystem, where human influence is strongest and predators like bears and wolves can cause serious trouble. The core of the ecosystem, in fact, could be kept at a maximum of wildness if we honestly addressed the edge issues—the ones that most commonly bedeviled G.Y.C.—and it was exactly to those most difficult issues that the experimental-population plan was designed to bring justice.

Later that afternoon, there was a vote, and the board was divided in three: a third on my side, a third for supporting the staff position, and a third undecided. I felt sick. I had long defended Louisa Willcox to her detractors, and I considered her a friend and an ally. (She and Honnold had even introduced me to Elizabeth Yates, who is now my wife.) But now Willcox was furious with me. Even Ed Lewis, my closest partner in my time as president, considered my appeal to have been an unjustified interference. I came away believing that G.Y.C. was damned well *going* to join in a feckless lawsuit that could prevent the very wolf reintroduction that we had worked for so hard for so long. They still believed there might be wolves out there somewhere.

And now the Cardwell wolf turns up. Cardwell, Montana, is situated about sixty-five miles northwest of the northwest corner of Yellowstone National Park, just south of Interstate 90—the line below which, according to the reintroduction rules, any wolf was to be considered a Yellowstone wolf.

This was August of 1994. The rule-making had just been signed in June—the final legal step. The aluminum kennels for shipping the wolves were being fabricated in Albuquerque, New Mexico. Forty radio collars had been ordered from Telonics in Mesa, Arizona. Trappers and legal agreements and aircraft were being lined up in Alberta. The pen sites were being selected, the pens designed, the materials bought. The wolf reintroduction was a done deal, dammit!

Joe Fontaine, the Montana wolf project leader for the U.S. Fish and Wildlife Service, in Helena, jumped in the car and sped to Cardwell to have a look at the wolf. The wolf was male, basic gray, seventy-eight pounds. But he had brown eyes. Fontaine's intuition told him that this was probably a wolf-dog hybrid, but the brown eyes were not diagnostic: wolves do have a wide range of facial appearance, and brown eyes, while uncommon, are not unknown.

Fontaine got a vet to fix the animal's trap-damaged foot. Then he put a radio collar on the wolf, turned him loose, and arranged for a couple of generous-spirited volunteers to have their own Telonics antenna and receiver.

For most of a month, the volunteers radio-tracked the Cardwell wolf from their car, and from time to time Fontaine would fly over the area to confirm their coordinates. If this was a wolf, he was a very odd one. He rarely moved more than a mile a day. As far as anybody could tell, he never killed anything. His injured foot was badly infected now, but somehow he kept moving within his tiny home range, eking out a life scavenging in dumps and boneyards.

Then suddenly he disappeared. Fontaine flew all over Montana looking for him, and eventually he found the wolf in wheat-and-barley-farming country along the Missouri River south of Helena. This was lousy wolf habitat, but the Cardwell wolf didn't seem to mind, and he got to be rather a well-known character around the neighborhood. He would let people come within thirty yards of him. Local ranchers would see him sleeping in the midst of their calves. But nobody ever saw him hunting, or even eating. Fontaine guessed maybe he was killing rats in the grain fields. Fontaine also figured by now that the Cardwell wolf was pretty surely not a pure wolf at all, and certainly not a wild one.

By mid-October, the Fish and Wildlife Service decided to go out and get him, take his collar off, and end the farce. They flew for hours, but once again the Cardwell wolf had vanished.

He has finally turned up today—six months later—in El Paso, Texas, approximately one thousand air miles from where he was last reported seen. The dog catcher found him by the side of the road, dead, run over by a car, still wearing his U.S. Fish and Wildlife Service radio collar.

The spot where the animal lay dead is not far from a breeding facility that produces wolf-dog hybrids, so the logical hunch is that this was all somebody's elaborate joke. Maybe the breeder's? Or maybe the bright idea of some merry Montana rancher who went down to Texas, got himself a wolf-dog to set loose, and then after a while picked him up and took the critter home? Seems like a lot of trouble for such an obscure prank.

One of Steve Fritts's study wolves made the longest move ever known to have been made by a wolf—549 miles, from northern Minnesota into central Saskatchewan.

Maybe the Cardwell wolf walked to Texas.

The Crystal Creek pack has made an abrupt and dramatic move. They are six miles outside Yellowstone Park, in the Shoshone National Forest, on the south slope of Hurricane Mesa, in the drainage of Crandall Creek, in deep snow and near precious little prey. Once again, a wolf pack has traveled into country that seems to make no sense—except perhaps in terms of its possible resemblance to their homeland in Alberta.

And once again, the Crystals have dumped Number Two. This is normal, I suppose, especially at this time of year, when home may soon be crowded with new arrivals, but what is it particularly about Two?

The Sodas killed a moose last night or this morning, and soon, as is their custom, moved on. A grizzly bear then took over, and then the coyotes, the birds, and the bugs. There is not much left of the moose carcass now—a smashed skull, the scattered mandibles.

The Sodas approach a bison, whose response is to stand there like a big brown rock until the wolves think of something else to do. Do you suppose that behind those beady, sleepy eyes, that bison brain is pounding with adrenaline, terror, rage? Bison are for me the hardest of Yellowstone's animals to get a feeling for. When Monsieur Touriste pushes in too close with his camera, as several unfailingly do every year (the French, for some reason, are overrepresented in the recent records of bison-related casualties), M. Bison tends to stand there blinking, without a sign of disturbance, until suddenly he explodes into a headlong charge and guts the poor bastard. The Soda Butte wolves sit and watch the bison a while longer, and he watches them. Finally they yawn, rise, and disappear into the shadows of the forest edge.

Doug Smith flies for hour after hour, but he still cannot find the Rose Creek pair.

# *Mysteries*

The Soda Butte wolves have become beautifully boring. Homebodies. Even their unceasing elk slaughter is getting dull.

Seven is still near Tower Junction with her dead elk, and Two is not far away, in the mid-Lamar. Neither, as far as we can tell, has shown the slightest interest in the other.

The Crystal Creek pack is now a good twenty miles outside the park, and at an inconceivable elevation—on the bleak flat summit of Beartooth Butte, some 10,500 feet above sea level. The weather up there is monstrous at this time of year; hundred-mile-an-hour winds and fifty below zero are common. There is very little in the way of wildlife on the Beartooth Plateau even in summer—a few rodents, a few mountain goats, a few little brown birds, an occasional grizzly bear, an only recently identified new subspecies of red fox—and in winter there is almost nothing but the fox. Nothing for a wolf to eat, nothing, that I can think of, for a wolf to do. But there they are, easily visible from the plane, lolling on the snow.

Again Doug Smith has flown long and far, and again has not found Nine and Ten. They have been missing for seven days now.

Smith sighs. "This is bad."

# Desperation

All morning the sky is low and gray. Wind slaps the thin hangar walls. Flying is impossible. Smith paces up and down. At last the weather breaks a little, and he takes hastily to the air.

He finds the Sodas still on their best behavior, no more than a few miles north of their pen. He must fly far to the north before he finds the Crystal Creek wolves. They have traveled twenty miles from Beartooth Butte since yesterday, in the worst possible direction. They have dropped down off the north edge of the Beartooth Plateau and are still headed north, along a ridge above the deep narrow canyon of Rock Creek. If this were a hundred years ago, they might have found extensive elk winter range where the canyon mouth opens to the prairies. Now, unfortunately, they will find the town of Red Lodge, Montana.

Smith flies back and forth and up and down, from Hayden Valley, in the center of Yellowstone Park, to the east side of the Absarokas and north up Slough Creek, up the Buffalo Fork, up Hellroaring, down the east, west, and main forks of the Boulder, up the Stillwater, down Rock Creek off the Beartooths, across the elk-thronged Northern Range, up the Paradise Valley to Livingston and still farther along the Yellowstone River, as far east and north as Big Timber, Montana. Nine and Ten cannot be found.

Tomorrow the wolf team will bring out two airplanes.

# *Footprints in the Snow*

APRIL 21, 1995

A call comes in from Red Lodge. An agent of the Montana Department of Fish, Wildlife and Parks has seen what he believes to be wolf tracks in the snow, just outside of town.

A quiet panic, not unmixed with exhilaration, grips our hearts. This is too far. Why should any of these wolves have abandoned the prey-rich and unpeopled elk winter ranges, unless they think they are headed back to Canada?

On the other hand, Red Lodge is better than Hinton. And only living wolves leave tracks.

The two airplanes lie in readiness at Gardiner, prepared to sweep back and forth across the entire northern Yellowstone region, and beyond if need be. Till now the biologists have been flying up and down the major drainages, basing their routes on what they believe they know of likely wolf travel patterns, which typically follow waterways or ridgetops. Now they will fly higher, on a comprehensive grid that will leave no tiniest creek or slope unsearched. But the weather is gusty, low, unflyable.

# Ill Tidings

Mark Johnson has been seeing to the wolves' well-being with loving care ever since the trapping in Canada began, but I can hardly look at him today without laughing in cynical mockery. He is so straight, so sincere, such a happy-face—as if his wonderful wolf project was going just *great*.

A group of zoology students from the University of Montana are visiting the park, and Johnson is putting on a slide show for them. Like Jim Halfpenny, Johnson has a bit of a Civil War look, thanks mainly to the abundance of beard, but behind the shrubbery there seems to be a sort of oh-boy innocence, which I would find touching if the wolf reintroduction had not gone so sour.

In a rapture of enthusiasm, Johnson recounts the contagion-minimizing wolf-shipping boxes he designed, and the painstaking weeks of selecting the pen sites and building the pens. The sites had to be level and hidden but accessible to humans in less than thirty minutes' walking, and then the park had to survey each site for possible rare plants and archaeological significance. The pen materials were lowered in by helicopter so as not to disturb the soil, and not to reveal to prying eyes a pathway to the captive wolves.

The pen configuration was designed not only to prevent the wolves from getting out but also to keep out the bullies of the Yellowstone wilds—bison and grizzlies. Hence the high-voltage electric wire around the outside. Johnson designed the pens to be cornerless, not only to discourage escape but also to make it less likely that dominant pack members could corner and kill a subordinate.

There would be a "security box"—biologese for doghouse—for each wolf, so they could hide from people or get away from other wolves. Also, if you needed to give a wolf a shot, you could chase him into the house and bolt the door, then open the hinged roof and jabstick the wolf from above or dart him with a blowgun.

From Johnson's point of view—or at least this is the impression he intends to convey—the project has been a wonderful success. The trapping went fine, the shipping went fine, the confinement was fine, the wolves are hunting wild prey, they are not killing livestock or one another, and they seem to be healthy. I remind myself, however, that the point of it all has been to restore wolves to Yellowstone, and two packs of three seem to be leaving.

The weather is still no good, but Smith cannot keep himself on the ground. Late in the day, wrenched and rocked in the angry wind, he flies back and forth across the snowy mountains, dark canyons, wide prairies. What he finds does no one's heart good.

Nine's daughter Seven has also left Yellowstone Park. She has headed due north up Hellroaring Creek into the Absaroka-Beartooth Wilderness, and she is still moving north.

And now the Sodas—the good, predictable, home-loving Sodas—have left the park as well, also to the north. They are already twenty miles north of the park boundary and are still going. They have passed over the crucial drainage divide separating parkward-flowing waters from north-flowing streams, and are moving down the drainage of the Stillwater River, which shoots through a steep wilderness canyon, largely devoid of game, until it begins to slow and meander through open grassland—elk winter range, private land, ranches. North of that lie many miles of easily passable prairie. There is not a significant topographic barrier between the Soda Butte pack and the land of their birth. There are, however, plenty of people with guns.

The weather over Red Lodge keeps it unapproachable, so Smith cannot locate the Crystals, and Nine and Ten are still unfound.

Of the fourteen wolves brought to Yellowstone in January, only one, Number Two, the timid Crystal Creek pup, remains inside the national park.

# A Man in a Truck

Bad weather. No flight.

Jim Halfpenny and I mull over the possible reasons for the nearly simultaneous movement of at least two packs, and probably three, so suddenly toward the north. The most obvious hypothesis is that snow conditions have prevented the wolves from getting over the jumble of the Beartooth and Absaroka ranges, and now that the snow has formed a walkable crust, they are simply doing what they have wanted to do since day one: go home.

There are alternative hypotheses. For example, this movement could be a random coincidence of random habitat exploration—three lemons coming up on the slot machine. Or it could be that the human presence in the Lamar has disturbed the wolves more than we realized, and they are just trying to get away from people, cars, noise. Maybe their movement has something to do with seeking isolation for denning, and this is actually a great thing—the imminent birth of a litter, two litters, three litters of pups. Two of the Soda Butte females are sexually mature, and both of them were in heat, and while it is rare it is not unknown for two litters to be born to one pack. What's more, good nutrition, which they have certainly had, is known to increase the odds of reproduction and to increase litter size. There could, then, not inconceivably, be four big litters of native-born Yellowstone wolves. Let's call it half a dozen each litter—

twenty-four pups. At this rate we'll be hitting recovery before the turn of the century. And Maybe Nine has secreted herself in a cave high in the mountains, and Ten has killed a moose just outside, and therefore they can spend their time inside the house together—with their new family—and that is why they are not coming through on the radio.

Maybe.

Between the emaciated and dwindling villages of Washoe and Bear Creek, Montana, a rutted two-track ranch road climbs southward up Scotch Coulee toward the old stagecoach line known as the Meeteetsee Trail, which rounds the muddy northern flanks of Mount Maurice and then descends to cross the windswept deserts east and south. Mount Maurice dominates the skyline south of the town of Red Lodge. It is a massive mountain, both broad and tall—ice on top, then subalpine spruce-fir forest, then lodgepole pine, then Douglas-fir mixed with spruce, then aspen and willow, and finally foothills of sagebrush and grassland. Across the Bear Creek highway to the north lie the ruins of the Smith coal mine, the site of Montana's deadliest industrial disaster, an underground fire in 1943 that killed seventy-four men.

Since then, this has been very lonesome country. Scattered here and there from Washoe to Bear Creek and beyond, abandoned mining shacks are rotting into the earth. Even in the towns, only a few decrepit houses remain occupied.

What sparse grass there is has just begun to green up. The snow that has brushed the Rock Creek canyon and Red Lodge just over the ridge to the west did not come this far into the weather-shadow of the mighty Beartooth Range. Snow rarely does; neither does rain; neither do people come this far. A few steers graze, widely scattered, through the rabbit-brush and greasewood, but the landscape is for the most part empty of both man and cow.

Red Lodge averages twenty-one inches of precipitation a year, but here on Bear Creek, only a few miles to the east, the average is eight. This is a land of dry washes and yellow clay buttes, of silences, wind, space, anonymity.

A man in a blue 1988 Ford four-wheel-drive pickup truck turns south off the highway onto the Scotch Coulee track. At this wettest moment of the year, the ruts are aswim in gumbo-brown water. The truck grinds slowly uphill past rusting mining equipment, broken bottles, a ruined railroad spur. A narrow feeder creek comes gurgling through a culvert beside which generations of people past caring have dumped generations of refuse. A little unpainted cabin clings to the brushy hillside, home to a friend of the man in the truck.

Past the cabin, the grade grows steeper, and the road deteriorates further. The soil is deep and fine-grained, the mud adhesive. Slipping, yawing, the truck claws up toward the high woodside meadows where black bears graze in the spring, on the northeast face of Mount Maurice. This is private land, property of the Sunlight Ranch Company—one of a complex of ranches owned by one Earl Holding, the president of Sinclair Oil and the founder of the Little America chain of truck stops—and the man in the blue pickup does not have permission to hunt here. It does not bother him to be trespassing, though. He has bear on his mind, a spring bear-hunting license in his pocket, and a scope-mounted Ruger M-77 7-mm magnum rifle on the seat beside him.

Fishtailing, slinging mud clots from its spinning wheels, the truck founders, high-centered on the hump between the ruts, dead stuck.

Chad McKittrick gets out and contemplates the brown-spattered fenders, the wheels sunk axle-deep. There is nothing else to do, in the gathering dusk, but shoulder his rifle and hike the two miles down the mountain to his friend Dusty Steinmasel's cabin.

It is a Sunday evening, and Steinmasel is at home. McKittrick's tale of muddy woe does not surprise Steinmasel, who has known him since high school in Red Lodge.

They try to free McKittrick's truck in the dark, but Steinmasel's Jeep Cherokee is no match for the April muck. He drives McKittrick home, and they agree to try again first thing in the morning, with McKittrick's other rig and some proper equipment.

# *Why?*

In the midst of what seems to be a mass exodus of wolves from Greater Yellowstone, Dave Mech returns—just in time for the shattering of premature conclusions. Mike Phillips climbs down out of the Super Cub to report on his morning of radio-tracking. The Soda Butte wolves have turned around—headed south, back upstream along the Stillwater. They seem to have traveled as far north as the Stillwater mining complex, a big compound of buildings, adits, heaps of platinum and palladium ore, settling ponds, houses, and round-the-clock hubbub. Apparently the Sodas found the neighborhood uncongenial.

The Stillwater is a fine place for wolves in the springtime—a broad canyon, no higher than six thousand feet at the bottom, mostly snow-free now, untrammeled by humans at this time of year, partly forest, partly meadow, and partly burned, and therefore richly grassy ungulate habitat. Most important, the Sodas are within a day's travel of an easy crossing of the Slough Creek drainage divide, which in turn would lead them, as they move downstream, back into the park.

The Crystal Creek pack has also turned around. They have backtracked with astonishing precision along the path they had taken toward Red Lodge, then up and over the ice-blasted heights of the Beartooth Plateau and Clay Butte, down across the Beartooth Highway and the upper Clark's Fork of the Yellowstone, around Hurricane Mesa, then finally to the ridge above Crandall Creek, exactly where they camped last week. If they continue this way, they will soon be back in the Lamar.

Seven, the Rose Creek pup, has also turned around. She has come back down Hellroaring Creek, and is less than a mile north of the park boundary.

Two, the Crystal homeboy, remains in the Lamar. In all the days of his freedom, he has yet to travel farther than three miles from his pen.

And Nine and Ten are found at last! Phillips radio-locates them, and then he sees them clearly, in a little snow-bright clearing on the north slope of Mount Maurice, just inside the Custer National Forest boundary—less than ten miles from Red Lodge, alive, and not headed farther north. Where have they been? Why has intensive radio-tracking day after day after day failed to find them? No one will ever know.

As Phillips flies in circles above them, Ten is moving around, but Nine stays solidly put the whole time. Could it be that she has denned?

The homing hypothesis lies crumpled on the wolf team's floor.

Where Mount Maurice slopes down toward Red Lodge, the upland forest gives way to aspen groves amid softly weeping talus jumbles; farther down, as the steepness shallows, lie the pastures of the Sunlight Ranch. The land has no cattle on it this early in the spring, nor cowboys, and it is teeming with deer, so it does seem plausible that Nine and Ten could safely settle there. Let them start eating deer, and maybe they will leave Mr. Holding's cattle alone. The Fish and Wildlife Service guys in Helena are proud of their northern Montana wolves who live in the midst of ranches and cows. The wolves are not killing stock, and the people are not killing wolves.

Phillips will not hear of it. "I'm supposed to be restoring wolves to the Greater Yellowstone Ecosystem," he says grimly. "I think you could question whether where Nine and Ten are is even inside the ecosystem. If it is, it's sure as hell on the edge of it. And it's nothing but downhill and wide open to the north and the east. Nothing but people and ranches and cattle and trouble."

Phillips looks out the window. Almost inaudibly, as though to himself, he murmurs, "Shit."

.    .    .

Chad McKittrick and Dusty Steinmasel, in McKittrick's number-two truck, a green 1978 Ford, return at seven-thirty in the morning to the mired pickup on Mount Maurice. They come armed with lumber, chains, shovels, axes, pry bars, a handyman jack, and McKittrick's customary just-in-case firepower, including a .44-caliber magnum revolver, a .22 rifle, and the Ruger 7 mm. They pile one-by-sixes and two-by-sixes behind the tires and try to lever them underneath. McKittrick, wheels spinning and motor roaring, rocks the blue truck back and forth as Steinmasel pulls with the green one. Steinmasel looks up to see a small single-engine airplane circling directly above them.

After an hour and a half of struggle, the stuck blue truck slithers free, and the mud-stained men sit quietly inside it to have an early-morning beer and talk about maybe going bear hunting later.

McKittrick is forty-one years old, pale, burly, high-cheekboned, short-necked, mustachioed, bald beneath his battered felt cowboy hat. He wears thick glasses over his narrow blue eyes. Steinmasel, forty-three, is as dark as McKittrick is pale, big, broad-shouldered, clean-shaven, with long, luxuriant brown hair pulled into a ponytail; he looks rather like an Indian but is not. McKittrick walks lightly, delicately. Steinmasel tends to lumber. They have both been around Red Lodge on and off since high school, seeing each other from time to time at the Snow Creek Saloon or another of the bars along Broadway—casual friends, no more, with not much in common but their station near the bottom of the continually upward-stretching socioeconomic scale of Montana.

Steinmasel works as a laborer for a concrete company. Divorced, but a good father to his two kids, he works hard, and keeps out of trouble. He is a bow hunter, a sportsman. McKittrick drifts in and out of trouble, in and out of jobs—freelance carpenter, oilfield roughneck, firewood cutter, collector of shed antlers. He is also a collector of firearms; some people in Red Lodge call him a gun nut. He is a lifelong bachelor, a regular at the Snow Creek Saloon, a friendly fellow who drinks a lot. He is a renegade from a strict Mormon family; two of his brothers were missionaries.

McKittrick starts the truck.

"Chad, look!" whispers Steinmasel hotly, pointing up the hill at something moving.

The door flies open, and McKittrick runs to the green truck and pulls out the Ruger. He settles the rifle butt against his shoulder and sights through the five-to-nine-power zoom scope, which is set at a magnification of five.

"That's a wolf, Dusty," he says. "I'm going to shoot it."

"Are you sure?" says Steinmasel. "It might be a dog."

"No," says McKittrick, "it's a wolf."

"Chad, no," pleads Steinmasel. "What if it's somebody's dog?"

"Yeah, right," says McKittrick. He takes aim.

About a hundred and forty yards away, Wolf Number Ten is walking slowly along a ridgeline, silhouetted clearly against the sky. Surely Ten sees the man with the rifle, but he is not afraid.

Number Ten was the only wolf who would run close to people when they came inside his pen in the park, the only wolf to leave his pen right after it was opened, the only wolf to stand in plain sight on the hill in the snow and howl at the people coming to feed him and his mate and her daughter. Whatever his experiences in Alberta may have been, Ten has shown little fear in Yellowstone, and he shows none now.

Steinmasel rummages for his binoculars. Just as he gets them into focus, he hears the shot. He sees the wolf spin around, bite at the wound high on his back, fall, kick his legs twice, and then lie still.

*"Why?"* Steinmasel cries out.

The single 7-mm magnum bullet has struck Number Ten in the upper chest cavity and ripped out through the other side, leaving massive lung hemorrhage and a shredded liver in its wake. McKittrick lays down the rifle and takes up his forty-four magnum pistol for the coup de grâce, but by the time McKittrick and Steinmasel reach him, Ten is dead.

There is no question now. This is not a dog. Ten is wearing a radio collar imprinted with the words NATIONAL PARK SERVICE and HINTON, ALBERTA, and bearing the name AURORA, each wobbly letter hand-painted in a different color by schoolchildren who thought this collar was bound for Idaho. In each of the wolf's ears is a red plastic tag marked FWS in white letters on one side and 10 on the other.

"This is a big fucking deal, Chad," says Steinmasel, who is scared, disgusted, and on the verge of throwing up. "We need to go to town and find somebody from Fish and Game and report this."

"No," replies McKittrick, "we can't report this. I'll go to jail. I can't do time."

"If we're not going to report it," Steinmasel tells his friend, "you're on your own. I don't have nothing to do with this. If we report it, I'm behind you a hundred percent. I'm a witness. It's an accident."

"No," says McKittrick. "I could go to jail."

It is nine o'clock in the morning. Steinmasel and McKittrick agree that more beer is called for. They drop one of the trucks at Steinmasel's cabin and head downhill in the other to the tiny crossroads of Belfry, Montana, to acquire a twelve-pack at Belfry Mercantile.

The wolf's body is still lying sprawled on the ridgetop. On the way to Belfry, McKittrick and Steinmasel realize that the radio collar is surely still transmitting. Steinmasel reminds McKittrick about the single-engine plane that was circling above them this morning. They drive back over the little-traveled Meeteetsee Trail and down the Scotch Coulee track to below the ridge where Ten lies dead.

Steinmasel hikes up to get the carcass. It is too heavy to carry, so he drags it downhill. "Here's your wolf," he says to McKittrick. "What are you going to do with him?"

Together the men pitch Ten's body into the back of the pickup. Steinmasel takes a wrench and unbolts and removes the radio collar. McKittrick slips off the red plastic ear tags. "I want him," says McKittrick. "Let's take him down to your garage and skin him."

"No fucking way, Chad," replies Steinmasel.

They find a secluded place back in some cottonwood and willow and string the wolf up with orange baling twine. McKittrick cuts off Ten's head—he wants the skull. Then he goes to work skinning the body. McKittrick is not much of a skinner, and Steinmasel grows impatient. He is thinking again of the plane. What if it comes back now? If that's one of those tracking planes, whoever was in it could follow the radio signal and see them from the air with the dead wolf. Finally Steinmasel helps finish the skinning. They pick up Ten's gleaming, blood-slick carcass by its big, densely furred feet and heave it into the brush below a red clay bank.

"At least let me hose down the cape at your house?" asks McKittrick.

They drive carefully down the Scotch Coulee track to Steinmasel's cabin. McKittrick sprays the blood from the raw pink underside of Ten's skin.

"I'll take care of the collar," says Steinmasel. "Smash it or something."

McKittrick stuffs Ten's head and hide into a plastic garbage bag, heaves it into the bed of his blue truck, and drives home. Steinmasel follows in McKittrick's green truck.

Behind McKittrick's house stands a cabin that he is building a bit at a time, whenever there comes a little money for materials and he has the energy. In the cold of the half-built cabin, where it will not spoil, Steinmasel helps McKittrick drape the wolf skin over a stepladder.

"We're right here," says Steinmasel. "Let's report it."

"No," replies McKittrick, "I can't do it."

"Will you at least leave me out of it? Like, a gentleman's agreement?"

"Okay. Sure." They shake hands on it.

McKittrick drives Steinmasel back to the cabin in Scotch Coulee.

Steinmasel tries yet again. "We can go up the canyon and take care of this right now"—meaning bring the carcass down and call the authorities.

"I'm going bear hunting," is McKittrick's only reply.

Dusty Steinmasel sits in his house contemplating the radio collar. He does not know that when a Telonics radio collar has not moved for more than five and a half hours, its usual rate of forty beeps per minute leaps to a rapid-fire hundred-plus. Even a sleeping animal moves around a little from time to time, so when the faster signal comes in, you know that either the collar has somehow come off or the wearer is dead. The signal is known as mortality mode.

Steinmasel assumes that the radio collar is still transmitting, and he knows that unless he destroys it it is going to continue. He gets out his world atlas and looks up Hinton, Alberta.

He hears a vehicle. He sees the lights. His heart clenches like a steel-jawed trap. It is only his neighbor, driving down out of Scotch Coulee.

He cannot live with this fear. He is in too deep already. He cannot bring himself to smash the radio collar. He wipes it down to get the fingerprints off. In the dark he walks down the rutted road toward the highway, to the culvert where the runoff-swollen creek rushes through. He drops the collar in. He does not know if the signal can be heard from underwater, but he hopes it can. He wants Chad McKittrick to be caught. He wants to be caught himself.

# *Ill Wind*

Steinmasel runs into McKittrick at the convenience store in Red Lodge. McKittrick has a copy of the Billings *Gazette* in his hand. There is nothing in it about a wolf being killed. "You take care of that collar?" McKittrick murmurs edgily.

"Yeah," Steinmasel lies.

Snow clouds blow in from the west. White ice-edged gusts whip against quivering aluminum wings at the Gardiner airstrip. Smith and Phillips sit by the phone, waiting for clearing weather, which does not come.

# Mortality Mode

Sun spills down the clay face of Mount Everts and finds its way inside every new green blade of grass on the velvety bench between the Gardner and Yellowstone rivers. Across my cabin-knoll at Above the Rest the south breeze from the Absaroka heights is stiff and chill, but when the wind rests the sun is warm. I wander down through the creek bottom in search of lee warmth. First phlox of the year, flat white stars. First buckwheat, dark gold buttons. In the mud a first buttercup. First grasshopper. First mosquito: ow. A meadowlark, the cowboy nightingale, fills the little aspen vale with melisma. A flicker rattles through the budding branches. An eagle, an immature golden, turns in a wide arc far overhead. Making a most remarkably un-avian sound—a perfect reproduction of a drumstick knocking on a hollow wood block—a raven wheels into a cleft in an orange cliff and lands on a heap of what passes in raven society for a nest, a slovenly pile of old sticks. Probably just been down to the airport for a hearty breakfast of shit soup.

When I return to the cabin, there is a message from Halfpenny on my answering machine. Doug Smith has landed, and the news is bad.

Flying over Rock Creek upstream from Red Lodge to see if Nine and Ten were still in that area, Smith picked up Number Nine's signal from the exact spot where she was the day before yesterday. Ten's collar, however, was transmitting in mortality mode.

The signal was faint, and vague, bouncing all over the place. Unwilling to believe that Number Ten could be dead, Smith told himself that the wolf might have slipped out of the collar somehow; that would explain the mortality signal. Then maybe somebody found the collar on the ground, and now the collar was inside a building; that would explain the low quality of the signal. There were plenty of buildings along Rock Creek. He kept flying, trying to figure out what was going on, but he never could get a decent location. He circled and circled, searching, disbelieving, his dread intensifying one agonized notch at a time. He was running out of gas.

At park headquarters all hell breaks loose. Frantic phone calls fly back and forth across the country. Do we call the secretary of the interior? The director of the Park Service? Do we wait till this is confirmed? This could be nothing. Nothing is certain till it is ground-truthed. Someone had better get over to Red Lodge pronto. Who? Park Service or Fish and Wildlife? Biologists or law enforcement? Do we tell the public or keep this quiet till we know something for sure? Whispered meetings cluster in the hallways. Intra-office tempers flare. Who has the right to know, who doesn't, who ought to have been notified before somebody else, what do we *do*?

Smith meanwhile is trying to stay calm, telling himself that this could all be a false alarm, worrying that he will be adjudged a conclusion-jumping alarmist. After all, the mortality signal could be nothing more than transmitter malfunction. Or maybe the collar is lying on the ground, beeping away while Ten goes about his business.

The Park Service's first instinct, true to its bureaucratic soul, is to declare the whole thing secret. But the wolf team in Helena has got to be told, and the Montana Department of Fish, Wildlife, and Parks. The director of the U.S. Fish and Wildlife Service, Mollie Beattie, a passionate wolf partisan, has made it clear that whenever something goes importantly wrong in this program, she is to hear about it without delay. Federal and state investigators must be brought in fast if there is to be any hope of catching the killer. If there is a killer, that is.

Mike Phillips and Doug Smith are already speeding toward Red Lodge in a government truck, so I call Wayne Brewster. He is incensed that I have found out about Ten already, and that I want more information. "I can't say anything to you, Tom," he says officiously, and rings off.

Brewster's boss, John Varley, is away at a conference. The park press officers will not take my call. I throw my laptop and some clothes in the back of the noble Pathfinder and make tracks for the scene of the crime. The road is narrow, icy in unexpected spots, treacherous; I speed whenever I dare, but it still takes me three hours.

As soon as they get to Red Lodge, Phillips and Smith are to meet up with Joe Fontaine, who is racing down from Helena, and Tim Eicher, a special agent from the Fish and Wildlife Service Division of Law Enforcement. A couple of Montana game wardens will also be there waiting for them. By the time they get organized, the investigative team will have only a few hours of daylight left, and snow—evidence-obliterating snow—is expected tonight.

Although they have the map coordinates from Smith's overflight, nobody is very confident about their accuracy because the signal was so funky. Usually a radio-location will tell you within two or three hundred yards where the signal is coming from—and under ideal conditions telemetry can be still more precise—but the signal that Smith got was so vague that they are going to have to search a wide area. The country is rugged, with few roads.

The weather closes in. Flying is out. They will have to try to home in on the ground. I fear, as do Phillips and Smith, that if they do not find Ten today they will never find him. All it takes is a good hammer, to smash the collar, and a shovel, to bury the body.

Under the experimental-population rule, it is legal to kill a wolf if you see it attacking your livestock, but you must report the killing within twenty-four hours. No such report has been filed. Therefore, even if somebody has killed Ten in the act of depredation, and the killer does not pick up the phone pretty soon, he will be a criminal at nine tomorrow morning. Under the Endangered Species Act, the killing of a protected animal is punishable by a fine of up to twenty-five thousand dollars and a prison term of six months. Possessing the dead animal is good for another twenty-five thousand and six months in stir. Transporting the body, oddly enough, because that crime is covered by the Lacey Act, can add a hundred-thousand–dollar fine and a year in prison.

.  .  .

Despite his Ohio birth, his Michigan education, and his master's degree in wildlife biology, U.S. Fish and Wildlife Service special agent Tim Eicher is the very image of the Western lawman. From the tip-top of his big cowboy hat or, if indoors, his gleaming bald dome, to his steady blue-eyed stare and his luxuriant handlebar mustache and down to the sharp-tipped toes of his high-heeled boots, everything about Eicher proclaims that this is not a man to be messed with. His voice is low, and hard. His words are spare, and precise. Just looking at him makes me feel like a teenager shoplifting condoms.

Eicher's stiff-necked cop taciturnity, while real enough, is underlain by a still quieter sense of antic humor, but what some wolf shooter is by God going to get is, in Eicher's own words, "a man hunter. And I don't fail. It may take time, but I get who I'm after. Always."

Agent Eicher and Carbon County sheriff Al McGill work their way along the Meeteetsee Trail, the road nearest to where Nine and Ten were last seen together, by Mike Phillips, in the early morning of the twenty-fourth, but their receiver picks up nothing. They start down the Bear Creek highway—toward Dusty Steinmasel's house—but it is ten o'clock by now, full dark, too late for the ravens and magpies that are the day-light beacons of a newly dead animal. Everybody is exhausted, and the sheriff and the special agent do not explore far enough down Bear Creek to pick up the signal there either.

Doug Smith and Mike Phillips stay out listening on a high ridge until eleven. There is no signal now from Ten's collar at all.

# The Radio Collar

Doug Smith takes to the sky at first light. Old, grainy snow streaks the greening foothills of Mount Maurice, but there is only a thin veil of new-fallen. The evidence, if any is to be found, remains unburied. Smith tunes in to Nine's frequency, and there she is, in a small clearing in the woods on the north slope of the mountain, just inside the national forest boundary, no more than five miles from Red Lodge, exactly where she was three days ago, with her mate. Damn, says Smith to himself, what a terrible place to den.

Now the Super Cub wheels northeastward, and Smith switches his receiver to 216.190, Number Ten's frequency. The signal is somewhat muffled, but louder and clearer than yesterday; it is still in mortality mode. Again Smith cannot home in on the precise location—maybe the signal is ricocheting, maybe the collar is indoors or under something—but as they tune in from different angles both the biologist and the pilot grow certain that the radio signal is coming from somewhere in the valley of Bear Creek.

Smith hastily draws a map of the area, showing as well as he can where he thinks the collar may be. Now Sheriff McGill, Tim Eicher, Joe Fontaine, and the state wardens can narrow the search for Ten on the ground. They drive over the snowy divide and down the Bear Creek highway into the desert. As they near a rutted old ranch road near the ruins of the Smith coal mine, the signal grows stronger.

About three miles downstream along the creek, an old-fashioned branding is under way. Mounted cowboys in full regalia are separating the cows and calves. They rope and tie the calves one by one, castrating the bull calves and tossing the glistening prairie oysters straight onto the iron-heating grill. They inoculate the calves, punch insecticidal plastic tags through their ears, sizzle the brand into heaving flanks with a red-hot iron, all to the music of death-certain bawling from the calves and the moans of their desolate mothers across the fence, to whom each year this terror is new. It is hard and dirty work amid the stink of panic-diarrhea and burned flesh. Branding is a great moment in the ranching year. The calves have made it out of winter, and money is on the hoof.

The herd is small, maybe fifty cow-calf pairs. This is not great cattle country. It is too dry, too hard, too cold. It is excellent deer habitat, however, with both whitetails and muleys plentiful. There are a few wintering elk as well. There is certainly enough game to sustain a family of wolves. There is certainly enough windswept solitude for a man to shoot one of them and for the shot never to be heard.

Sheriff McGill well knows that there are plenty of possible wolf killers within a short drive of this lonely road in the desert. Along Rock Creek above Red Lodge, where the land is lush and game is abundant, the houses are lined up in almost suburban density. Plenty of candidates there. Then there is Red Lodge itself, not twenty minutes' wolf trot downstream, or ten by motor vehicle—nineteen hundred humans, mostly peace-abiding certainly, but also including at least a few with itchy fingers and some long-simmering grudge against the government or the enviros or whomever else they might choose to see the wolf as symbolizing. At a café on Broadway in Red Lodge, a lawyer friend of mine who has done a fair amount of freelance prosecution for the state, including a number of poaching cases, leans forward confidentially over his cup of coffee: "I can name you a couple good suspects right off the bat."

The mortality signal grows still stronger. The urgent beeping leads the search team south off the Bear Creek highway and up a narrow, muddy track between sage-covered hills pocked with melting snow. Two hundred yards in, they come to a little feeder creek running through a culvert beneath the road. The signal is now so intense that Fontaine removes the aerial from his receiver. Several scruffy young cottonwoods rise from the bank. Garbage and old mining debris are scattered up the hillsides and downstream. The spring runoff water is high, sluicing through fast and hard.

The signal is coming from somewhere in the culvert. Tim Eicher pulls on his rubber hip boots and goes in, wading up from the downstream end, hunched double against the rushing, painfully cold stream, feeling with his hands in the black water. As he comes back into the light at the upstream end of the culvert, Eicher's hands close on the radio collar. He emerges wearing his sunny I-don't-fail grin.

Telonics radio collars are made to take a beating. The transmitter is encased in a waterproof fiberglass shell. The neck band is of heavy double-layered leather, three inches wide and almost half an inch thick. Its ends overlap between two stainless steel plates secured with stainless steel nuts and bolts. This one has been unbolted—something a wolf cannot do. And a person cannot take one of these collars off a wolf unless the wolf is either drugged or dead. Ten is dead, and not of natural causes.

A mud-spattered Jeep Cherokee turns in off the Bear Creek highway, grinds up the Scotch Coulee road, and stops at the congregation of lawmen. Dusty Steinmasel, on his way home, climbs out. Wonders what's going on.

Tim Eicher studies Steinmasel intently: shoes, trousers, belt, shirt, jacket, hands, rings, height, weight, chin, mouth, nose, eyes, hair, hat. Steinmasel is wearing a cap bearing the legend BACA LANDING CATTLE COMPANY. Eicher served eight years as a game warden in New Mexico, and he knows the Baca family, and he knows the ranch manager, and, by God, come to think of it, he knows Dusty Steinmasel! Used to work there. Eicher even recognizes Steinmasel's yellow Jeep Cherokee.

"I remember you," says Eicher, smiling, stepping forward with his hand out.

Steinmasel is nervous, his gaze furtive as he shakes the man hunter's hand. He remembers Eicher too. "Hi," says Steinmasel, and points up the road beyond. "I live just up there."

"Have you seen anything unusual lately?" asks Eicher. "Anybody coming through? Particularly Monday?" Eicher believes that Ten was killed on Monday the twenty-fourth because the next day was too stormy and snowy for your typical lazy-ass poacher to be out and about.

Nothing unusual, Steinmasel avers, nobody through for at least a week. Just himself and his neighbor Dave Oxford.

Tim Eicher teaches interrogation techniques to up-and-coming officers, so he knows what to look for. First, he says, you have to decide which of three types of person you are dealing with: visual, auditory, or feeling. Your visual type will look upward when you question him, and tend to say things like "I see." The auditory person will tend to look sideways when questioned, and say, "I hear you." The feeling type tends to keep his eyes downcast under questioning, and his remarks will refer to his feelings. Eicher will not reveal his technique for determining whether the person is telling the truth, except to say that it has to do with involuntary eye movements—so involuntary that nobody can control them even if he knows the trick.

Eicher knows instantly that Steinmasel is lying.

A little later, Steinmasel's neighbor, Dave Oxford, the only other person living in Scotch Coulee, drops by to see what all the fuss is about.

Eicher asks Oxford if he has seen anybody around or anything unusual. Not really, says Oxford. Oxford's face is open, his eyes unevasive. Oh—he did see Chad McKittrick on Monday, when he and Dusty went up the hill to get Chad's truck unstuck.

Ah.

Eicher walks up the road past Steinmasel's cabin and on uphill for a couple of miles till he comes to a place where he can see that a vehicle was stuck in the mud. What his gut and his training have already told him, evidence now confirms: Dave Oxford was telling the truth, and Dusty Steinmasel was not.

Meanwhile the Soda Butte pack remains in the upper reaches of the Stillwater River, deep within the wilderness. They seem to be moving around less and less. This really does look like denning. We do not even know which female wolf will turn out to be the mother.

Seven is not picked up on the radio, but nobody is particularly worried about her. She travels almost as little as Two. As far as this year's reproduction is concerned, she is irrelevant anyhow.

And bless those Crystals' timorous hearts! After their epic journey to Red Lodge and back to their hideout at Crandall, the Crystal Creek wolves have returned to Crystal Bench and the halcyon security of Yellowstone National Park. They have covered three hundred miles. They continue past the pen, down the lower Lamar to Tower Junction, where elk are many and young Two is still noodling around, getting fat.

# A Bad Place

Nine still has not moved. If she gives birth now, she will be in an impossible position. If Ten were alive, he could go out and kill something, masticate the meat to a dense, high-protein pulp, and regurgitate it for her. She in turn would put that food directly toward the production of milk. In time, the pups would begin to share in the predigested prey, and then Nine would be able to go out and stretch her legs and hunt, with Ten home babysitting.

None of that can happen now. If Nine were to leave her pups and go out to hunt, even in a deeply dug den they could be smelled out and carried off by predators, particularly coyotes and hibernation-famished bears, those species being accomplished excavators. Left alone in this raw, wet weather, the tiny, thin-pelted newborns could easily freeze to death. Little animals—little anythings for that matter—have more surface in relation to their mass than big ones, and thus the small ones lose heat more quickly. On the other hand, if she did not hunt, her milk would dry up and the pups would starve.

What is to be done? Do you go in and crawl all over Mount Maurice trying to find her and maybe her den and risk displacing her away from the pups? A highly stressed mother wolf might well abandon her young. Or do you just cross your fingers, hold your breath, and leave her alone? Will she be okay where she is, or should you try to trap her and get her out of this bad neighborhood? Ten's assassin is still out and about.

A dark comic scenario suggests itself. Suppose Nine dens on private land. Suppose also that the owner of the land is the person who killed Ten. The wolf killer would then qualify for the Defenders of Wildlife reward of five thousand dollars for the first private land owner to host a denning mother wolf. Ha ha.

As of this morning there is also a reward from the Fish and Wildlife Service, of one thousand dollars, for information leading to the conviction of the person or persons responsible for Ten's, as they call it, "disappearance." So if the guy turns himself in, he is already six thousand bucks to the good toward paying his own fine for violating the Endangered Species Act.

Mike Phillips is not amused. He is very unhappy about Nine. "How long was Ten here before he got killed?" demands Phillips.

The answer, allowing for twenty miles of travel per day, is one week, max.

"But I see every problem as an opportunity!" Phillips booms, in his best argument-with-an-unseen-opponent tone. "This sets the stage for some magnificent management! Ten won't have died in vain! *I* say we wait a few days, just long enough to be sure Nine has denned, and then we go in there and we get her and we move her right back to the park so she can have those puppies there and they can grow up in peace! Or maybe they're already born—we just go pick up the whole kit and caboodle!"

You mean—put her back in the Rose Creek pen? And feed them there until the pups can fend for themselves?

"Hell, yes!"

Mightn't that be months?

"So what?"

Ed Bangs, thinking things over in Helena, away from the heat of the crisis, is not so sure. It is Bangs's nature to take things one step at a time, avoiding haste and its perils. At least externally, he is the very model of an easygoing guy; within, let us say he is deliberate. "First of all, even denning doesn't tell us we're going to have pups. She may think she's pregnant, but pseudopregnancy is fairly common. Even if she does have pups, I'm inclined to leave her right where she is. Look at our Augusta pack, just a little ways west of Great Falls. That female has denned for the last four years in the midst of fifteen hundred cow-calf pairs, and they didn't lose but two calves last year. I'm also worried that feeding those pups in the pen could habituate them to humans, and then they might lead their mother near people and she might abandon them before they're ready to take care of themselves. She might even wander back to Red Lodge looking for her mate and leave the pups behind."

Phillips, the model opposite of easygoing, makes a bad-persimmon face, then explodes. "That's ridiculous! That Augusta country is nothing like where Nine is! We're talking about thousands of people right next door to her! And who cares if the pups are habituated to people? If they're in the park, they're going to be safe. Plus it would add to the park experience. Everybody's always wondering if visitors are going to be able to see wolves. Well, if Nine's puppies lost their fear of people, people would see them, wouldn't they? Anyway, I don't think habituation is very likely. The only way anybody ever really tames a wolf is by handling it constantly from practically the day it's born. We'd be bringing in food only a couple times a week and then leaving. They'd grow up wild! I think we've got a fantastic opportunity here to show the world that we can and we will manage these wolves!"

Snow is falling heavily in the Red Lodge country. Footprints, tire tracks, cigarette butts, beer cans, spent shells and bullets, and the skinless body of Wolf Number Ten disappear beneath the all-erasing whiteness.

After strong hints from the U.S. Fish and Wildlife Service that they can handle this situation very well, thank you very much, the National Park Service biologists have gone home. When a wolf leaves the park, it seems, the wolf comes back under F.W.S. jurisdiction.

Phillips grants this, grudgingly. As soon as he gets back to Mammoth Hot Springs he is working the phones, finding out what the wolf biologists of the world think should be done about Nine. He is not shy about volunteering his own opinion.

Joe Fontaine remains in Red Lodge to look for Nine's den and to try to persuade neighboring land owners that having wolves among their cows is not going to be a problem. He will drink weak coffee at their kitchen

tables, citing chapter and verse on northern Montana, Minnesota, maybe
Europe. He will talk low rates of depredation, no land use restrictions,
instantaneous response from Animal Damage Control in the unlikely
event of trouble.

And his listeners? I can see those closed-in faces below hat-flattened
gray hair, those noncommittal nods, the diffident wife transmitting elo-
quent nonverbal messages to her stolid husband. Fontaine cheerfully
claims to have had a lot of good experience with Montana ranchers, but
might he not be sitting at the kitchen table with the guy who pulled the
trigger on Ten? Might he not therefore better pay heed to his personal
security?

Joe Fontaine is a very big guy, an iron pumper from the look of him,
with a manner of quiet self-assurance and intense reserve. He does not
look like somebody you want to piss off. The rancher at the table would
probably also suppose that behind Fontaine lay hidden cadres of law
enforcement combing through Red Lodge, where rumors spread through
the bars like plague. "I think I'll be okay," says Fontaine softly, with a
quick flash of grin.

# John Weaver

Black-footed ferrets were thought to be extinct until a small, isolated population was found alive in 1981 on a ranch in Greater Yellowstone, near Meeteetsee, Wyoming. Those few ferrets, on that one site, were almost certainly the very last of a species that evolution had taken millions of years to fashion. The ferrets have been struggling through a captive breeding program that has been plagued by accidents, disease, and human error. In 1996, a small number of their heirs, reintroduced into protected habitat, did give birth in the wild, but the black-footed ferret remains the most endangered mammal in North America; the poverty of genetic variation in the handful of captive breeders does not augur well for the future.

Have the wolf's friends been good enough friends to the ferret? What will the wolf have cost us? The conservation community has been in political decline for years in this region, where for some people we have replaced the Communists as the ire target of choice. In spite of 10(j), in spite of the Defenders of Wildlife compensation fund and all the other concessions, the wolf has not made us more popular in the communities of Greater Yellowstone, and the national anti-conservation forces single out the wolf reintroduction as the perfect example of the Endangered Species Act's spendthrift romanticism.

The very objects of conservation have become uncertain. It is ruefully amusing to see the disarray. An illustrative issue in Greater Yellowstone is the controversy over bison. Yellowstone Park's bison have increased in number, and have learned to use the groomed snowmobile trails as easy conduits to less crowded pastures—often on private ranchland. Those ranches' owners are nearly all convinced that the bison will infect their cattle with brucellosis, despite the absence of proof. In response to the ranchers, for the last several years, the state of Montana has met the bison influx with rifle fire. Several hundred bison are shot every year, and the meat is shipped to poor Indians. (A lot of Indians are excited about reestablishing bison herds on the reservations, and so would prefer these gifts on the hoof, but capturing and moving a wild adult bison is a task few people in their right mind would wish to take on.) The Greater Yellowstone Coalition and other conservationists deplore the slaughter. But even leaving aside the brucellosis scare—I mean, let's imagine that there is no such thing as brucellosis—what are the ranchers supposed to do when these fur-bearing tanks bust through the fences they have paid for, chase away the horses they depend on, and eat grass meant for conversion into beef and therefrom into their very livelihoods? And if the conservationists don't mind big-game hunting—and most don't—why does the buffalo shooting upset them so much? It is not as though the population is dying out; quite the opposite. This is just one example of the reigning confusion.

The fact of the matter is that a lot of conservation is at heart sentimental. We have our favorites—wolves, say—and our favoritism is sometimes grounded in science, sometimes not. I think we can say with safety that the return of the wolf has strengthened the Yellowstone ecosystem, but we cannot say with safety that bison absolutely do not transmit brucellosis to cattle, for there has yet to be a proper controlled experiment. Between cows and bison, we prefer bison, which are romantic, ferocious, and natural. Between the destruction of wolf habitat by houses, cars, and ranching on one hand and the preservation of wolf habitat by our heroic selves on the other, we unerringly choose the latter. We also drive cars, we live in houses built in what used to be sensitive wildlife habitat (sometimes till the moment we got there), and we avidly consume the products of the most destructive system of agriculture the world has ever known.

How many species have gone extinct in tropical forests in the twenty years since we started working for the return of the wolf? What else might we have done with all that money? What could we have said that might have averted the acrimony among the wolf's own friends? What could we have imagined to make this a time of unmarred glory? What is absent that should be present now?

Sometimes, in the Lamar to chronicle the onset of the wolves' first Yellowstone spring, I sense one such absence. John Weaver is not here. If anybody can be said to have been *meant* to be here now, it is Weaver. I always assumed that he would have the job that Mike Phillips now has, project leader. Weaver did apply for the second slot, project biologist, the job Doug Smith got. Smith is terrific, no doubt of it, but one wonders why Weaver, with all his qualifications and his years of experience, lost out. Nobody will come right out and say it, but I suspect that there was some personal or political conflict somewhere in the shadows.

Weaver was bitterly disappointed. He had just earned his doctorate with a dissertation that seemed fitted like a Savile Row suit to the Yellowstone reintroduction: "Ecology of Wolf Predation amidst High Ungulate Diversity in Jasper National Park, Alberta." The abundance and diversity of wolf prey in Yellowstone are very much like those in the Canadian Rockies. Weaver's data from a well-established wolf pack would have made a perfect comparison with the colonizing packs of Yellowstone. He may even have known some of the Yellowstone wolves personally, for his study area reached to the outskirts of Hinton.

Weaver had studied predator-prey relationships in the coyote population of Jackson Hole. He had been an assistant to the legendary wildlife biologist George Schaller in his study of the jaguar in the Pantanal of Brazil. As an endangered species biologist for the Bridger-Teton and Targhee national forests in the nineteen-seventies, Weaver had had to face the grizzly bear population crash that followed the closing of the Yellowstone garbage dumps, and he walked without losing his balance the thread-thin line between effectiveness in the bureaucracy and the pitiless demands of the bear. A less determined person would have decided that he did not fit in a Forest Service hell-bent on timber harvest and road building. Weaver knew that the seven national forests in the Greater Yellowstone region controlled much more grizzly habitat than the two national parks did, and that the forests had not been treating that habitat very well, and he did not hesitate to say so.

In the seventies and early eighties, Forest Service biologists were giving up right and left in fury or frustration, their data twisted to "get out the cut," their recommendations ignored. Not seldom, the biologists were harassed (especially the women), transferred to irrelevant desk jobs, or forced out altogether. In that less than congenial environment, Weaver chose not to quit but to speak up for the grizzly bear and other declining species. He established new nesting pairs of peregrine falcons all over Greater Yellowstone. He gave Renée Askins her start. He sifted through the historical records and the ecosystem itself to show that there were in fact no wolves here. As a member of the ill-fated interagency Wolf Management Committee formed in 1990, he tried to fashion a recovery plan that not only would satisfy the states but also would work. Backroom politics—on both sides—finally tore the committee apart, but Weaver had once again sought the middle way, trying both to mollify the wolf's opponents and to get the wolf on the ground.

In the event, all such perfect preparation did not bring him to Yellowstone. Instead he took on another mission fraught with political risk: leading a project to reintroduce grizzly bears to central Idaho—Chenoweth country. Trying to avoid the hatred and suspicion that have haunted the wolf project, and Yellowstone grizzly bear management too, Weaver decided to start where the inveterate enemy of the grizzly bear's recovery lay in wait: among the people who must live with the bear. He brought ranchers, logging company executives, biologists, and enviros to the same table, with the shared goal of a viable population of grizzly bears in a place from which they had been expunged generations ago. Then intra-agency conflict exploded, and when the smoke cleared, Weaver was gone. The struggle to return the grizzly bear to Idaho continues without him.

Whatever may have been his disappointments, Weaver charges onward. His latest thing is lynx. He had noticed an intriguing structural and proportional resemblance between the skeleton of a lynx and that of a snowshoe hare, the lynx's principal prey. He thinks there may be something previously unknown to be teased out of that. He and his wife have also raised a lynx by hand as a pet. Chirp is huge, with hind legs almost two feet long and feet like giant cheeseburgers, four inches across. She is as gentle as a lap kitty, though it took nearly round-the-clock handling throughout her infancy and youth to produce such tameness. When Weaver goes into her chain-link cage, all twenty-eight pounds of her bounds to his shoulders and purrs. Weaver takes Chirp into the mountains, puts a radio collar on her, and follows along, taking notes, as she hunts.

John Weaver is not in Yellowstone today, but his legacy is, in the form of wolves.

# Hank Fischer

April 30, 1995

Having ordinary citizens make management decisions about endangered species is a dangerous idea. Every time a bullet slams into a grizzly bear, it does so, after all, as the result of a citizen's management decision. Yet Hank Fischer, northern Rockies representative for Defenders of Wildlife, clings to this dangerous idea. He wants to see the Idaho grizzly restoration led by citizens. Not only would the bears be loosed under the experimental-nonessential banner, allowing liberally for the removal of trouble bears, but the critical decisions and ruling policy would be made by a committee of seven citizens of Idaho, five citizens of Montana, one member of an Idaho-based Indian tribe, and only two Feds. The secretary of the interior would appoint the citizens on the basis of their governors' recommendations.

A group response to Fischer from seven regional conservation groups runs along the lines of "bad for bears, bad for conservation . . . sets dangerous precedents . . . unfettered by biological reality . . . classifying habitat based on political whim . . . nothing to prevent the governors from picking only political friends and industry cronies . . . look no further than Idaho governor Phil Batt's recent filling of the state slot on the Cabinet-Yaak/Selkirk Grizzly Subcommittee [with] an executive from Crown Pacific Timber. . . ."

Remember: this is the same Hank Fischer who loved the idea of

10(j)—the experimental-nonessential designation that "downlists" a rein-troduced population of an endangered species—because it was going to minimize illegal killing of wolves; the same who thought 10(j) would hurry up the public hearings by defusing the opposition; the man who took the government's side in the no-10(j)-wolves-in-Idaho lawsuit brought against it by fellow enviros. This is also the Hank Fischer whose strategy of nonconfrontation got the wolf on the ground; who instituted the private fund for compensation of livestock losses; who (with like-minded others) may be inventing a new and more effective philosophy of conservation.

It looks to me as though his Idaho grizzly proposal is meant to be provocative. Its potential for political manipulation really is too great a risk. I have a lot of other quibbles with it, too, but never mind. Innovation always makes mistakes. Never mind, either, that the factions of the wolf schism are still mad at each other. And I don't mean the organizations, I mean the people—the age-old spectacle of human nature squashing human reason like a bug.

Here is the problem with Fischer's bear plan. Grizzly bears and resource exploitation are often truly in conflict, and if there is ever to be a self-sustaining grizzly metapopulation in the northern Rockies, the resource-extraction industry is going to have to make some sacrifices. The math, the genetics, and the unforgiving necessities of grizzly bear conser-vation are surely harder to understand than people's need for wood or wealth; complex interactions of unrelated influences can make small grizzly populations extremely vulnerable to extinction. Yet the conflict between bear and industry is what Fischer's citizen-managers would have to decide. Without guaranteed scientific representation on the com-mittee, the Idaho grizzly project could easily run off the rails at high speed. Remember the self-immolation of the grizzly bear recovery com-mittee of 1990—on which Hank Fischer so unhappily served.

Yet conservation has no hope whatever without a broader social base. There is a lot of happy talk about toxic sites in the ghetto and suchlike, but the fact of the matter is that conservation remains in great part a gen-teel, chic, and exclusive reserve for highly educated rich white people— People Like Us. The earnest manner of concern for the toxified ghetto is itself a badge of belonging. The dreadlocked, vegetarian young Jacobins who style themselves "dirtbags" are often the children of the grandees they abhor, and share with them the habit of moral absolutism.

Most of the non-belongers outside the conservation movement's pale do not think very often of grizzly bears or wolves. Yet the laws of our nation mandate the conservation of endangered species, and those laws are not the work only of the cultural élite. The people at large do, it seems, share the conservation groups' ideals. In occasional elections the people at large also express their irritation at the pettiness, the self-righteousness, and the vanity of conservationists whose sole concept of success is the winning of battles, victory over evil.

I am not suggesting that conservation add affirmative action to its agenda, recruiting Joe Sixpacks and Chicano migrant workers. I am asking only for some serious attention to the principle embodied in Hank Fischer's developing approach to conservation, because the virtuous-victory model has lost too many battles.

The principle has been demonstrated beautifully in game theory, in which the ultimate advantage of a certain form of reciprocal altruism seems to have been mathematically proved. This amazing proof is the product of a computer program called TIT FOR TAT, written by the Canadian game theorist Anatol Rapaport. TFT lives inside a larger program that matches program against program until each has faced every other two hundred times. Then there is another round, in which the programs are all represented in proportion to their scores in the first game. Before long, there are only a few survivors—the fittest. It is very much like natural selection. The ultimate winner, no matter how many rounds are played, is always TIT FOR TAT.

TFT is only five lines of code long. Its economy has the simplicity of the sublime. In his book *The Moral Animal*, Robert Wright describes how TIT FOR TAT works:

> On the first encounter with any program, it [TFT] would cooperate. Thereafter, it would do whatever the other program had done on the previous encounter. One good turn deserves another, as does one bad turn.
>
> The virtues of this strategy are about as simple as the strategy itself. If a program demonstrates a tendency to cooperate, TIT FOR

TAT immediately strikes up a friendship, and both enjoy the fruits of cooperation. If a program shows a tendency to cheat, TIT FOR TAT cuts its losses; by withholding cooperation until that program reforms, it avoids the high costs of being a sucker. So TIT FOR TAT never gets repeatedly victimized, as indiscriminately cooperative programs do. Yet TIT FOR TAT also avoids the fate of the indiscriminately *un*cooperative programs that try to exploit their fellow programs: getting locked into mutually costly chains of mutual betrayal with programs that would be perfectly willing to cooperate if only you did. Of course, TIT FOR TAT generally forgoes the large one-time gains that can be had through exploitation. But strategies geared toward exploitation, whether through relentless cheating or repeated "surprise" cheating, tended to lose out as the game wore on. Programs quit being nice to them, so they were denied both the large gains of exploitation and the more moderate gains of mutual cooperation. More than the steadily mean, more than the steadily nice, and more than various "clever" programs whose elaborate rules made them hard for other programs to read, the straightforwardly conditional TIT FOR TAT was, in the long run, self-serving.

TIT FOR TAT begins with the Golden Rule, in other words, and will continue to do unto others as it would have them do unto it for as long as the others reciprocate. If the others only know that the TFT strategy will inevitably prevail, they will adopt it as their own, and an earthly paradise of unceasing Golden-Ruling will ensue. The first time the other takes a swing at TIT FOR TAT, however, TFT abandons the Golden Rule and slugs back.

Hear this phrase again: "getting locked into mutually costly chains of mutual betrayal with programs that would be perfectly willing to cooperate if only you did." Sound familiar? Can human nature ever absorb the wisdom of TFT well enough to practice it?

And: your first move is always supposed to be cooperation, but in real life, where does the game "begin"? Isn't almost every conservation conflict actually some ancient battle, incapable of being re-begun? I wonder if Rapaport has tried introducing TFT into a war already well under way.

Maybe this is where the human part must come in, the part called faith. What if we arbitrarily proclaim *right now* to be the beginning of the game, and offer cooperation, and thereafter follow the simple rules of TIT FOR TAT?

Thinking in this light about Fischer's citizen committee, and the whole business of community-based conservation, I wonder whether a little training in conflict resolution—in advance of the conflicts—mightn't be a good idea. It does sound like less fun than beating up on the Forest Service, but it could lead somewhere we have not been able to go in our battle gear.

Hank Fischer's opponents among the enviros will tell you that the wolf reintroduction is under way *in spite of* the conciliatory sacrifices he so warmly supports. Maybe 10(j) has won no ranchers' hearts, but I know that it attracted political support where that support was most needed.

The experimental-nonessential designation also enabled the exercise of a subtle and perhaps more powerful influence, namely, the withdrawal of political opposition. Total reversal of a popular stand is political hemlock. The provisions for ranchers to protect their livestock themselves—to *use* those cherished rifles in their pickup racks—gave many politicians the out they had to have. There were people who could have raised one hand and stopped the whole thing cold. I am thinking particularly of the former governor of Wyoming, Mike Sullivan, who may have liked the idea of wolves in Yellowstone but certainly dared not say so. And I am thinking of that state's quirky, crafty, unpredictable, and charming senator, Alan Simpson. Simpson loves to bash the (liberal, touchy-feely, sissy) Park Service, and for years he had delighted in bashing the wolf plan. Then it started looking a lot more popular than he had thought. After the selection of the 10(j) alternative, both Sullivan and Simpson quietly kept their heads down.

Conciliation can be painful, but it will be much less so when it can be biologically targeted. There are areas where there is ample ecological "give," and others where there is none. We can afford the loss of Number Ten—but we cannot afford to lose Nine. The same is true of grizzly bears, only more so: especially in a small population, every female is of critical value. Even in Yellowstone, only a few female grizzlies survive long enough to keep the population going. In any given year, only a handful give birth. Population modeling has established that an average loss of more than one female Yellowstone grizzly per year would send the population crashing toward zero.

Think, then, what a risk there is in Fischer's citizen-management plan. But think, too, of the Yellowstone wolves. Is it fair to say that they are here because Hank Fischer worked so hard for a plan that allows them to be shot?

He shrugs. It is not modesty that prevents the heroes of the wolf story from taking credit; it is a recognition of the complexity of the story, the multiplicity of the actors. What could he say? The shrug is just right.

# *Turf*

MAY 1, 1995

It is no longer a hypothesis but a settled fact that Nine has denned on Mount Maurice. She is hardly moving at all. Telemetry, the abundance of her footprints around one focal point, and the absence of her footprints anywhere else all show that she is occupying an area of less than an acre. She seems to be okay: Doug Smith has seen her from the air, slipping through the trees around what must be her den site, vivid against the snow.

Joe Fontaine is going to be hauling in roadkill for her starting today, coming close enough, he hopes, that she will find the food but not so close, we all pray, that she will be displaced. Especially given the loss of her mate—given that terror, and ongoing dread, and the loss of all help and companionship—it is quite possible that if she is further disturbed she will abandon the den, choosing to save herself and her future contributions to the gene pool over the survival of these particular pups. If they exist.

Before the Fish and Wildlife Service biologists in Helena decide on the next move, they want to know whether this is a pseudopregnancy. If it is, there will be no point in spending a lot of time and money on Nine. If, on the other hand, she has given birth, then hers will be very important pups indeed. Montana's senator Conrad Burns smells votes in the unquenched fury of the wolf haters. He and his slash-and-burn allies are threatening to take their machetes to any further reintroduction of wolves. If Burns succeeds, pups from the mating of Nine and Ten could bear much of the responsibility for founding a Yellowstone population.

The outlook for the other two packs makes the burden of Nine's conjectural offspring still heavier. The Crystals are acting thoroughly unparental, running up and down and all around the Lamar. The Sodas are anybody's guess; there are signs both pro and con. On one hand, female Fourteen is sticking close to one place in the upper Stillwater. But if she does have pups, we will not know for quite a while yet, simply because the putative den site is so deep in the backcountry. No one dares ski in, for fear that she might abandon her den. On the other hand, neither of the Soda Butte pack's adult females has ever bred before; Fourteen is only two years old. Pseudopregnancy seems just as likely as the real thing.

There is ugly talk in the bars of Red Lodge. One old fellow has been complaining that one of the wolves killed one of his horses. In fact this dead horse cannot have been a wolf kill, for Nine has not budged, and she is the only wolf anywhere near, but in the bars who believes that?

Nine's tiny home range takes in a piece of private ranchland, and Fontaine has been diligently cultivating the ranch manager. The manager has promised to keep all his gates securely locked against intruders, and he seems, says Fontaine, somewhat intrigued to have a wolf on his place, though not exactly delighted.

It is becoming clearer that Fontaine and his F.W.S. colleagues would like to see Nine stay here, even if she does have pups. Among the northern Montana wolf packs they are so proud of, there has been very little depredation on livestock, and when there has been trouble Carter Niemeyer and his A.D.C. troops have responded quickly and effectively. Defenders of Wildlife has compensated the ranchers for the full value of their losses. And let's face it, at least some of this is a turf thing. Everybody wants a piece of the return of the wolf to Yellowstone.

Mike Phillips wants Nine back and he wants her *now*. He and Doug Smith are also stinging over the latest message from Helena: the Fish and

Wildlife Service has engaged a plane locally and will take over the aerial monitoring of Wolf Number Nine. Phillips and Smith are kindly requested not to fly the area anymore, for fear that their circling might reveal Nine's location to persons unhealthily interested therein. The new plane wouldn't? So nobody flies.

# Sitting in Wait

On top of the Fish and Wildlife Service's initial one-thousand-dollar reward and Defenders' five thousand, the National Audubon Society is now offering another five thousand dollars for information on Number Ten's killer, and an organization in California called Sea Shepherd, which I thought was about marine mammals, has kicked in two thousand more. That makes thirteen thousand bucks.

The tips, the leads, the rumors, the absolutely certain accusations are piling up on Tim Eicher's desk. "It's too much fucking money," he complains. "When I get the guy, he's going to want a jury trial, and in a district where the median income is twenty thousand dollars, that thirteen thousand is going to be a problem. Any jury here is going to know people will lie for thirteen thousand dollars."

And why isn't Eicher prowling the bars of Red Lodge incognito, meeting with secret informants, Sherlock-Holmesing the scene of the crime? Why is he sitting behind his desk in Cody?

"Something will come up. A hunter has to be patient."

There is pressure on Tim Eicher. His bosses, all the way up to the U.S. Fish and Wildlife Service director, Mollie Beattie, want this crime solved *now*. His phone rings not only with the fantasies of reward hunters and the lies of grudge bearers but also with official and unofficial "encouragement" from well up the chain of federal command. So how does all that heat affect him?

Eicher leans back in his chair with his hands behind his head. Beneath the big mustache his lips part at the corner with a single soft smack, as though around an invisible toothpick. "I don't give a shit about pressure."

Because Ten's radio collar was hidden in an obscure culvert which only someone who knows that landscape well would think of, Eicher is confident that his man is a local. Some night the guy is going to get drunk in some bar and brag about killing that wolf. Somebody who could use thirteen thousand bucks and might even not be sympathetic is going to hear him. "There's going to be one phone call," the special agent says flatly.

He will not say so, but I think Eicher is counting on that too-big reward to draw Dusty Steinmasel toward the telephone late some remorse-ridden evening.

# Natives

Joe Fontaine is hiking through the mottled, crumbling, knee-deep snow down the north face of Mount Maurice with a Telonics receiver and a hand-held antenna. When he picks up Number Nine's signal, he does not move straight toward her, but rather veers to the side, to get the signal from another bearing. Thus, by triangulation, he can locate her precisely without coming too close and disturbing her. He moves into the forest quiet as a cat.

The *tock-tock-tock* in Fontaine's headphones grows louder. He is homing in on her. She is close. Downhill, the snow has drifted deep, and the forest is thick where several small streams race out of the heights. Along these watercourses grow large Englemann spruces and a dense riparian understory of alder, willow, bog birch, and hawthorn. Nothing as well hidden as a wolf bed will be visible once these deciduous plants come into leaf, which will be soon. Fontaine needs to find Nine soon.

If she does have pups, they will be the first native-born Yellowstone wolves in over sixty years.

It is about thirty-five degrees, and overcast. Fontaine can see the whole town of Red Lodge spread below him, not five miles away. He walks east, trying to circle wide around the wolf. He sees wolf tracks leading away, but they might not be fresh; he elects to stay with the greater immediacy of telemetry. He sees a day bed scooped into the snow, wolf-sized, near a tall old spruce tree.

He hears a faint mewing. He is three yards from the big spruce. Nine's signal is strong, but she seems to be moving away fast. Has he displaced her from the day bed—from a den? He hears the mewing again, close, but still he cannot find it. He lifts a low, snow-hugging bough of the spruce tree. In the near-darkness back against the trunk he sees a squirming, whimpering mass of baby wolves—newborns, their eyes still closed. He counts seven, and thinks there may be eight.

# YELLOWSTONE
## Doubt

# A Tirade

MAY 4, 1995

Phoning in from Gardiner first thing in the morning to see how the field-work and the investigation are coming along, I happen to catch Joe Fontaine in his room at the Super 8 Motel in Red Lodge, and so I am among the first to know.

I call Norm Bishop at Yellowstone Park, and his shout of joy half deafens me.

Hank Fischer, in Missoula, reacts with characteristic reserve: "That's great" is all he says. He's only spent fifteen years trying to get here.

Jim Halfpenny lets fly a whoop.

Ed Bangs is quietly pleased, but he is also facing a problem: Nine and her pups are on private land, land that will have young cows on it this summer. Ecosystems do not really have edges, but for jurisdictional pur-poses you have to assign some sort of reasonable limit, and this wolf family has to be said to be pretty close to the edge. They are dangerously close to people with guns. Even if they survive here and establish a terri-tory, the eventual dispersers from the pack are just as likely to head north and east into ranch country as to colonize unoccupied habitat in the wild-lands to the south and west. Bangs is beginning to agree with Mike Phillips that moving Nine and her litter back to the Rose Creek pen is the only thing to do.

Phillips himself at this moment is flying over the other wolves, and is not expected back until three this afternoon, so he still does not know that Nine has given birth, or that Helena has endorsed his proposal to move her back into the park, or that he is being asked to fly again, in case she decides to move.

Phillips locates Nine's yearling Seven, still on her own and apparently thriving, up Hellroaring Creek about five miles north of the park.

The Crystal Creek wolves remain in the Lamar. He sees both alphas digging, as they have been doing here, there, and everywhere, enlarging coyote dens and tearing into old ground squirrel burrows. They have dug at least five holes big enough to serve as dens, but the alpha female is not settling down. Indeed she is unusually restless.

He finds that four of the Soda Butte wolves have moved up the Stillwater and back over the drainage divide toward the pack. In the high headwaters of Pebble Creek, no more than a mile or two above the park boundary, the Sodas have killed an elk. Fourteen has stayed behind in the Stillwater, precisely where she has been now for days. As soon as they have gorged themselves on elk meat, the rest of the pack return to her quickly.

Now, at last, the Soda Butte pack's situation is clear. Fourteen is the alpha female, and she has denned in the remote upper valley of the Stillwater River, a perfect place for it. Her packmates are bringing food to her and perhaps another litter of native Yellowstone wolves.

At ten minutes to three, I hear an airplane motor from my little aerie at Above the Rest. I rush outside, and there is the Super Cub tilting in toward the airstrip. I jump into the muddy, mile-worn, but ever-eager Pathfinder and race down the hill, skidding around a lumbering Winnebago and blasting on through the Gardiner motel strip.

Phillips is leaning against his truck chatting with the pilot, still in his flight suit, when I give him the news about Nine.

She has pups, Mike. Seven or eight. Joe found them.

His reaction is not quite the jubilation I expected. "This is ludicrous! Did Joe go in there on foot? I bet he went in there on foot. Didn't see the mother? Of course he didn't. He displaced her. She may abandon those puppies!"

Phillips wanted to trap her first, and then go in to see if there were pups. But might not a trapping operation also have risked displacing her?

Why not just keep leaving carcasses, protect the site, and see how it works out? I neglect to mention Bangs's nascent change of heart. To move or not to move Number Nine has been the subject of some frank exchanges of views.

"Oh, perfect!" roars Phillips, his bright red face clashing with his light blond hair. "Sure, let's leave them there right where Ten was killed. Has everybody forgotten about Ten? We picked up Nine and Ten on the radio on April 13, on Wolverine Creek, in the upper Slough drainage. Then they went off the air for the next eleven days, until we found them right outside Red Lodge. Let's assume they'd left Wolverine right away, and that they traveled at the same rate as the Crystal pack, which was about fifteen miles a day. That puts them in Red Lodge on April 16 at the earliest. And that means that Ten lasted no more than eight days! How do you think that bodes for Nine? Mr. Bullet is still out there walking around. And where do you think those wolves are going to go as soon as they can travel? I'll lay money they're going to go north or east out onto those flats. Over and over again, wolves settle where people are—not because of the people but because they like river valleys, the same as people do. What kind of future do you think they'll have out there, in the middle of people and houses and livestock? We're supposed to be establishing a wolf population in the Greater Yellowstone Ecosystem, not out on the plains of Montana! This is fucking ludicrous! You can write that down. Put it in your damn book.

"I'll bet anything he went in there on foot and spooked her off those pups. I know that site. We've got a radio location of less than an acre. And unless there's something wrong with my telemetry, you just couldn't see those pups unless you were right up on them—the vegetation is that thick. And if you're right up on them, and you claim to be a biologist, you're an asshole."

Phillips knows that what is to be done about Nine is ultimately Helena's or even Washington's call, but he is not exactly resigned to simply stepping back from the decision. "I want Mike Finley to know what this is going to mean, and Mollie Beattie, and Bruce Babbitt. Tom, these wolves may be the only chance we ever get! I have absolutely no assurance that we're going to get more wolves next year. What's Nine supposed to do next February? Mate with a coyote? A dog? She can't mate with one of the pups, because they won't be sexually mature yet. This is absurd.

"Moving her would be a piece of cake. Maybe you wait four or five weeks, till the pups are strong and their eyes are open and they don't have to nurse all the time. Meanwhile, all that time you're watching exactly how she approaches the carcasses you're leaving, and you start setting fake trap sets along the way. She's going to travel a predictable route, and then when the time comes you just set traps all along it. You put a transmitter on each one, and you monitor them twenty-four hours a day. When the trap goes off, you wait about an hour while her foot swells up, so you're sure she can't pull out, and then you go in, get her out of the trap, and stuff her in a kennel. The puppies are just lying around helpless. All you have to do is pick them up. Four hours later, she's back in the pen.

"We've been figuring she had already whelped, and we've all been talking about what should be done. Varley doesn't think they should stay there! Mech doesn't think they should stay there! But *they*"—by which I believe he means Bangs and Fontaine—"they don't listen to Mech. That whole operation was one big cluster-fuck till Dave arrived and got those people organized. He's only the person who knows the most about wolves in the world! Why listen to him! Excuse me? This is total bullshit, Tom."

He's loud. He's abrasive. He is also smart, dedicated, and hard-working, and in this case, I believe, he is right.

In time, in the knowledge that for the foreseeable future he must work with Joe Fontaine and Ed Bangs, and with consciousness of his own passionate nature, Mike Phillips's ire will cool toward regret. He is beginning, these days, to think of times to come, after the wolf project is safely in bed. He is thinking big—of global conservation strategies, of forming a mega-coalition of all the major American conservation groups, of leveraging government's native timidity with private initiatives and private money. For all his temper, this is a man devoted to doing good. In time he will make up with Joe Fontaine, for the sake of the wolves.

The Lamar, so austere in winter, is extravagantly alive this afternoon. Swallows wheel through clouds of hatching caddis flies above the glittering river. Two pairs of trumpeter swans are moving slowly together across one small pond—probably embroiled in nasty territorial dispute, but to a sap like me a visual poem, of crystalline symmetry. On a death-silvered riverside, cottonwood's crown, perch two bald eagles, surveying their green estate. Bugs are buzzing. Sandhill cranes are gargling somewhere. Spring peepers, out in the marsh, are peeping.

And lo and behold, here is Mike Phillips, with a pair of fat aeronautical headphones on his head. How many hours a week does the citizenry get out of this not very highly paid employee? He raises his antenna and scrunches his face up, listening. He points, the first evidence that he has even noticed my presence beside him. "They're just over that ridge," he whispers. "Five has been up and down through here all week. Today they've been hanging at this one little spot."

Yellowstone Park historian Paul Schullery and his visiting mother pull over. Schullery sets up his tripod and spotting scope. Doug Frank, a young Syracuse professor who is studying herbivory on the Northern Range, appears.

"We've got to go up," says Phillips.

Does he think we can see the den?

"Maybe."

Phillips and Frank climb like mountain goats up the densely sage-brushed, rubbly, and very steep hillside, leaving the rest of us quickly behind. Schullery and I stop to breathe, our hearts thundering in our throats. I look upslope, and Phillips is little more than a dot. He has apparently seen nothing, for he is still climbing. I decide to wait right here till he sees something. I gawk around. Something is moving down the ridge. Two somethings. Holy smoke: grizzly bears. A big one following a little one, the big one dark, the little one reddish. Schullery—who, being the author of *The Bears of Yellowstone*, ought to know—thinks the big one is a male with his springtime hormone surge coming on. The big bear hurries forward, closing the gap between them, and, sure enough, sniffs avidly at the smaller bear's bottom.

They angle toward us. I consider what to do if they keep coming. The nearest tree is, oh, say a mile away? Honoring the better part of valor, we descend. The bears glance at us and change direction.

As I turn back toward the valley to look once more for the wolves across the river, I think I see a flash of black back and feathery tail disappear behind the third ridge to the south—a wolf, a wolf! Well, maybe. We wait, and see no further sign.

The valley is rapidly filling with shadow. Phillips has not found the den. On the other hand, earlier this eventful day, he has seen the complete sequence of a wolf kill for the first time in his life—just out there. Four, the big black alpha male of the Crystal Creek pack, approached a cow elk head on, without attacking, apparently just to get her attention until Five, his mate, could sneak up behind and sink her teeth into the elk's back leg. At that instant Four sprang forward and bit solidly into the throat. For about fifteen seconds the elk stood still, her neck raised high despite the big wolf hanging from it, and then she fell, dead.

# The Body

Evert Armstrong, a mechanic and maintenance man on the Sunlight Ranch, is out looking for shed elk antlers along the Scotch Coulee track when he smells dead animal. He follows the stench to a body lying between a bush and a steep red clay bank, entangled in orange baling twine. Something has been eating on the carcass; the whole rib cage is stripped bare. The animal has no head. The body had been skinned, but crudely: the four feet and four cuffs of ankle fur are intact. Those gigantic feet could be nothing else. This is a wolf.

Armstrong calls his boss, ranch manager Paul Ranschau, and Ranschau calls his range detective, Pat Cunningham. Cunningham, a former sheriff's deputy, thinks it was probably a rancher or a cowboy who shot the wolf—that's who uses baling twine. Ranschau realizes that a criminal investigation on the Sunlight Ranch is going to be a major hassle. They *could* just bury the carcass and avoid the whole thing. He has no particular love for wolves. But Ranschau also believes that the law is the law. He picks up the phone and calls Carbon County sheriff Al McGill, and the sheriff calls Tim Eicher.

When Eicher arrives at the corpse he notices that the red clay bank has a recently excavated hole in it. The hole goes deep. There are wolf tracks in and out. There is only one possible interpretation of all this. Before she fled to the security of the spruces uphill to give birth, Nine came and dug this den beside the dead body of her mate.

# Rattling Dusty's Chain

May 10, 1995

Leo "Grasshopper" Suazo, a crack interrogator up from the Denver office, joins Tim Eicher for a visit to Dusty Steinmasel.

"Were you up the Scotch Coulee road on the evening of April twenty-third?" demands Eicher in his flattest official tone.

Nope.

"Were you up the Scotch Coulee road on the morning of April twenty-fourth, helping Chad McKittrick get his blue Ford truck unstuck?"

No, sir.

"You know who killed that wolf, Dusty."

Well, all right, he was up there with Chad that morning, but he doesn't know who killed the wolf. He himself sure didn't.

Tim Eicher and Grasshopper Suazo share a flicker of eye contact. They both know that Steinmasel is lying.

Eicher figures he can wait a little longer for his phone to ring, and the special agents bid good-bye to a very rattled Dusty Steinmasel.

# The Phone Call

This is Saturday, so Eicher is not in the office when Steinmasel calls, as Steinmasel surely intends. He leaves a message on the answering machine. He, uh, forgot to tell Eicher about the black Chevy. He wants to talk.

Eicher picks up his messages and suspects straight off that there is no black Chevy. He gets in his unmarked but obvious government truck and drives to Red Lodge.

The man hunter exudes calm; the hunted man is tied up in knots. Steinmasel tells the story truthfully, Eicher believes, and in meticulous detail—up to the moment when he and McKittrick are standing over Number Ten's body. There, suddenly, he goes vague. He says that after McKittrick shot the wolf, he, Steinmasel, went straight home, and then he was so upset he went out, uh, fishing. He never handled the body, or the collar. When he went back to look at the dead wolf again that afternoon, it was gone, and there were new tire tracks leading uphill toward the Mee-teetsee Trail.

Eicher knows that Steinmasel is lying about the afternoon, but he remains pretty sure that the details of the killing in the morning are true. He has enough information now for a search warrant on Chad McKittrick.

"All I need now, Dusty, is for you to write all this up in your own words," Eicher says casually to Steinmasel, "then sign it."

# *Lies and Truth*

May 14, 1995

Dusty Steinmasel drives through Red Lodge and out to Chad McKittrick's house to confess that he has ratted. McKittrick is quiet, forgiving, and plastered. Steinmasel mentions that he has left himself out of the story entirely, as they had previously agreed. The affidavit which he has written out makes no mention of his having retrieved the carcass, having helped McKittrick skin it, or having transported the pelt and the head to McKittrick's house. The false story concealing those facts is itself a federal felony.

McKittrick nods gloomily. "I'm sorry I got you involved," he says. "I've been out here drunk for the last two weeks while you been running around paranoid." He pauses for a long moment. "I'm glad it's over."

Steinmasel calls Eicher to tell him that the affidavit is ready.

# The Search

Tim Eicher and his supervisor, Commodore Mann (he is not the head of a
yacht club; that's his name), are at federal court in Billings, Montana,
bright and early. They present to Judge Jack Shanstrom an Application
and Affidavit for Search Warrant.

Eicher has laid out his case in six terse pages. "Based on the fore-
going," the application concludes,

> the affiant has probable cause to believe that evidence of the illegal
> take, possession, and transportation of wolf #R10 will be found at
> the property of Chad McKittrick, located in Palisade Basin Ranches
> subdivision, Tract 21, near Red Lodge, Carbon County, Montana;
> said property being fruits, instrumentalities, and evidence of a vio-
> lation of the Endangered Species Act and the Lacey Act, and con-
> sisting of a wolf hide, wolf hair and blood, a wolf skull and/or wolf
> parts, a 7-mm magnum rifle and 7-mm ammunition, a leather rifle
> scabbard, knife(s), axe(s), small metal plate(s) and two bolts, 1x6
> and 2x6 boards, and orange baling twine, said property being
> fruits, instrumentalities, and evidence of violations of the Endan-
> gered Species Act, 16 USC 1538(a) (G), 50 CFR 17.84(i) (3) and (5)
> and the Lacey Act, 16 USC 3372 (a) (1).

Warrant in hand, Eicher, Mann, and two other Fish and Wildlife Service special agents, Roy Brown and Ron Hanlon, make for Red Lodge, sixty miles away. There they hook up with Sheriff McGill, Montana agent Kevin Nichols, and a sheriff's deputy who will sit in the car down the road for backup in case of trouble. In convoy, they head for McKittrick's.

Thanks to Steinmasel's visit last night, McKittrick is expecting them. He greets the intimidating contingent of lawmen and firepower with what seems almost like gratitude. But he also looks very nervous, and Eicher knows that nobody whose home is being minutely searched for criminal evidence is likely to feel particularly peaceful, and he knows that McKittrick is not Carbon County's most stable individual. While the others comb through the house, Eicher takes McKittrick out for a little walk-and-talk. Eicher does not take notes, and he is not carrying a tape recorder; he is, however, wearing a loaded pistol. They go down and check out the trout ponds. They hit a few golf balls. McKittrick talks freely about the shooting, but he maintains that he thought Wolf Number R-Ten was a feral dog. (The R in Ten's full name as written on his radio collar is for the red tags that were punched through the ears of all the wolves bound from Hinton to Yellowstone; the Idaho wolves had blue ear tags.)

Inside, meanwhile, the searchers find the Ruger M-77 rifle under the sofa, with three live rounds of ammunition inside. Eicher brings McKittrick in, and the suspect escorts his captors to the wolf's hide and severed head in the half-built cabin out back.

Chad McKittrick is charged with killing Wolf Number R-Ten, possessing the remains, and transporting them.

Ten's head, hide, and body will be frozen and then shipped to the U.S. Fish and Wildlife Service forensics laboratory at Ashland, Oregon.

In the lab, forensic mammalogist Bonnie Yates will introduce Ten's head into a colony of flesh-eating beetles, where it will stay until the skull is perfectly clean, white, and free of stink. Then she will measure the cranium, jaw, and teeth. Her morphometry will confirm that it is the skull of a gray wolf.

Molecular biologist Stephen Fain will subject Ten's flesh and hair to

three sorts of DNA testing. A nucleotide sequence analysis of mitochondrial DNA isolated from the body recovered at Scotch Coulee will determine that it can have come only from a member of the species *Canis lupus.*
A polymerase chain reaction will prove that the dead wolf was a male. A
comparison restriction analysis will show that the hide and head and
flesh all belonged to the same animal, and also that the dead male wolf's
DNA matches precisely that of the plug of flesh punched out of Number
Ten's ear at Hinton and kept frozen for precisely such a situation as this.

Veterinary pathologist Richard Stroud will remove the tiny Personal
Identification Tag from Number Ten's skin. The P.I.T., scanned by
a laser-driven reader, will confirm the wolf's identity. An X ray will
find bullet fragments inside Ten's thorax in a pattern typical of a high-
powered rifle wound. Stroud will find that the shrapnel completely
destroyed the wolf's liver and lungs; a 7-mm magnum is an awesome
weapon. The greater part of the bullet continued on through the
abdomen and out the other side. It has never been found.

As opinions roll in from the various far-flung wolf biologists who are
the project's informal consultants, there is consensus between Helena and
Mammoth: Nine and the pups will be moved back into the park.

Each delivery of roadkill has been left in the same place near the
makeshift den to which Nine has moved her brood. Like any other wolf,
Nine likes to follow a familiar route whenever she can; she has gone to
dinner along the same path every time. The biologists have tricked her.
Doug Smith, Joe Fontaine, and Carter Niemeyer, the wolf-trapping
maestro of Animal Damage Control, have set five steel-jawed leghold
traps into the ground along the travelway between Nine's maternal headquarters and the feeding site. They cover the traps with dirt and duff.
Any possible telltale odor is nicely disguised by a lavish application of
Number Ten's scat collected from the Rose Creek pen, as well as some of
Niemeyer's reeking secret formula. In classic crude-but-effective fashion,
well suited to these days of budget cutbacks, each trap is connected by a
string to a simple radio transmitter about the size of a flashlight. When
the trap springs, the string pulls a magnet off the transmitter, and it starts
emitting a rapid-fire beep. These transmitters have been pirated from

Telonics radio collars; what is now the good-news beep was in its previous incarnation the mortality mode.

Each radio transmits on a different frequency, and each will be checked every two hours around the clock. The night clerk at the Super 8 does the wolf team a welcome favor by volunteering to run the radio trapline when even wolf biologists prefer to be asleep.

# *Home*

The cold steel jaws slam shut on Number Nine's leg. Imagine the pain. Imagine the terror. If you will attribute to a wolf a conception of futurity, imagine Nine's despair—her mate dead, her pups squealing with panic. The squeals subside to weak desolation. She quiets, knowing she is soon to die.

Nine does not know that in fact her luck has taken a sudden one-eighty toward the good. She does not know that her friends Doug Smith, Mark Johnson, Joe Fontaine, and Carter Niemeyer are at this moment—four o'clock in the morning—prying themselves out of bed down at the Super 8.

By five-thirty she is fast asleep in a shiny aluminum kennel in the back of a government pickup, with tranquilizer surging through her synapses. She gets a shot of penicillin and vitamins. Mark Johnson examines Nine and declares her to be in fine condition, maybe just a little skinny. Despite the generous portions of elk and deer meat she has been served, her weight is down from the ninety-eight pounds she weighed at Hinton to eighty-five.

The trackers, including the excited clerk from the motel, now go in search of the pups. They follow Nine's trail to the new den site she has recently established, which is little more, again, than a depression in the snow, and oh, shit. The pups are not there.

She must have moved them, probably only last night. Where? For two hours, three, stretching into four, Joe Fontaine leads the team on an anxious search for the big spruce under which he first found the pups, where he hopes she may have taken them. Doug Smith is certain that the litter will not be there: he has several radio-locations of Nine in the same place, and it is far from Fontaine's spruce tree. Fontaine persists nonetheless, and this is his operation, so the others go along. Finally they find the nest beneath the spruce tree. No pups. No sign of recent occupancy.

Now what? Number Nine and her eight pups constitute over 40 percent of the Yellowstone wolf population. This early in the game, every individual animal is precious.

At eleven-thirty in the morning, after six and a half hours of slogging through gunky snow and gunkier mud, Joe Fontaine woofs his soft maternal wolf-grunt for the thousandth time, and this time he hears a whimpering. They have found the den, though it is hardly worthy of the term. This den is even more makeshift than the old one—no more than a scooped-out depression beneath one of the few trees in a talus slide—obviously new, and made in haste. Surrounded by that jumble of broken rock, it is certainly in a well-protected location.

The motherless pups flee clumsily but quickly at the sight of these dreadful invaders, wriggling into dark, deep interstices between the rocks. The terrified pups are not easy to get hold of. Sometimes the men must reach into some crack all the way up to their armpits. In time they have seven little wolves, but the eighth, if there is one, remains hidden and now silent in some crevice, nobody knows where. At last a probing stick touches something soft, yielding, breathing, definitely alive—pika? hibernating marmot? baby wolf? The longest arm in the bunch cannot quite reach. Doug Smith tries a pair of leatherman's pliers. Stretching to the limit of his long arm, with a guy on each leg trying to ram him up the hole, Smith clamps hold of the soft fuzzy thing and drags Nine's eighth pup into the first day of her new life.

Mark Johnson examines the pups and draws a little blood from each. They all look great—healthy, bright-eyed, squirming, making their dissatisfaction loudly apparent. Seven of them are black; one is brownish gray shading toward black. All weigh between four and five pounds. Four are male and four are female.

The pups roam loose around the helicopter as Nine, now recovered from her drugging, sniffs at them from inside her metal box. The wolves and their unrecognized benefactors skim the Beartooth Plateau, a roadless, buildingless, white, black, and blue winter wasteland of ice and rock spangled with frozen lakes. They pass over Cooke City. The dense forest of upper Soda Butte Creek rolls by beneath, and then the wide bright green meadows of the Lamar.

The helicopter comes to earth at the Rose Creek pen. How quick, how short a trip this is for a human in a flying machine, how long and how profound a distance for a wolf! The men stuff the pups one by one into the would-be den they have made inside the pen, a lean-to of logs and spruce boughs. They open the door of the kennel. Nine bounds out to kiss her family and breathe the well-remembered scent of what had better now be home.

The federal magistrate in Billings releases Chad McKittrick without bail. He orders McKittrick to stick close to home—Carbon and Yellowstone counties only—and keep his hands off firearms, please?

# YELLOWSTONE

## Justice

# Northern Rockies Wolf Reduction Project

JUNE 12, 1995

"The chances of visitors seeing wolves in Yellowstone are very slim," warns the quasi-newspaper *Yellowstone Today*, which is handed through the driver's window of every park visitor's vehicle when it enters the park.

Well, it looks as though nobody told the Crystal Creek pack. More than two thousand people have seen them in the Lamar valley, usually across the river to the south, some miles from the road. That distance is good for the wolves, but not for photography. The serious wolf groupies cruise slowly up and down the valley each dusk and dawn, glassing the flatlands with high-powered binocs, then station themselves in pullouts and up the steep hillsides with tripod-mounted spotting scopes and long telephoto outfits.

When the wolves appear, word zizzes along the network like neurons firing. Within minutes, a throng of puffing, down-swaddled wolf lovers has gathered at the vantage point. Two dozen people see the Crystals and a grizzly bear disputing custody of an elk carcass. The wolves howl, they wrestle, they play chase, they hunt, they stroll, they sleep. Longtime wolf watchers—those who have been at it for more than, oh, ten days—resent the intrusion of the Johnny-come-latelies who had to read about this in the newspapers. Rangers are wading into Gordian traffic knots now known as wolf jams. The Crystal Creek wolves, still minus Number Two, are showing themselves, on average, two days out of every three.

The number of visitors coming through the other gateways to Yellowstone Park has increased less than 3 percent over last year, while the number coming through Cooke City is up 22 percent. Wolf T-shirts and teacups and belt buckles are flying off the shelves at Lone Wolf Mercantile and the other kitsch emporiums in Cooke. Hank Fischer's *Wolf Wars* has been rushed to publication and is selling like sixty; it can be found even at Safeway supermarkets, the only honest-to-God book in the magazine rack. Junk mail hawking wolf tchotchkes is clogging up mailboxes across America. The "Northstyle" catalogue features the Phantom of the Forest T-shirt ("Twilight. The elusive wolf pads silently through the pines"), the Alpha Wolf Necktie ("confidently poised on 100% silk"), and the Wolf Collage Collection, comprising matching bomber jacket, duffel, and travel pouch of Olefin Tyvek®.

Of the fifteen wolves released in Idaho, only one is known to be dead, the one shot next to Eugene Hussey's dead calf. Another headed north out of radio-tracking range. The other thirteen are doing fine. Most of them have remained within the Idaho wilderness, though several have wandered over the Bitterroot divide into Montana from time to time. There have been a number of reports of depredation on livestock, the better part of them coming from the area around Salmon, but none has turned out to be the work of wolves.

As was expected with such young wolves and a hard release, no pups have been born in Idaho this spring. But three new male-female pairs have formed, and more can be expected before next winter's mating season. The wolves have been seen most often in precisely the places from which reports of wolf sightings most commonly came in the years before the reintroduction, but not one uncollared wolf has been spotted. It is virtually certain now that there are no native breeding packs in central Idaho. (Yet the lawsuit drags on regardless.)

The Crystal Creek wolves are still digging. They have dug dens all up and down the Lamar, several of which are visible from the road. But there are no Crystal pups, and it is too late to hope for them. Five's frantic craving for a den and her countervailing restless inability to settle down in one have been classic symptoms of a pseudopregnancy. Number Five has always been strongly dominant over Number Four, the putative alpha male, an imputation now worth reconsidering: perhaps Four is Five's son.

In a landscape of rolling Tuscan grainfields south of Siena, a group of farm workers approach an abandoned *casale* (an old type of farm house) to rest in the shade at the end of the day. A—no—yes—a *wolf* bounds out of the ruins and disappears into the wheat. This is less than a hundred yards from the Via Cassia, the ancient highway linking Siena to Rome.

They call the chief game warden, and he calls Luigi Boitani, whose country house is not far away. Boitani and the warden go in to investigate. They find a litter of six wolf pups in the house.

Boitani advises leaving them alone, in the hope that the displaced mom will return. She does so that night, moving all six to a new den site, perhaps, chuckles Boitani, another abandoned *casale*.

Coming too fast around a curve in the mountains near Cooke City, Chad McKittrick careens off the highway and rolls his truck. The highway patrol takes its sweet time getting over the Beartooth Pass, which is still snowpacked and icy. By the time the lawmen arrive, McKittrick has crawled out of the wreckage and gotten a lift to town. He is now in one of the bars, drunk. Because it cannot be determined whether he got drunk in the bar or was already drunk when he had the accident, McKittrick will not be charged with driving under the influence.

He is wearing a big knife, two pistols, and a T-shirt emblazoned with the words NORTHERN ROCKIES WOLF REDUCTION PROJECT. The cab of his pickup is full of beer bottles. The officers confiscate a total of nine guns.

They know that McKittrick is facing federal charges for killing a wolf, and they know that he is within ten miles of the Lamar valley, which has been in all the papers and all over the local TV news since the Crystal Creek pack began putting on their spectacle, but the highway patrolmen never report the accident, the T-shirt, or the nine firearms to the U.S. attorney in Billings.

JULY 4, 1995

Perhaps in declaration of his personal independence, Chad McKittrick, back home in Red Lodge, rides his horse in the parade down Broadway. He is wearing his pistol and his Northern Rockies Wolf Reduction Project shirt. Later, McKittrick charges into a bar still on horseback. Both he and the horse are asked to leave.

# Innocence and Inexperience

The Lamar is a place of wind. The chinooks pour down from the south off Specimen Ridge and the Mirror Plateau, buffeting the valley with vernal gusts even in deep January, sweeping windward hill faces clean of snow. Sleet comes stinging out of the northeast in angled slashes down Soda Butte Creek. Blue northers bring blizzard and whiteout out of the high Absaroka nearly any time of year. Warm southwesterlies wheel northwest in a hurrying arc becoming hammerheaded blasts of gale. The wind is here even when you cannot feel it: even on the stillest and most golden summer day, great fluffy clouds stream overhead at eagle speed.

But rarely does the Lamar know a wind like that which blows on July 29, 1995. It is of the hammerhead type, sunny Doctor-Jekyll southwest transmogrified in half an hour into arctic Mister-Hyde northwest, beneath a bruise-black sky. The violence lasts only half an hour, but that is enough to topple two big Douglas firs on top of the Rose Creek pen's chain-link wall.

Nine and the pups manage to keep out of the way, but the fence lies smashed beneath the fallen trees, and the resulting torsion has opened a pup-sized hole at ground level. The pups are big gangly adolescents now, twenty-five to thirty pounds apiece, all legs and feet, but already they are looking like *wolves*, and wolves like to explore. By the time the biologists discover what has happened, all eight pups have escaped.

They are still too young, however, to be very brave explorers. When the wolf team returns later in the day—with Mike Phillips howling to try to get the escapees to reveal their hideaway—three of the pups rush back into the pen to be with their mom; the rest crowd against the fence near her.

The team withdraws, hoping maybe the rest of the pups will crawl back in. But the next morning, so much for that: there are only two pups inside with their mother. The hole is patched. Hav-a-Hart traps and big kennel traps are set.

The next day, there are three pups in the pen. Unless that third pup has learned teleportation, he must have climbed up the steeply angled trunk of the fallen Doug-fir lying across the crushed top rail of the fence, picked his way among the dense and broken branches, and thence dropped down in.

Mike Phillips, ever on the lookout for optimistic opportunity, figures that the half-down tree will make a perfect one-way door for the pups still outside: while the tree is evidently climbable from the bottom, jumping back up to where it overhangs the pen is another matter.

The biologists set out padded leghold traps with radio-transmitter alarms. A week of trapping nets only one more pup. Four in, four to go.

The next morning there are only three wolf pups in the pen. What is going on here?

Another pup is trapped and put inside, the gray female. The score is four and four again. Then *she* gets out. This is unbelievable. The only possible explanation is that these pre-adolescent, supposedly clumsy wolves have been making the leap straight up onto the tangled, unsteady, supposedly impassable jumble of splintered limbs of the fallen tree, threading their way through, and then skidding down the trunk to freedom. Phillips's "one-way door" is in fact wolf-pup monkey bars. A chain-saw slices up the Douglas fir, putting an end to the monkey business.

The leghold traps get two more pups. The biologists establish an observation point on a distant hill, and soon see that the three pups left outside have no desire to abandon the security of home and family. Every morning, they make their way to shady bed sites in the aspens, never more than a quarter mile from the pen, and there they sleep the days away; at evening they come back to the pen, to spend their nights divided from siblings and mother only by woven wire. Given this stabilization into habit, a new strategy emerges, viz., How about we just leave the poor critters alone? The electric fence must stay turned off; fingers are crossed that no impetuous buffalo bull will decide to take a shortcut through the pen. Routine resumes: roadkill twice a week, occasional glimpses of the three fugitive pups.

This will continue until the end of the early high-country hunting season in the fall, when hunters flock to the park boundary to ambush elk migrating out toward winter range. Meanwhile, we can only hope that no grizzly bear, coyote pack, or redneck rifleman will try to take advantage of the innocence and inexperience of the Rose Creek pups.

The time of year has come when wolf packs establish what the biologists call rendezvous sites. A rendezvous site is a place where everybody knows to gather, a temporary headquarters, often in the remoter reaches of the pack's territory. At the slightest sign of threat, the rendezvous site will be moved. Pups of the year can travel easily now, but they still know little of the world. Their hunting education will start in the fall, when prey is more vulnerable and the pups' adult teeth have come in. Till then, they are permitted to mess around with mice and such in the rendezvous site, and are strictly forbidden to stray.

Several times now, Mike Phillips and Doug Smith have seen the Soda Butte pack from the air moving between rendezvous sites. The strapping, bold three-year-old black-and-silver male Twelve has not been acting like an alpha in the slightest; the elderly blue wolf Thirteen leads the way. Female Fourteen follows, followed by her subordinate sister Eleven and a single pup.

Chad McKittrick attends Quarter Beer Night (25¢ per beer, that means) at the Snow Creek Saloon in Red Lodge. Near the Meeteetse Trail bridge over Rock Creek, just south of town—about five miles from where he killed Number Ten—he passes a sheriff's patrol car so close that he brushes the deputy's arm. The cops pull him over and tell him to get into the backseat of the patrol car. He asks if he can take a pee first. They say okay. McKittrick plunges into the roadside brush and hightails it for glory.

The officers plunge in after him. Thanks to the Quarter Beers, the chase is short. They search his pickup and find marijuana. McKittrick is charged with possession of dangerous drugs, reckless driving, driving under the influence of alcohol, and resisting arrest. He is released on bond.

As summer wanes, McKittrick starts hollering and waving his guns at people whom he considers to be driving too fast past his house. From time to time he is seen shooting randomly into the air, often wearing a black cowboy hat and no shirt. He threatens a neighbor's dog's life. Federal Express refuses to deliver to anybody in the neighborhood until somebody does something about this madman with the guns and the hat. McKittrick's admirers in the bars buy him drink after drink after drink. He gives autographs all around, sometimes offering his famous signature without being asked.

U.S. magistrate Richard Anderson rules that McKittrick has violated the principal term of his release from federal custody, namely that he not break any federal, state, or local law while awaiting trial. Anderson orders that McKittrick be held in jail while the court studies his psychiatric evaluation.

President Bill Clinton, his wife, Hillary, and their daughter, Chelsea, visit the Rose Creek pen in a hailstorm. Mike Phillips pries off the lid of one of the security boxes so they can get a gander at a couple of cowering wolf pups.

# Resumption, Rebeginning

FALL 1995

The elk are moving down from the mountains. The grass of the Lamar is brown; the last asters wither. The brief gold glory of the aspens is past. Grizzly bears have finished robbing the red squirrels' caches of pine nuts. The bears' long winter sleep awaits the big snow that will seal them into their dens, and until then they are in the throes of the pre-hibernation lunacy known as hyperphagia—insatiable night and day, frantically storing up fat, bold beyond reason. A big old griz, drawn in on the scent of the roadkill left at the Rose Creek pen for the three of Nine's heirs still outside, could make hors d'oeuvres of those know-nothing pups.

There is a new wolf outside the pen. Number Eight, one of the Crystal Creek yearlings, has been hanging around for weeks, making friends with Nine's pups and eyes at Nine. Eight is now seventeen months old, not quite old enough to be deemed an adult, but old enough to know that he likes this big black female a lot, and old enough to do the job of an adult male wolf this winter.

It is time to put radio collars on the pups in the Rose Creek pen and then to set the pack free. And what the *hell*? There are not five but six wolf pups inside. One of them—hard to say which—has climbed the ten-foot chain-link fence to drop in for a visit.

Twelve Montanans—quiet, unassuming, attentive, clearly unused to being watched so hard—sit in the jury box for two and a half days at the federal district court in Billings, hearing the testimony of Dusty Steinmasel, Tim Eicher, and Chad McKittrick. The defendant continues to claim that he thought Number Ten was a dog. Steinmasel testifies that McKittrick knew perfectly well that he was shooting a wolf. The jury's deliberation lasts an hour and fifteen minutes.

Chad McKittrick is found guilty of killing a member of a threatened species, guilty of possessing its remains, and guilty of transporting it.

Sentencing will come later, after an investigation into McKittrick's personal history, character, and recent behavior. Unfortunately for this book, that report will not be made public.

The Crystal Creek yearling Number Eight is waiting for the Rose Creek pack when the pen is opened, and Number Nine promptly accepts him as her new mate. Eight and Nine and the eight pups have settled in the mid-Lamar, claiming title to the valley from the river north. The Crystal pack sticks respectfully to the south side. The Soda Buttes visit the Lamar occasionally, but they are spending most of their time in the upper Stillwater and the headwaters of Slough and Pebble creeks, in the Absaroka-Beartooth Wilderness just north of the park. All three packs have settled in what now must be called territories. Home ranges. Homes.

Not one of these wolves has killed one head of livestock. Not one has tried to go home. They have given us nine native young. These are Yellowstone wolves now.

# YELLOWSTONE
## Death and Birth

# Travels and Travails

Out for a stroll with his master along the West Rosebud River, twenty-five miles south of Absarokee, Montana, a dog named Smoker, who has been trained to track mountain lions, picks up a scent and races away. Smoker follows his nose into the midst of the Soda Butte pack, who tear him to pieces.

A United Parcel Service van heads home from Christmas deliveries in Silver Gate and Cooke City. The night is black as ink. Wolf Number Twenty-two, one of the pups of Nine and Ten, bounds across the Lamar valley road and slams into the flank of the dark brown truck. By the time the sorrowing driver finds him, Twenty-two is dead.

In either an expulsion or a bold dispersal, the alpha manqué, Twelve, has left the Soda Buttes. At first he moves indecisively back and forth across the north face of the Beartooths. Then he seems to make up his mind. He skirts Red Lodge and travels rapidly south along the eastern front of the Absarokas, following the blurry ecotone between the arid, windswept ranchlands and the mountain wilderness.

Number Three has also left his pack, the Crystals, and has turned up in the middle of the heavily peopled but game-rich Paradise Valley, the broad golden course of the Yellowstone River running north out of the park. He passes many cows and calves on his way through the valley, but he pays them no heed. Near Emigrant, Montana, there is a compound of pens housing a number of privately owned wolves, whom Three—sociable and curious, as almost all wolves are—comes to visit.

Then a rancher near Dry Creek, about three miles from the captive-wolf facility, reports one of his sheep missing and another injured. A pair of Great Pyrenees dogs—a breed originally developed to protect sheep from wolves—has been killing sheep all summer around Emigrant, but the rancher at Dry Creek believes that the black wolf whom several of the neighbors have seen is to blame. Mike Phillips, Doug Smith, and Animal Damage Control rush in.

A.D.C. finds a dead sheep on the ranch and concludes that the rancher is right: this is the work of a wolf, not a dog. Two other sheep from the same band are missing.

Number Twelve, the Soda disperser, is radio-located in the wilderness headwaters of the South Fork of the Shoshone River, giving a wide berth to Cody, Wyoming.

A helicopter, an A.D.C. sharpshooter, and a nifty new nonlethal wolf-control gadget called a net gun make short work of Number Three on the ranch at Dry Creek. Mike Phillips puts him in the Rose Creek pen till the wolf teams can finish arguing about what to do with him. Phillips wants to mate Three with one of the female wolves soon to arrive from Canada. Ed Bangs and Steve Fritts in Helena consider such a pairing a recipe for a sheep-killing information lineage.

Number Twelve passes Dubois, Wyoming, still headed south. He has covered sixty-five straight-line miles, over some of the most rugged terrain in North America, in the past two days.

The Soda Butte pen is disassembled, then rebuilt on the Blacktail Deer Plateau, a wide savanna reach of the Northern Range, as rich in wildlife as the Lamar. A new, fourth pen will provide for the first wolf release on the west side of the park, on Nez Perce Creek, in the geyser basin near Old Faithful. After a trouble-free journey from British Columbia, the first shipment of eleven new wolves arrives.

The capture of whole packs in Canada has proved even more difficult this year than last. More matchmaking, therefore, is in store. An unacquainted male and female meet in the Blacktail pen, and do not kill each other. A mother and her two big pups go to Crystal Bench also accompanied by a candidate for alpha male; they accept him without demur. The pen at Nez Perce Creek gets an alpha pair and three of their offspring—the only intact pack this year, and veteran bison killers all.

The Helena opinion wins out. After eleven days in the Rose Creek pen, Number Three boards a southbound truck for his resettlement in the Pelican valley, several mountain barriers distant from Dry Creek and its sheep.

Six more wolves arrive from Canada. Another fatherless family, an alpha female and her three pups, meet another prospective alpha male in the Rose Creek pen. The last British Columbian wolf, the seventeenth this year, is a fourth subordinate member of the bison-killing pack, which he rejoins, no doubt rejoicing, at Nez Perce.

Five days after his release, Number Three arrives at White Lake, in the headwaters of Pelican Creek. Two days later he is near Tower Junction, twenty-eight miles to the north. The day after that he is at Dailey Lake in the Paradise Valley, twenty-four miles farther north. The ranch at Dry Creek reports one sheep attacked, though not killed.

The next morning, Number Three is hanging around the Dry Creek ranch house in plain sight. The owners have brought all their sheep into a dog-guarded paddock. The wolf sniffs his way blithely around the perimeter. Three has definitely got his mojo working: the guard dogs demonstrate submissive behavior toward him. Animal Damage Control gears up again.

A.D.C. arrives the next day, but high winds prevent a radio-tracking flight, and the agents call off the search. As evening falls, Three returns to Dry Creek. He plays for a while with one of the dogs, then sets about harassing the horses. The rancher chases him out of the barnyard.

In the morning a helicopter hovers over the wolf. Animal Damage Control agent Jim Hoover leans out and, in accordance with the rules for reintroduction of a nonessential-experimental population, fires two shotgun blasts into Wolf Number Three.

On the Horse Creek road near Daniels, Wyoming, about twenty miles west of Pinedale, a snowmobiler finds Soda Butte wolf Number Twelve shot dead.

Idaho wolf Number Four, an adult female, is found dead along Rock Creek, east of Missoula, Montana. Necropsy indicates that she was killed by a mountain lion.

Idaho Six and Eight have formed a pair, as have Idaho Nine and Sixteen and Idaho Five and Ten. Idaho female Fifteen has also found a mate, an uncollared wolf, probably a disperser from the north. Idaho Seven, Eleven, Twelve, and Fourteen are within five miles of one another near Blue Joint Meadows, just over the state line inside Montana; they may or may not have become a pack. Idaho Two has not been radio-located since November. Idaho Seven, from whom not a beep had been heard since last July, has turned up safe and sound at Lost Trail Pass, on the Idaho-Montana border. The signal of Idaho Three has not been heard for almost a year; transmitter failure is a possibility, but more likely she is dead.

As John Weaver is handling a shipping kennel, one of the new Idaho wolves bites him so hard that his thumb is broken. Although the chance is very small that the medical examination in Canada could have failed to detect rabies, the rules require that the wolf be put to death.

Twenty other new wolves are released on the Middle Fork of the Salmon River in central Idaho.

Federal magistrate Richard Anderson sentences Chad McKittrick to three months in the Yellowstone County Detention Center and a subsequent three months at the interestingly named Alpha House in Billings. The six months of imprisonment will be followed by a year of "supervisory release," during which the wolf killer will be subject to surprise drug tests, random searches of his property, and all-around close watching. The court recognizes McKittrick as indigent, but warns him that as soon as he starts earning an income he will be expected to pay the United States of America ten thousand dollars in restitution, which the judge figures to have been roughly the cost of the capture, transportation, handling, medical care, custody, feeding, release, and monitoring of Wolf Number Ten.

# The Return of the Wolf
# to Yellowstone

Ranchers along the Beartooth Front, citing the Soda Butte pack's killing of Smoker the dog, ask Judge William F. Downes to stay the release of the seventeen new wolves now confined in the Yellowstone pens. The court's reply:

> ... *It is ORDERED that Plaintiffs' motion for a preliminary injunction is hereby DENIED.*

On a ranch near Meeteetse, Wyoming, coyotes have come to feed on a heap of storm-killed calves. A cowboy with a rifle picks off the coyotes one by one. This is perfectly legal. He then discovers—or "discovers"—that one of the dead coyotes is a hundred-pound, radio-collared female wolf: Number Eleven, the second unlucky disperser from the Soda Butte pack.

Because Eleven was in no way threatening livestock, the cowboy has violated the Endangered Species Act, but because he has turned himself in, he will only be fined.

The Montana ranchers apply to the Tenth U.S. Circuit Court of Appeals in Denver for a stay of the wolf release, pending their appeal of Judge Downes's denial of their plea for an injunction.

Having heard nothing about any appeal until a phone call from me alerts him to its imminent possibility, and remembering only too well the same court's behavior last year, Doug Smith excuses himself abruptly, jumps in his truck, and hurries to open the Nez Perce and Rose Creek pens.

The alpha female of the Nez Perce wolves, Twenty-seven, and her three daughters leave almost immediately. The alpha male and the male pup do not. Nor do the five wolves at Rose Creek see any reason to hurry out.

Two days later, the alpha male at Nez Perce leaves the pen, but the pup still refuses to budge. The biologists go in and harry him out.

So as not to intrude on wolves already living in the neighborhood, the two in the Blacktail pen—strangers two months ago, ardent mates today—are moved to a temporary enclosure near the Lone Star geyser, not far south of Old Faithful. This pen is small, and open at one end: its purpose is merely to keep the wolves together while they are coming out from under the drugs that sedated them during their move. They are free to leave at their leisure. This pair and their offspring will be known as the Lone Star pack.

To the Montana ranchers the federal appeals court in Denver replies in one sentence:

*The application for injunction and emergency stay is DENIED.*

The Nez Perce alpha female and her three daughters are moving fast, north and east past Cooke City, while the alpha male and the one male pup head north toward Mammoth. This puts them sixty miles apart and still diverging. All our hope for bison-killing wolves is vested in these veterans. This is a problem.

Because the northern and central parts of the park are already so crowded with wolves, the wolf team's plan for the four in the Crystal Bench pen is to helicopter them into remote backcountry near Heart Lake, in the south-central part of the park. But bad weather keeps the chopper grounded, and the biologists figure that since the Nez Perce wolves have all traveled so far from their pen, it will serve. They put the wolves inside and leave the gate open. Henceforth these four will be known as the Chief Joseph pack, after the great Nez Perce chief who in 1877 led his people through these very mountains in flight from slaughter in western Montana, toward slaughter in central Montana.

Pre-technological humans cannot be restored to Yellowstone. Yet think how powerful their influence on this ecosystem must have been. They hunted nearly every animal here, herbivore and carnivore alike, fish and fowl. They set fires to reinvigorate the grasslands and keep forest encroachment at bay. They were even more dangerous than grizzly bears to those whom they considered intruders. (On their way through the park in 1877, the Nez Perce refugees shot a number of tourists.) Now what has the grizzly bear become, and the elk, and the wolf, in the absence of their ancestral rival, companion, and killer, the Indian? The closest we can come now are the well-intentioned computer models and best guesses of our ecosystem managers, ever besieged by whatever the latest in politics is, and three million tourists a year.

After eleven wary days, the wolves in the Rose Creek pen leave it. The pack is named for the mountain above Rose Creek, Druid Peak.

The Lone Star female is found dead, her hind legs badly burned, having fallen through the thin mineral crust of a boiling hot spring. There are six dead pups in her womb.

Montana's senator Conrad Burns announces that two hundred thousand dollars of the wolf project's budget has been diverted to a study of whirling disease in rainbow trout.

Five, the Crystal alpha female, dens in the southern Lamar, but again this year she bears no young.

The Druid Peak wolves, whose pen lay squeezed between the territories of the Crystal Creek and Rose Creek packs, find unclaimed space in the upper reaches of Slough Creek, some twenty miles to the north. They show no sign of denning.

The Chief Joseph pack keeps moving, exploring, never settling in one place for long—evidence that they too will produce no young this year.

The Lone Star male remains a loner, roaming far and wide: into the Idaho wheat-and-potato country on the back side of the Tetons, down and back up the Wyoming Range, north to Old Faithful and the hot springs, the place of his widowing.

And remember Number Two, the shy, slow Crystal Creek pup who wouldn't leave the pen, then couldn't find his pack, then wandered the mid-Lamar alone, coming near to Nine's daughter Seven again and again but never quite meeting up with her? Well, Number Two and Number Seven are the first of Yellowstone's new wolves to become a mating pair in the wild, and are, therefore, the first naturally formed Yellowstone wolf pack in seventy years. In a den in the heart of their territory on the Blacktail Deer Plateau, Seven gives birth to three pups. Henceforth they will be known as the Leopold pack, in honor of Aldo Leopold, the first to dream of the return of the wolf to Yellowstone.

Fourteen, the Soda Butte alpha female, dens on private land near Red Lodge—on the ranch of one of the Republican candidates for Montana's one seat in the U.S. House of Representatives. She also gives birth to three pups.

The Nez Perce alpha male and his son continue north into the Paradise Valley. The female subordinates split with their mother, then split again into two and a loner; all three spend much of the spring dangerously near Red Lodge. The Nez Perce alpha female, Twenty-seven, on the north face of the Beartooths, in a den she has dug all alone, gives birth to five pups.

The wolf team would very much like to bring the scattered Nez Perces back together in a pen in the park and see if a second try at acclimation might keep these precious bison killers put. After all, the same thing worked with Nine last year.

Number Nine herself and her new mate, ex-Crystal Number Eight, along with the seven yearlings surviving from Nine and Ten's ill-starred honeymoon last year, are using a surprisingly small area in the northern Lamar. Nine and Eight have three new pups, bringing the Rose Creek pack to an even dozen.

Number Four is killed by the Druid Peak pack in an invasion of the Crystal pack's territory. With the alpha male dead in battle, one son executed, two dispersed, and no new pups or recruits, the Crystal Creek pack is down to Five and her two-year-old Six, and Five seems to have been injured in the fight with the Druids.

Although the Soda Butte pack remains on private ranchland, surrounded by cows and near sheep, too, their record remains spotless.

Nevertheless, the Fish and Wildlife Service team in Helena decrees that the Sodas must be spared the perils and temptations of the Beartooth Front. The old blue alpha, Thirteen, and the pack's sole pup from last year (a female, we now learn) are helicopter-darted. The alpha female, Fourteen, escapes. Mike Phillips crawls into the den to extract her three new pups. The next day, Fourteen is caught in a leghold trap. Phillips parks the Sodas in the Crystal Bench pen while he decides what to do with them next. The two-year-old male, Fifteen, remains at large.

After their victory over the Crystal Creek pack, the Druid Peak wolves seem to have imperial ambitions. They trespass next on Rose Creek territory, and another bloody battle ensues. Rose yearling Twenty is fatally injured, and both the Druid Peak alphas are badly hurt.

## SUMMER 1996

A wolf kills two calves near Cascade, Idaho, and is promptly trapped by Animal Damage Control. The A.D.C. agents intend only to move the young wolf, but he drags the steel leghold trap into a stream and drowns. Other than this single incident, Idaho wolf depredation has been nil. New pairs continue to form; there may be as many as twelve.

The Chief Joseph alpha female is run over by a tractor-trailer truck on U.S. 191 where it cuts through the western side of Yellowstone Park.

The attempt to reunite the Nez Perce pack continues, quixotically. The alpha male is near Mammoth Hot Springs, no longer accompanied by his son; that male yearling and his lone-roving sister somehow find each other across opposite sides of the ecosystem and travel together in the Absarokas (not far from our ranch, though no one in the valley reports seeing them). When they venture west into the Paradise Valley, they spook a rancher, get captured, and are incarcerated in the venerable Rose Creek pen. Their two sisters spend a while exploring Sunlight Basin, east of the park, then head-to-hell-and-gone-south, into the Teton Wilderness and the headwaters of the Yellowstone. Alpha female Twenty-seven is by now totally trap-wise. She changes dens, moves her pups, dives into cover at the slightest sound of aircraft or whiff of humanity. She begins a dalliance with the Soda Butte two-year-old Fifteen, and together they start sneaking down to a ranch at night to kill sheep, which they refuse to dignify by eating.

Fifteen is finally trapped, and is slapped into custody in the Nez Perce pen. Twenty-seven, having lost her partner in crime, quits killing sheep. One of her new pups is caught in a trap set for her. The pup's shattered leg is amputated; he will spend the rest of his life at the Wildlife Science Center in Forest Lake, Minnesota. Week after week, the wolf team holds Fifteen in reserve for Twenty-seven. They catch another of Twenty-seven's pups, this time without injury, and he joins Fifteen in the Nez Perce pen.

Forest fire rages across the Beartooth Front. Twenty-seven and her pups move south into the wilderness, and the trappers give up. After the fires have passed through, the wolves return.

Ten orphan pups from northern Montana—their parents having been executed for livestock depredation—join the Nez Perce brother and sister in the Rose Creek pen.

So. Twelve wolves there at Rose Creek. The three-legged pup in rehab. The six Soda Buttes in the Crystal Bench pen. Number Fifteen and the Nez Perce pup at Nez Perce. Twenty-one Yellowstone wolves in captivity.

"What are we doing?" Mike Phillips groans. "I'm starting to feel like a damned zookeeper."

One of the Soda Butte pups dies mysteriously, with no visible evidence of illness or injury. His mother and father, his yearling sister, and his two surviving siblings are released near where the upper Yellowstone River flows into Yellowstone Lake, and soon the Soda Butte five are released to make a home there.

The Nez Perce alpha male is still alone, while his ex-mate, the untrappable Twenty-seven, and her three remaining pups seem quite at home on the Beartooth Front.

The Lone Star alpha male, on another long-range wander, strikes up a romance with one of the hitherto inseparable Nez Perce sisters, and the couple settles down together in the vast, uninhabited (by wolf or man) Thoroughfare country, in the upper Yellowstone drainage.

The five members of the Leopold pack—Seven, Two, and their three pups—remain at home on the Blacktail Deer Plateau.

The widowed alpha male of the Chief Joseph pack and his two year-ling daughters have ceased their peregrinations, and seem to have estab-lished a territory in the northwest corner of the park.

After months of lone roaming, the male Chief Joseph yearling is accepted into the bloodthirsty Druid Peak pack, whose alphas have recovered from their war wounds. The five original Druids and the new one have bullied their way into the central Lamar and staked out a big, choice territory there.

No fools, the two wolves who are all that is left of the Crystal Creek pack have shifted their home range slightly south, to the Mirror Plateau and the upper Lamar, well out of the Druid gang's way.

The eleven wolves of the Rose Creek pack—Number Nine, Number Eight, their three pups, and Nine's six surviving yearlings—are at home in the western Lamar, keeping out of trouble.

The young Nez Perce female left alone by her sister's elopement to the Thoroughfare pops up at the Nez Perce pen, where her baby brother is imprisoned with Fifteen. The latter, ever amorous, seems to take a shine to her. Accompanied by his young cellmate, Fifteen is set free to pursue this latest romance. Five days later, along the Firehole River, the male pup is hit by a car. Fifteen and the yearling female take up domestic life.

Only the Rose Creek pen remains occupied, by the two Nez Perce yearlings and the ten new arrivals from northern Montana. They will all be released together in the winter, to take their chances as, it is hoped, a pack. Lacking any formal education, these twelve young wolves will be entering a chancy world, one filling rapidly with highly skilled competition.

There are forty free, wild wolves in the Greater Yellowstone Ecosystem: five fully established packs, two others nearly so, two new likely pairs—and more soon to come.

To Tuscany's "You must find out for yourself," Yellowstone whispers in reply, "Now I understand." Our newfound love of the wolf is as rational as our forebears' hatred. The wolf wolf lovers love and the wolf wolf haters hate are both truths.

The black-footed ferret must have prairie dogs to eat, but the prairie dogs, because they eat so much grass, are incompatible with cattle ranching; the ferret, therefore, will persist, if it does, only in reserves. The grizzly bear must have space, solitude, wilderness; the grizzly persists only in reserves. But Yellowstone and Tuscany have taught us that we, even ranchers, can live with the wolf, and the wolf can live with us, in the ordinary world, even nearby, often unknown.

Shall it be so? Shall wildness persist in the heart of civilization? We can choose.

Civilization began with agriculture, which enabled higher human reproductive and survival rates and higher human densities. Every stage in civilization's history has been marked by an increase of our species' success in self-propagation. We have been so successful in latter days that we must set aside land not yet dominated by the machinery of civilization—"the wild"—in order to preserve those of our fellow species which would otherwise be destroyed.

The altering of nature has long been the essential work of civilization. This work frees civilized people from drudgery; there are then time and prosperity enough for the recognition, creation, sharing, and love of beauty.

Nature teaches us the patterns of beauty. As the natural grows more rare, we value it the more. Notions of the sublime and the sacred emerge. *I am drawn to beauty as a tree is drawn to light or an animal to water*, says the artist, in whom we see ourselves.

Civilization sometimes damages the beauty it treasures. To stop Hitler, we bomb Dresden. To bring agriculture to the American West, we extirpate the wolf and subjugate the Indian. To propagate itself, civilization damages nature. We repair the damage when we can, and the act of restoration adds its own, new beauty. Heartbreak mirrors its opposite, love. The restored *Pietà* of Michelangelo behind safety glass in St. Peter's Basilica in Rome is more beautiful to me than it was before Laszlo Toth smashed Mary's face with a hammer.

Civilization's next great success in self-propagation ought to be another alteration of nature—an alteration, paradoxically, of the human species' natural, blind urge to produce as many successful offspring as possible. The result will be the noblest restoration in our history. A strong and courageous civilization can enable the persistence of the wild, and, hence, the persistence of beauty. Beauty is destroyed only when civilization weakens into barbarism, world war, genocide, despair. Civilization and beauty die together.

Whether the end, when it comes, will take the form of an unbearable superfluity of people or of the extinction of the human species—by war, plague, poison, or an asteroid, in a hundred or a hundred thousand years—the death of civilization will be attended by the disappearance of the wolf from Yellowstone.

Autumn 1996

The Lamar is gold, dry, silent, still, a place of absences. Summer has gone, taking its people with it. The bluebirds are gone, and the kestrels. The elk are still in the mountains. The wind, though soft, whispers, "Winter." This keeps happening, time passing, loss, death.

This will never happen again. This moment, this history, has passed, is past. The river mirrors its golden bank, a line of black trees, the dimming silver sky. At the side of the road a man stands alone, telling himself what he is seeing, what he has seen, telling himself that he must remember it all, aching for the words in which to remember. All this, all this. Why should he be weeping? Below the indistinct horizon move the shadow-silhouettes of wolves.

# A READER'S BIBLIOGRAPHY

I have annotated certain sources of particular interest, sometimes with quotations from them, sometimes with my own remarks.

## BOOKS

Allen, Durward L. *Wolves of Minong: Their Vital Role in a Wild Community.* Boston: Houghton Mifflin, 1979. The story of the pioneering study of the wolves of Isle Royale, by its founder.

Bass, Rick. *The Ninemile Wolves.* Livingston, Mont.: Clark City Press, 1992.

Boitani, Luigi. *Dalla parte del lupo: La riscoperta scientifica e culturale del mitico predatore.* Milan: Editoriale Giorgio Mondadori, 1986.

Casey, Denise, and Tim W. Clark, eds. *Tales of the Wolf.* Moose, Wyo.: Homestead, 1996.

Cheney, Dorothy L., and Robert M. Seyfarth. *How Monkeys See the World: Inside the Mind of Another Species.* Chicago: University of Chicago Press, 1990.

Clark, Tim W. *Carnivores of the Greater Yellowstone Ecosystem: Selected Readings.* Collected for a course at the Yellowstone Institute, 1994.

Cook, Robert S., ed. *Ecological Issues on Reintroducing Wolves into Yellowstone National Park.* Denver: U.S. Department of the Interior, National Park Service, 1993. See individual articles in the journal section, below.

Corbet, Gordon. *The Mammals of Britain and Europe.* London: William Collins, 1980.

Dekker, Dick. *Wolf Story: From Varmint to Favorite; and: the Wolves of Jasper.* Edmonton: BST Publications, 1994.

Despain, Don G., ed. *Plants and Their Environments: Proceedings of the First Biennial Scientific Conference on the Greater Yellowstone Ecosystem,* Yellowstone National Park, Wyo., September 16–17, 1991. See individual articles in the journal section, below.

Despain, Don G. *Yellowstone Vegetation.* Boulder, Colo.: Roberts Rinehart, 1990.

Dillard, Annie. *Pilgrim at Tinker Creek.* New York: Harper's Magazine Press, 1974.

Ferguson, Gary. *The Yellowstone Wolves: The First Year.* Helena, Mont.: Falcon Press, 1996.

Fischer, Hank. *Wolf Wars.* Helena, Mont.: Falcon Press, 1995.

Fox, Michael W. *Behaviour of Wolves, Dogs, and Related Canids.* Malabar, Fla.: Robert E. Krieger, 1971.

Grady, Wayne. *The World of the Coyote.* San Francisco: Sierra Club Books, 1994.

Greater Yellowstone Coalition. *An Environmental Profile of the Greater Yellowstone Ecosystem.* Bozeman, Mont.: Greater Yellowstone Coalition, 1994.

————. *Sustaining Greater Yellowstone: A Blueprint for the Future.* Bozeman, Mont.: Greater Yellowstone Coalition, 1994.

Griffin, Donald R. *Animal Minds.* Chicago: University of Chicago Press, 1992.

Grooms, Steve. *The Return of the Wolf.* Minocqua, Wis.: NorthWord Press, Inc., 1993.

Haines, Aubrey L. *The Yellowstone Story: A History of Our First National Park.* Yellowstone National Park, Wyo.: Yellowstone Museum and Library Association, 1977.

Harrington, Fred H., and Paul C. Paquet, eds. *Wolves of the World: Perspectives of Behavior, Ecology, and Conservation.* Park Ridge, N.J.: Noyes Publications, 1982. See individual articles in the journal section, below.

Hoffman, Paul. *That Fine Italian Hand.* New York: Henry Holt and Co., 1990.

Jepson, Tim. *Wild Italy.* San Francisco: Sierra Club Books, 1994.

Jordan, William R., III, Michael E. Gilpin, and John D. Aber, eds. *Restoration Ecology: A Synthetic Approach to Ecological Research.* Cambridge: Cambridge University Press, 1987.

Keiter, Robert B., and Mark S. Boyce, eds. *The Greater Yellowstone Ecosystem: People and Nature on America's Wildlands.* New Haven: Yale University Press, 1991.

Klinghammer, Erich, ed. *The Behavior and Ecology of Wolves.* New York: Garland STPM Press, 1979. See individual articles in the journal section, below.

Leopold, Aldo. *A Sand County Almanac.* London: Oxford University Press, 1949.

Leslie, Robert Franklin. *In the Shadow of a Rainbow: The True Story of a Friendship Between Man and Wolf.* New York: W. W. Norton, 1974.

Link, Mike, and Kate Crowley. *Following the Pack: The World of Wolf Research.* Stillwater, Minn.: Voyageur Press, 1994.

Lopez, Barry Holstun. *Of Wolves and Men.* New York: Charles Scribner's Sons, 1978. A wonderful book.

MacArthur, Robert H. *Geographical Ecology: Patterns in the Distribution of Species.* Princeton: Princeton University Press, 1972.

MacArthur, Robert H., and Edward O. Wilson. *The Theory of Island Biogeography.* Princeton: Princeton University Press, 1967. The seminal text of the biological field most crucial to conservation in our time.

McNamee, Thomas. *The Grizzly Bear.* New York: Alfred A. Knopf Inc., 1984.

————. *Nature First: Keeping Our Wild Places and Wild Creatures Wild.* Boulder, Colo.: Roberts Rinehart, 1987.

Meagher, Margaret Mary. *The Bison of Yellowstone National Park.* Scientific Monograph Series. Washington, D.C.: National Park Service, 1973.

Mech, L. David. *The Way of the Wolf.* Stillwater, Minn.: Voyageur Press, 1991. For a quick introduction to the basics of wolf biology, this is the book.

———. *The Wolf: The Ecology and Behavior of an Endangered Species.* Minneapolis: University of Minnesota Press, 1970. Still the best compendium of wolf biology.

———. *The Wolves of Isle Royale.* Washington, D.C.: National Park Service, 1966.

———. *Wolves of the High Arctic.* Ely, Minn.: International Wolf Center, 1992.

Milstein, Michael. *Wolf: Return to Yellowstone.* Billings, Mont.: *Billings Gazette,* 1995.

Murray, John A., ed. *Out Among the Wolves: Contemporary Writings on the Wolf.* Anchorage: Alaska Northwest Books, 1993. An excellent anthology.

Nabhan, Gary Paul. *Songbirds, Truffles, and Wolves: An American Naturalist in Italy.* New York: Pantheon Books, 1993.

Nielsen, Leon, and Robert D. Brown, eds. *Translocation of Wild Animals.* Milwaukee: The Wisconsin Humane Society, 1988.

Paquet, Paul, and Arlin Hackman. *Large Carnivore Conservation in the Rocky Mountains.* Toronto: World Wildlife Fund, 1995.

Pennino, Luciano. *Paestum and Velia.* Salerno: Plurigraf, 1990.

Peters, Roger. *Dance of the Wolves.* New York: McGraw-Hill, 1985.

Peterson, Rolf O. *Wolf and Moose Studies on the Kenai Peninsula, Alaska, 1976–80.* Report to the U.S. Fish and Wildlife Service.

———. *Wolf Ecology and Prey Relationships on Isle Royale.* Scientific Monograph Series. Washington, D.C.: National Park Service, 1977.

———. *The Wolves of Isle Royale: A Broken Balance.* Minocqua, Wisc.: Willow Creek Press, 1996.

Phillips, Robert L., and Charles Jonkel, eds. *Proceedings of the 1975 Predator Symposium.* Missoula: Montana Forest and Conservation Experiment Station, University of Montana, 1975.

Promberger, Christoph, and Wolfgang Schröder, eds. *Wolves in Europe: Status and Perspectives.* Proceedings of the workshop "Wolves in Europe: Current Status and Prospects," Oberammergau, Germany, April 2–5, 1992.

Quammen, David. *The Song of the Dodo.* New York: Scribner, 1996. The definitive explanation of the global biodiversity crisis, and a wonderfully gripping narrative.

Russell, Sharman Apt. *Kill the Cowboy: A Battle of Mythology in the New West.* Reading, Mass.: Addison-Wesley, 1993.

Savage, Candace. *Wolves.* San Francisco: Sierra Club Books, 1988.

Seton, Ernest Thompson. *Lives of Game Animals.* Garden City, N.Y.: Doubleday, Doran, 1929.

Simonetti, Gualtiero, and Marta Watschinger. *Erbe di Campi e Prati.* Milano: Arnaldo Mondadori Editore, 1994.

Singer, Francis J., compiler. *Grazing Influences on Yellowstone's Northern Range.* Yellowstone National Park, 1990. See individual articles in the journal section, below.

Steinhart, Peter. *The Company of Wolves.* New York: Alfred A. Knopf, 1995.

United States Congress, Office of Technology Assessment. *Harmful Nonindigenous Species in the United States.* Washington, D.C.: U.S. Government Printing Office, 1993.

United States Department of the Interior, Fish and Wildlife Service. *The Reintroduction of Gray Wolves to Yellowstone National Park and Central Idaho: Final Environmental Impact Statement.* 1994.

Walker, Stephen. *Animal Thought.* London: Routledge and Kegan Paul, 1983.

Weaver, John L. *Ecology of Wolf Predation amidst High Ungulate Diversity in Jasper National Park, Alberta.* Ph.D. thesis, University of Montana, 1994.

Wilkinson, Kathleen. *Trees and Shrubs of Alberta.* Edmonton: Lone Pine, 1990.

Wilson, Edward O. *Biophilia.* Cambridge: Harvard University Press, 1984. "Our natural affinity for life—biophilia—is the very essence of our humanity and binds us to all other living species."

———. *The Diversity of Life.* Cambridge: Belknap Press, 1992. Why all this stuff matters.

Wright, Robert. *The Moral Animal.* New York: Pantheon Books, 1994. "Why we are the way we are: the new science of evolutionary psychology." Indispensable insight into human nature.

Yellowstone National Park. *Wolves for Yellowstone?* Two-volume report to the U.S. Congress, 1990 and 1992.

Zimen, Erik. *The Wolf: A Species in Danger.* New York: Delacorte Press, 1981.

## MAGAZINES, NEWSPAPERS, AND TECHNICAL JOURNALS

Certain papers presented at conferences or published in book-length collections are referenced by the shorthand terms explained below.

**Cook:** Papers collected in Robert S. Cook, ed., *Ecological Issues on Reintroducing Wolves into Yellowstone National Park,* 1993.

**GYE-1:** Papers collected in Don G. Despain, ed., *Plants and Their Environments: Proceedings of the First Biennial Scientific Conference on the Greater Yellowstone Ecosystem,* Yellowstone National Park, Wyo., September 16–17, 1991, as well as other papers presented at that conference.

**GYE-2:** Papers presented at the conference "Greater Yellowstone Predators: Ecology and Conservation in a Changing Landscape," September 24–27, 1995, Yellowstone National Park, Wyo.

**Klinghammer:** Papers collected in Erich Klinghammer, ed., *The Behavior and Ecology of Wolves,* 1979, first presented at the "Symposium on the Behavior and Ecology of Wolves," Wilmington, N.C., May 23–24, 1975.

**Singer:** Papers collected in Francis J. Singer, ed., *Grazing Influences on Yellowstone's Northern Range,* 1990.

**WH2000:** Papers presented at the conference "Wolves and Humans 2000: A Global Perspective for Managing Conflict," Duluth, Minn., March 9–12, 1995.

**WW:** Papers collected in Fred H. Harrington and Paul C. Paquet, eds., *Wolves of the World,* 1982.

Allen, Durward L., and L. David Mech. 1963. "Wolves Versus Moose on Isle Royale." *National Geographic,* February.

Allendorf, F., S. Mills, and S. Forbes. 1995. "Genetic Considerations for Carnivore Populations." Paper presented at the conference "Greater Yellowstone Predators: Ecology and Conservation in a Changing Landscape," September 24–27, Yellowstone National Park, Wyo., henceforth to be referenced as GYE-2.

Anderson, Jay E. 1991. "A Conceptual Framework for Evaluating and Quantifying Naturalness." *Conservation Biology,* September.

Arnold, Sandra L. 1995. "An Alaskan Perspective on Wolf 'Control' and the Wildlife Decision-Making Process in Alaska." Paper presented at the conference "Wolves and Humans 2000: A Global Perspective for Managing Conflict," Duluth, Minn., March 9–12, henceforth to be referenced as WH2000.

Asa, Cheryl S., Eric K. Peterson, Ulysses S. Seal, and L. David Mech. 1985. "Deposition of Anal-Sac Secretions by Captive Wolves." *Journal of Mammalogy* 66, no. 1.

Askins, Renée. 1995. "The Wolf Fund: A Beginning and an End." *International Wolf,* summer.

Bangs, Edward E. 1991. "Return of a Predator: Wolf Recovery in Montana." *Western Wildlands,* spring.

———. 1995. "Reintroducing Wolves to Yellowstone and Central Idaho." WH2000.

Bath, Alistair J. 1987. "Attitudes of Various Interest Groups in Wyoming Toward Wolf Reintroduction in Yellowstone National Park." M.S. thesis, University of Wyoming.

———. 1987. "Countywide Survey of the General Public in Wyoming in Counties Around the Park Towards Wolf Reintroduction in Yellowstone National Park." Report to the National Park Service.

———. 1987. "Statewide Survey of the Wyoming General Public's Attitude Towards Wolf Reintroduction in Yellowstone National Park." Report to the National Park Service.

———. 1991. "Public Attitudes in Wyoming, Montana and Idaho Toward Wolf Restoration in Yellowstone National Park." In *Transactions of the 56th North American Wildlife and Natural Resources Conference.*

Bath, Alistair J., and Thomas Buchanan. 1989. "Attitudes of Interest Groups in Wyoming Toward Wolf Restoration in Yellowstone National Park." *Wildlife Society Bulletin* 17, no. 4.

Bath, Alistair J., and C. Phillips. 1990. "Statewide Surveys of Montana and Idaho Resident Attitudes Toward Wolf Reintroduction in Yellowstone National Park." Report to Friends of Animals, National Wildlife Federation, Fish and Wildlife Service, and National Park Service.

Bean, Michael J. 1991. "Populations, Experimental Populations, and the Listing and Delisting of Species." A legal analysis by the chairman of the wildlife program of the Environmental Defense Fund.

Berger, Joel. 1990. "Pregnancy Incentives, Predation Constraints, and Habitat Shifts: Experimental Evidence for Wild Bighorn Sheep." *Animal Behaviour* 41.

———. 1991. "Greater Yellowstone's Native Ungulates: Myths and Realities." *Conservation Biology,* September.

Berger, Joel, and John D. Wehausen. 1991. "Consequences of a Mammalian Predator-Prey Disequilibrium in the Great Basin Desert." *Conservation Biology,* June.

Bergerud, A. T., W. Wyett, and B. Snider. 1983. "The Role of Wolf Predation in Limiting a Moose Population." *Journal of Wildlife Management* 47, no. 4.

Billings, W. D. 1991. "The Effects of Global and Regional Environmental Changes on Mountain Ecosystems." In Despain, Don, ed., *Plants and Their Environments: Proceedings of the First Biennial Scientific Conference on the Greater Yellowstone Ecosystem* (see books section, above), henceforth to be referenced as GYE-1.

Bishop, Norman A., compiler. 1992. "Yellowstone Wolf Answers: A Second Digest." Yellowstone National Park document.

———. 1995. "Converting Prey to Greater Biodiversity." *International Wolf*, summer.

Bjorge, Ronald R., and John R. Gunson. 1983. "Wolf Predation of Cattle on the Simonette River Pastures in West-Central Alberta." In Carbyn, L. N., ed., *Wolves in Canada and Alaska*. Edmonton: Canadian Wildlife Service Report no. 45.

———. 1989. "Wolf, *Canis lupus*, Population Characteristics and Prey Relationships near Simonette River, Alberta." *Canadian Field-Naturalist*, July–September.

Block, Günther E. 1995. "Renovation of Livestock Guarding Dog Management in Slovakia and the Use of Livestock Guarding Dogs as Defenders Against Wolves and Stray Dogs in Germany." WH2000.

Bobek, Boguslaw. 1995. "Status, Distribution, and Management of the Wolf in Poland." WH2000.

Boitani, Luigi. 1982. "Wolf Management in Intensively Used Areas of Italy." In Harrington, Fred H., and Paul C. Paquet, eds. *Wolves of the World: Perspectives of Behavior, Ecology, and Conservation*, (see book section, above) henceforth to be referenced as WW.

———. 1989. "Viva il lupo!" Interview in *Defenders*, May–June.

———. 1992. "Ecological and Cultural Diversities in the Evolution of Wolves–Humans Relationships." Manuscript.

———. 1995. "The Italian Way of Saving Wolves and Shepherds." WH2000.

———. 1996. "Il ritorno del lupo." *Airone*, January.

Boitani, Luigi, and Erik Zimen. 1975. "The Role of Public Opinion in Wolf Management." In Klinghammer, Erich, *The Behavior and Ecology of Wolves*, 1979 (see book section, above), henceforth to be referenced as Klinghammer.

Bowermaster, Jon. 1994. "Cry Wolf." *Bazaar*, March. A profile of Renée Askins.

Bowser, Gillian. 1990. "Winter Foraging Behavior of Elk and Bison in Yellowstone National Park, Wyoming." In Singer, Francis J., *Grazing Influences on Yellowstone's Northern Range* (see book section, above), henceforth to be referenced as Singer.

Boyce, Mark S. 1993. "Predicting the Consequences of Wolf Recovery to Ungulates in Yellowstone National Park." In Cook, Robert S., ed., *Ecological Issues on Reintroducing Wolves into Yellowstone National Park* (see book section, above) henceforth to be referenced as Cook.

———. 1995. "Assessing Models for Carnivore Conservation and Management." GYE-2.

———. 1995. "Brucellosis and the Future of Greater Yellowstone." *Yellowstone Science*, winter.

Boyd, Diane K. 1995. "The Role of Wolf Dispersal and Human Tolerance in Successful Recolonization." WH2000.

Boyd, Diane K., Robert R. Ream, Daniel H. Pletscher, and Michael W. Fairchild. 1994. "Prey Taken by Colonizing Wolves and Hunters in the Glacier National Park Area." *Journal of Wildlife Management,* April.

Brewster, Wayne G., Norman A. Bishop, and Paul Schullery. 1995. "The EIS: A Complex Decision Made." *International Wolf,* summer.

Brewster, Wayne G., Norman A. Bishop, Paul Schullery, and John Varley. 1995. "The Public Has Spoken: Wolves Belong in Yellowstone." *International Wolf,* summer.

Brussard, Peter F. 1991. "The Greater Yellowstone Ecosystem." *Conservation Biology,* September.

Brussard, Peter F., Dennis D. Murphy, and Reed F. Noss. 1992. "Strategy and Tactics for Conserving Biological Diversity in the United States." *Conservation Biology,* June.

Burk, C. John. 1973. "The Kaibab Deer Incident: A Long-Persisting Myth." *BioScience,* February.

Burkett, Douglas W., and Bruce C. Thompson. 1994. "Wildlife Association with Human-Altered Water Sources in Semiarid Vegetation Communities." *Conservation Biology,* September.

Carbyn, Ludwig N. 1982. "Coyote Population Fluctuations and Spatial Distribution in Relation to Wolf Territories in Riding Mountain National Park, Manitoba." *Canadian Field-Naturalist* 96.

———. 1983. "Wolf Predation on Elk in Riding Mountain National Park, Manitoba." *Journal of Wildlife Management* 47, no. 4.

———. 1987. "Gray Wolf and Red Wolf." In Novak, M., J. A. Baker, M. E. Oebard, and B. Malloch, eds., *Wild Furbearer Management and Conservation in North America.* Toronto: Ontario Trappers Association and Ontario Ministry of Natural Resources.

Chadwick, Douglas. 1987. "Manitoba's Wolves: A Model for Yellowstone?" *Defenders,* March–April.

Chapple, Steve. 1993. "What Is a River Worth?" *The New York Times,* 30 August.

Chase, C. H., R. A. Hartford, and R. C. Rothermel. 1991. "GIS Documentation of the 1988 Greater Yellowstone Area Fire Growth." In GYE-1.

Christian, Freddy W. 1995. "Scent Marking by Wolves by Use of Urine and Feces in Relation to Dominance Hierarchy." WH2000.

Ciucci, Paolo, and L. David Mech. 1992. "Selection of Wolf Dens in Relation to Winter Territories in Northeastern Minnesota." *Journal of Mammalogy* 73, no. 4.

Clark, Tim W., Elizabeth Dawn Amato, Donald G. Whittemore, and Ann H. Harvey. 1991. "Policy and Programs for Ecosystem Management in the Greater Yellowstone Ecosystem: An Analysis." *Conservation Biology,* September.

Clark, Tim W., A Peyton Curlee, and Richard P. Reading. 1996. "Crafting Effective Solutions to the Large Carnivore Conservation Problem." *Conservation Biology,* August.

Clark, Tim W., S. Minta, and P. Kareiva. 1995. "Yellowstone as a Model System for Understanding Carnivores." GYE-2.

Clark, Tim W., Paul C. Paquet, and A. Peyton Curlee. 1996. "General Lessons and

Positive Trends in Large Carnivore Conservation." *Conservation Biology*, August.

*Clementine.* 1995. Special issue on the New World Mine. Autumn.

Cohen, Joel E. 1995. "How Many People Can the Earth Support?" *The Sciences*, November–December. "The answers depend as much on social, cultural, economic and political choices as they do on constraints imposed by nature."

———. 1995. "Population Growth and Earth's Human Carrying Capacity." *Science*, 21 July. "Human choice is not captured by ecological notions of carrying capacity that are appropriate for nonhuman populations."

Coles, W. H. 1995. "Model of Wolf and Moose Dynamics on Isle Royale." WH2000.

Conniff, Richard. 1994. "Healthy Terror." *Atlantic Monthly*, March. "We are in danger of turning what's left of the planet into a petting zoo."

Cook, S. Joyelle. 1995. "Conflicting Actors and Controversial Issues: Wolf Conservation and Management in Lands Adjacent to Parks and Protected Areas." WH2000.

Cottenoir, Leo. 1995. "Yellowstone's Last Wolf, 1943." *International Wolf,* summer. Interview with the man who killed it.

Coughenour, Michael B. 1991. "Elk Carrying Capacity on Yellowstone's Northern Winter Range: Preliminary Modeling to Integrate Climate, Landscape, and Nutritional Requirements." In GYE-1.

Coughenour, Michael B., Francis J. Singer, and James Reardon. 1991. "The Parker Transects Revisited: Long-Term Herbaceous Vegetation Trends on Yellowstone's Northern Winter Range." In GYE-1.

Cowley, Geoffrey. 1996. "The Roots of Good and Evil." *Newsweek,* 26 February. "[Chimpanzee] males achieve dominance not through sheer force but through shrewd politics."

Crabtree, Robert L., and P. Moorcroft. 1995. "Wolf Density in Relation to Prey and Landscapes." GYE-2.

Crabtree, Robert L., and John D. Varley. 1995. "Ecological Role of the Coyote on Yellowstone's Northern Range." GYE-2.

Curlee, A. Peyton, and Tim W. Clark. 1995. "Nature's Movers and Shakers." *Defenders,* spring. "In the functioning of ecosystems, predators such as wolves, otters, and even starfish play a pivotal role."

Curnow, Edward E. 1969. "History of the Eradication of the Wolf in Montana." M.A. thesis, University of Montana.

Davis, Leslie B., Stephen A. Aaberg, and Linda Scott Cummings. 1991. "Northern Rocky Mountain Paleoecology in Archeological, Paleobotanical, and Paleoethnobotanical Perspective." In GYE-1.

Dawidoff, Nicholas. 1992. "One for the Wolves." *Audubon,* July–August. Profile of Renée Askins and the Wolf Fund.

DelGiudice, Glenn D., Francis J. Singer, and Ulysses S. Seal. 1990. "Physiological Assessment of Winter Undernutrition in Elk of Yellowstone National Park." In Singer.

Derr, Mark. 1996. "The Dog-Wolf Connection." *Natural History,* March.

DeVelice, Robert L., Gerald J. Daumiller, Patrick S. Bourgeron, and John O. Jarvie. 1991. "Bioenvironmental Representativeness of Nature Preserves: Assessment Using a Combination of a GIS and a Rule-Based Model." In GYE-1.

Diamond, Jared. 1993. "Cougars and Corridors." *Science,* 2 September.

Dowling, Thomas E., W. L. Minckley, Michael E. Douglas, Paul C. Marsh, and Bruce D. Demarais. 1992. "Response to Wayne, Nowak, and Phillips and Henry: Use of Molecular Characteristics in Conservation Biology." *Conservation Biology,* December.

Egan, Timothy. 1994. "New Gold Rush Stirs Fears of Exploitation." *The New York Times,* 14 August.

Ewing, Roy, and Jana Mohrman. 1990. "Report on 1989 Suspended Sediment and Turbidity in the Yellowstone River and Selected Tributaries from Yellowstone Lake, Yellowstone National Park, Wyoming, to Tom Miner Basin, Park County, Montana, Following the 1988 Wildfires." In Singer.

Farnes, Phillip E. 1990. "Development of a Scaled Index of Winter Severity for Animal Studies in Yellowstone National Park." In Singer.

Fischer, Hank. 1995. "Defenders of Wildlife's Role in Yellowstone Wolf Recovery." *International Wolf,* summer.

Fleischner, Thomas L. 1994. "Ecological Costs of Livestock Grazing in Western North America." *Conservation Biology,* September.

Fontaine, Joseph A. 1995. "Wolf Recovery Progress in Montana." WH2000.

Forbes, Stephen H., and Diane K. Boyd. 1996. "Genetic Variation of Naturally Colonizing Wolves in the Central Rocky Mountains." *Conservation Biology,* August.

Frank, Douglas A. 1991. "Plant-Ungulate Ecology of Grasslands on the Northern Range of Yellowstone National Park." GYE-1.

Frank, Douglas A., and Samuel J. McNaughton. 1990. "Interactive Ecology of Plants, Herbivores, and Climate in Yellowstone's Northern Range." In Singer.

———. 1993. "Evidence for the Promotion of Aboveground Grassland Production by Native Large Herbivores in Yellowstone National Park." *Oecologia* 96.

Frankham, Richard. 1995. "Inbreeding and Extinction: A Threshold Effect." *Conservation Biology,* August.

Fritts, Steven H. 1982. "Wolf Depredation on Livestock in Minnesota." Washington, D.C.: U.S. Fish and Wildlife Service.

———. 1983. "Record Dispersal by a Wolf from Minnesota." *Journal of Mammalogy* 64, no. 1.

———. 1988. "Wolf Distribution and Road Density in Minnesota." *Wildlife Society Bulletin* 16.

———. 1991. "Wolves and Wolf Recovery Efforts in the Northwestern United States." *Western Wildlands,* spring.

———. 1993. "Controlling Wolves in the Greater Yellowstone Area." In Cook.

———. 1993. "Reintroductions and Translocations of Wolves in North America." In Cook.

———. 1995. "Despite Concerns, Acquisition Is a Success." *International Wolf,* summer.

———. 1995. "The Past, Present, and Future of Wolf Recovery in the Rocky Mountains and Pacific Northwest." WH2000.

———. 1995. " 'Soft' and 'Hard' Release: Planning the Reintroduction." *International Wolf,* summer.

Fritts, Steven H., and Edward E. Bangs. "Gray Wolves." GYE-2.

Fritts, Steven H., Edward E. Bangs, and James F. Gore. 1994. "The Relationship of

Wolf Recovery to Habitat Conservation and Biodiversity in the Northwestern United States." *Landscape and Urban Planning* 28.

Fritts, Steven H., and Ludwig N. Carbyn. 1995. "Population Viability, Nature Reserves, and the Outlook for Gray Wolf Conservation in North America." *Restoration Ecology* 3, no. 1.

Fritts, Steven H., and L. David Mech. 1981. "Dynamics, Movements, and Feeding Ecology of a Newly Protected Wolf Population in Northwestern Minnesota." *Wildlife Monographs*, October.

Fritts, Steven H., William J. Paul, and L. David Mech. 1984. "Movements of Translocated Wolves in Minnesota." *Journal of Wildlife Management* 48, no. 3.

———. 1985. "Can Relocated Wolves Survive?" *Wildlife Society Bulletin* 13.

Fritts, Steven H., William J. Paul, L. David Mech, and David P. Scott. 1992. "Trends and Management of Wolf-Livestock Conflicts in Minnesota." Washington, D.C.: U.S. Fish and Wildlife Service.

Gee, C. Kerry, Richard S. Magleby, Warren R. Bailey, Russell L. Gum, and Louise M. Arthur. 1977. "Sheep and Lamb Losses to Predators and Other Causes in the Western United States." Washington, D.C.: U.S. Department of Agriculture, Economic Research Service.

Gese, Eric M., and L. David Mech. 1991. "Dispersal of Wolves (*Canis lupus*) in Northeastern Minnesota, 1969–1989." *Canadian Journal of Zoology* 69.

Gilbreath, Jennifer D. 1995. "The Red Wolf and Private Lands." WH2000.

Grothe, S., R. L. Crabtree, E. M. Gese, K. Hatier, and H. D. Picton. 1995. "Winter Ungulate Carrion and Landscape Influences on Coyote Behavior and Population Demographics on Yellowstone's Northern Range." GYE-2.

Gunson, John R. 1983. "Wolf Predation of Livestock in Western Canada." In Carbyn, L. N., ed., *Wolves in Canada and Alaska*. Edmonton: Canadian Wildlife Service Report no. 45.

———. 1983. "Wolf-Ungulate Predation in North America: Review of Major Studies." Alberta Energy and Natural Resources, Fish and Wildlife Division.

———. 1995. "Canadian Transplants." *International Wolf,* summer.

Haber, Gordon C. 1995. "A Critical View of Wolf Control in Alaska and the Yukon." WH2000.

———. 1996. "Biological, Conservation, and Ethical Implications of Exploiting and Controlling Wolves." *Conservation Biology*, August.

Hadley-Barnosky, Elizabeth A. 1991. "Grassland Change over 2000 Years in Northern Yellowstone Park." In GYE-1.

Halfpenny, Jim. 1993. "Tracking Wolves: A Scientific Approach." Gardiner, Mont.: A Naturalist's World.

Halfpenny, James C., and Diann Thompson. 1996. "Discovering Yellowstone Wolves: Watcher's Guide." Gardiner, Mont.: A Naturalist's World.

Halfpenny, Jim, Diann Thompson, and Norm Bishop. 1996. "Tracking Wolf Recovery." Gardiner, Mont.: A Naturalist's World.

Harrington, Fred H., and L. David Mech. 1979. "Wolf Howling and Its Role in Territory Maintenance." *Behavior* 68.

———. 1982. "An Analysis of Howling Response Parameters Useful for Wolf Pack Censusing." *Journal of Wildlife Management* 46, no. 3.

———. 1982. "Patterns of Homesite Attendance in Two Minnesota Wolf Packs." In WW.

Harrington, Fred H., and L. David Mech. 1982. "Wolf Pack Spacing: Howling as a Territory-Independent Spacing Mechanism in a Territorial Population." *Behavioral Ecology and Sociobiology* 12.

Harrington, Fred H., L. David Mech, and Steven H. Fritts. 1983. "Pack Size and Wolf Pup Survival: Their Relationship Under Varying Ecological Conditions." *Behavioral Ecology and Sociobiology* 13.

Harrington, Fred H., Paul C. Paquet, Jenny Ryon, and John C. Fentress. 1982. "Monogamy in Wolves: A Review of the Evidence." In WW.

Henne, Donald R. 1975. "Domestic Sheep Mortality on a Western Montana Ranch." In Phillips, Robert L., and Charles Jonkel, eds., *Proceedings of the 1975 Predator Symposium* (see book section, above).

Henshaw, Robert E. "Can the Wolf Be Returned to New York?" In WW.

Henshaw, Robert E., Randall Lockwood, Richard Shideler, and Robert O. Stephenson. 1979. "Experimental Release of Captive Wolves." In Klinghammer.

Hillis, T. L. 1995. "Changes in Reproductive Parameters of Wolves, *Canis lupus*, during a Caribou, *Rangifer tarandus*, Population Increase in the Central Canadian Arctic." WH2000.

Holmes, Roger. 1995. "Issues and Alternatives Surrounding Future State Management of Wolves in Minnesota." WH2000.

Huber, Djuro. 1995. "Wolves in Croatia: Status and Perspectives." WH2000.

*International Wolf.* Many issues.

International Wolf Center. 1995. "1995 World Status Report." Technical Publication #292.

―――. 1995. "A World of Wolf Gifts." Catalog.

Jackson, Sally Graves, and John A. Kadlec. 1991. "Relationships Among Breeding Songbirds, Willows, and Browsing by Elk and Moose in and Around Northern Yellowstone National Park." In GYE-1.

Jimenez, Michael D. 1995. "Impacts of Humans on Recolonizing Wolves in Ninemile, Montana." WH2000.

Jobes, Patrick C. 1991. "The Greater Yellowstone Social System." *Conservation Biology*, September.

Joslin, Paul. 1982. "Status, Growth, and Other Facets of the Iranian Wolf." In WW.

―――. 1995. "Are Differences in Wolf (*Canis lupus*) Densities Between Alaska and Minnesota Mainly Attributable to Variations in Wolf Management Policies?" WH2000.

Kareieva, Peter. 1993. "No Shortcuts in New Maps." *Science,* 23 September. Describing a new mapping system—"gap analysis"—which overlays distribution of animal species on a map of habitat types.

Keiter, Robert B., and Patrick T. Holscher. 1990. "Wolf Recovery Under the Endangered Species Act: A Study in Contemporary Federalism." *Public Land Law Review* 11.

Keiter, Robert B., and Harvey Locke. 1996. "Law and Large Carnivore Conservation in the Rocky Mountains of the U.S. and Canada." *Conservation Biology*, August.

Keith, Lloyd B. 1983. "Population Dynamics of Wolves." In Carbyn, L. N., ed., *Wolves in Canada and Alaska*. Edmonton: Canadian Wildlife Service Report no. 45.

Kellert, Stephen R. 1985. "The Public and the Timber Wolf in Minnesota." Unpublished report, Yale University.

———. 1985. "Public Perception of Predators, Particularly the Wolf and Coyote." *Biological Conservation*, 31, pp. 167–89.

Kellert, Stephen R., Matthew Black, Colleen Reid Rush, and Alistair J. Bath. 1996. "Human Culture and Large Carnivore Conservation in North America." *Conservation Biology*, August.

Kelly, Michael. 1995. "The Road to Paranoia." *The New Yorker*, 19 June. On the scary delusions of the radical right.

Knight, Dennis H., and Linda L. Wallace. 1989. "The Yellowstone Fires: Issues in Landscape Ecology: A Landscape Perspective Is Necessary in Resolving the Difficulties of Natural Area Management." In Singer.

Knight, Richard L., George N. Wallace, and William E. Riebsame. 1995. "Ranching the View: Subdivisions Versus Agriculture." *Conservation Biology*, April.

Knopf, Fritz L., and Fred B. Samson. 1994. "Scale Perspectives on Avian Diversity in Western Riparian Ecosystems." *Conservation Biology*, September.

Kohn, Bruce E. 1995. "Impacts of Highway Development on Timber Wolves in Northwestern Wisconsin." WH2000.

Lane, John R., and Cliff Montagne. 1991. "Comparison of Soils Inside and Outside of Grazing Enclosures on Yellowstone National Park's Northern Winter Range." In GYE-1.

Lawrence, Deron E., and G. Wayne Minshall. 1991. "Short- and Long-Term Changes in Riparian Zone Vegetation and Stream Macroinvertebrate Community Structure." In GYE-1.

Lenihan, M. L. 1987. "Montanans Ambivalent on Wolves." Montana Poll, Bureau of Business and Economic Research, School of Business Administration, University of Montana.

Lime, David W., Barbara Koth, and James C. Vlaming. 1993. "Effects of Restoring Wolves on Yellowstone Area Big Game and Grizzly Bears: Opinions of Scientists." In Cook.

Lorenz, Jay R. 1986. "Raising and Training a Livestock-Guarding Dog." Oregon State University Extension Service, Circular 1238, April.

Ludwig, Donald, Ray Hilborn, and Carl Walters. 1993. "Uncertainty, Resource Exploitation, and Conservation: Lessons from History." *Science*, 2 April. Recommendations: "1) Include human motivation and responses as part of the system to be studied and managed. 2) Act before scientific consensus is achieved."

Mack, John A., and Francis J. Singer. 1993. "Population Models for Elk, Mule Deer, and Moose on Yellowstone's Northern Winter Range." In Cook.

———. 1993. "Using Pop-II Models to Predict Effects of Wolf Predation and Hunter Harvests on Elk, Mule Deer, and Moose on the Northern Range." In Cook.

Maguire, Lynn A., and Christopher Servheen. 1992. "Integrating Biological and Sociological Concerns in Endangered Species Management: Augmentation of Grizzly Bear Populations." *Conservation Biology*, September.

Mallonee, Jay S., and Paul Joslin. 1995. "Traumatic Stress Disorder in an Adult Wild Captive Wolf." WH2000.

Mann, Charles C. and Mark L. Plummer. 1993. "The High Cost of Biodiversity." *Science*, 25 June.

———. 1995. "Are Wildlife Corridors the Right Path?" *Science*, 1 December. ". . . Corridors are not always self-evident. . . . Ted Case, an ecologist at UC San Diego, says that ecologists usually define corridors by vegetation types—strips of forest land between the lawns of suburban developments, for instance—but species such as salamanders may follow different trails. 'I'm not as sure they are responding to vegetation types, rather than microbes in the soil or fungus or ants.' "

Marston, Richard A., and Jay E. Anderson. 1991. "Watersheds and Vegetation of the Greater Yellowstone Ecosystem." *Conservation Biology*, September.

Maskarinec, Gary S. 1991. "Native Plant Die-offs." In GYE-1.

Maughan, Ralph. 1995–96. "Ralph Maughan's Wolf Report." On the Internet at www.poky.srv.net/~jjmrm/maughan.html. See the Continuing Information section of this bibliography, below.

McLaren, B. E., and R. O. Peterson. 1994. "Wolves, Moose and Tree Rings on Isle Royale." *Science*, 2 December.

McNamee, Thomas. 1982. "Trouble in Wolf Heaven." *Audubon*, January. About the Isle Royale wolf project and Rolf Peterson.

———. 1986. "Yellowstone's Missing Element." *Audubon*, January.

———. 1992. Testimony at a hearing of the Committee on Energy and Natural Resources, U.S. Senate, on behalf of the Greater Yellowstone Coalition, the Montana and Wyoming chapters of the Sierra Club, and the Wilderness Society, September 19.

———. 1992. "Yellowstone's Missing Wolves." *Defenders*, November–December.

McNaught, D. A. 1985. "Park Visitor Attitudes Toward Wolf Recovery in Yellowstone National Park." M.S. thesis, University of Montana.

McNaughton, Samuel J. 1996. "Grazing and Yellowstone." Interview in *Yellowstone Science*, winter.

Meagher, Mary, and Margaret E. Meyer. 1994. "On the Origin of Brucellosis in Bison of Yellowstone National Park: A Review." *Conservation Biology*, September.

Mech, L. David. 1975. "Population Trend and Winter Deer Consumption in a Minnesota Wolf Pack." In Phillips and Jonkel (see book section, above).

———. 1975. "Some Considerations in Re-establishing Wolves in the Wild." In Klinghammer.

———. 1977. "Wolf-Pack Buffer Zones as Prey Reservoirs." *Science*, 21 October.

———. 1982. "The IUCN Wolf Specialist Group." Includes a "Draft Table of Information for World Conservation Strategy for the Wolf, 1979." In WW.

———. 1987. "Age, Season, Distance, Direction, and Social Aspects of Wolf Dispersal from a Minnesota Pack." In Chepko-Sade, B. D., and Z. Halpin, eds., *Mammalian Dispersal Patterns*. Chicago: University of Chicago Press.

———. 1988. "Longevity in Wild Wolves." *Journal of Mammalogy* 69, no. 1.

———. 1990. "Who's Afraid of the Big Bad Wolf?" *Audubon*, March. Regarding the risk of wolf attack on humans.

———. 1992. "Daytime Activity of Wolves During Winter in Northeastern Minnesota." *Journal of Mammalogy* 73, no. 3.

————. 1993. "Details of a Confrontation Between Two Wild Wolves." *Canadian Journal of Zoology* 71.

————. 1993. "Resistance of Wolf Pups to Inclement Weather." *Journal of Mammalogy* 74, no. 2.

————. 1993. "Updating Our Thinking on the Role of Human Activity in Wolf Recovery." U.S. Fish and Wildlife Service Information Bulletin.

————. 1994. "Buffer Zones of Territories of Gray Wolves as Regions of Intraspecific Strife." *Journal of Mammalogy*, February.

————. 1995. "The Challenge and Opportunity of Recovering Wolf Populations." *Conservation Biology*, April.

————. 1995. "Territoriality and Fertility in Wolf Packs with Vasectomized Males." WH2000.

————. 1995. "Wolf Realities: What Wolves Mean Now, and What They Will Mean in the Future." *Yellowstone Science*, summer. Interview.

Mech, L. David, Steven H. Fritts, Glenn L. Radde, and William J. Paul. 1988. "Wolf Distribution and Road Density in Minnesota." *Wildlife Society Bulletin* 16, no. 1.

Mech, L. David, and H. H. Hertel. 1983. "An Eight-Year Demography of a Minnesota Wolf Pack." *Acta zoologica fennica* 174.

Mech, L. David, and Patrick D. Karns. 1977. "Role of the Wolf in a Deer Decline in the Superior National Forest."

Mech, L. David, R. E. McRoberts, R. O. Peterson, and R. E. Page. 1987. "Relationship of Deer and Moose Populations to Previous Winter's Snow." *Journal of Animal Ecology* 56.

Mech, L. David, Thomas J. Meier, and John W. Burch. 1991. "Denali Park Wolf Studies: Implications for Yellowstone." *Transactions of the 56th North American Wildlife and Natural Resources Conference.*

Mech, L. David, Michael E. Nelson, and Ronald E. McRoberts. 1991. "Effects of Maternal and Grandmaternal Nutrition on Deer Mass and Vulnerability to Wolf Predation." *Journal of Mammalogy*, February.

Mech, L. David, and Roger B. Peters. 1977. "The Study of Chemical Communication in Free-Ranging Mammals." In D. Müller-Schwartze and M. M. Mozell, eds., *Chemical Signals in Vertebrates.* New York: Plenum.

Mech, L. David, and Ulysses S. Seal. 1987. "Premature Reproductive Activity in Wild Wolves." *Journal of Mammalogy* 68, no. 4.

Mendelssohn, H. 1982. "Wolves in Israel." In WW.

Merrill, Evelyn, Jon Hak, and Nancy Stanton. 1991. "Responses of Nematodes to Ungulate Herbivory on Bluebunch Wheatgrass and Idaho Fescue in Yellowstone National Park." In GYE-1.

Messier, François. 1984. "Moose-Wolf Dynamics and the Natural Regulation of Moose Populations." Ph.D. dissertation, University of British Columbia.

Milinski, Manfred. 1993. "Cooperation Wins and Stays." *Science*, 1 July. Describing the victorious Tit-for-Tat solution of the Prisoner's Dilemma.

Miner, Norton R. 1971. Letter from the state supervisor of the Montana Division of Wildlife Services to Glen Cole, chief of biological research at Yellowstone National Park. Miner reported two observations of a wolf feeding on a deer. In the first observation, an outfitter and guide from Big Timber took a potshot at the animal, and missed. The second sighting, in the valley where I now live, was by our ranch manager's grandfather.

Minta, S., P. Kareiva, and M. Soulé. 1995. "Is There a Theory of Carnivore Ecology?" GYE-2.

Moffat, Anne Simon. 1996. "Biodiversity Is a Boon to Ecosystems, Not Species." *Science,* 15 March.

Moore, Peter D. 1996. "Hunting Ground for Farmers." *Nature,* 22 August. Wildlife habitat management by Europeans five thousand years ago.

Moran, G., and J. C. Fentrass. 1975. "A Search for Order in Wolf Social Behavior." In Klinghammer.

Morell, Virginia. 1996. "Life at the Top: Animals Pay the High Price of Dominance." *Science,* 19 January. Chemical indicators show stress levels higher in dominant mongooses and wild dogs than in subordinate individuals—contrary to the widely accepted view that subordinates worry and stew about their social position while the alphas pick their teeth.

Mueller, Christine. 1989. "The Reintroduction of Wolves to Yellowstone: The Legislative and Legal History." Senior thesis, University of California at Santa Cruz.

Murphy, Sue Consolo, and Donay D. Hanson. 1993. "Distribution of Beaver in Yellowstone National Park, 1988–1989." In Cook.

Nelson, Michael E., and L. David Mech. 1981. "Deer Social Organization and Wolf Predation in Northeastern Minnesota." *Wildlife Monographs,* July.

———. 1985. "Observation of a Wolf Killed by a Deer." *Journal of Mammalogy* 66, no. 1.

———. 1991. "Wolf Predation Risk Associated with White-Tailed Deer Movements." *Canadian Journal of Zoology* 69.

Newmark, William D. 1995. "Extinction of Mammal Populations in Western North American National Parks." *Conservation Biology,* June.

Niemeyer, Carter. 1995. "Precapture Operation—Snaring and Radio-Collaring of 'Judas' Wolves." *International Wolf,* summer.

———. 1995. "Wolf Damage Management in Relation to Wolf Recovery." WH2000.

Norland, Jack E., and Francis J. Singer. 1990. "Effects of the 1988 Fires on the Northern Range: 1989 Forage, Productivity, Winter Elk Habitat Use, and Snow Relations." In Singer.

Noss, Reed F., Howard B. Quigley, Maurice G. Hornocker, Troy Merrill, and Paul C. Paquet. 1996. "Conservation Biology and Carnivore Conservation in the Rocky Mountains." *Conservation Biology,* August.

Nowak, Ronald M. 1992. "The Red Wolf Is Not a Hybrid." *Conservation Biology,* December.

Oosenbrug, Sebastian M., and Ludwig N. Carby. 1982. "Winter Predation on Bison and Activity Patterns of a Wolf Pack in Wood Buffalo National Park." In WW.

Ovsyanikov, Nikita. 1995. "Does the Russian Wolf Suffer 'Perestroika'?" WH2000.

Packard, Jane M., and L. David Mech. 1983. "Population Regulation in Wolves." In Bunnell, F. L., D. S. Eastman, and J. M. Peek, eds., *Symposium on Natural Regulation of Wildlife Populations.* Moscow: University of Idaho Forest, Wildlife, and Range Experiment Station, Proceedings 14.

Packard, Jane M., L. David Mech, and Ulysses S. Seal. 1983. "Social Influences on Reproduction in Wolves." In Carbyn, Ludwig N., ed., *Wolves in Canada: Their*

*Status, Biology, and Management.* Edmonton: Canadian Wildlife Service Report no. 45.

Packard, Jane M., Ulysses S. Seal, L. David Mech, and Edward D. Plotka. 1985. "Causes of Reproductive Failure in Two Family Groups of Wolves (*Canis lupus*)." University of Minnesota, Veterans Administration Medical Center, Patuxent Wildlife Research Center, and Marshfield Medical Foundation.

Paine, Robert T. 1969. "The *Pisaster-Tegula* Interaction: Prey Patches, Predator Food Preference, and Intertidal Community Structure." *Ecology*, Autumn. "The pattern of species occurrence, distribution, and density are disproportionately affected by the activities of a single species of high trophic status. I have labelled these 'keystone species.' "

Palomares, F., P. Gaona, P. Ferreras, and M. Delibes. 1995. "Positive Effects on Game Species of Top Predators by Controlling Smaller Predator Populations: An Example with Lynx, Mongooses, and Rabbits." *Conservation Biology*, April.

Paquet, Paul C. 1989. "Behavioral Ecology of Sympatric Wolves (*Canis lupus*) and Coyotes (*Canis latrans*) in Riding Mountain National Park, Manitoba." Ph.D. dissertation, University of Manitoba.

Parker, Warren T., and Michael K. Phillips. 1991. "Application of the Experimental Population Designation to Recovery of Endangered Red Wolves." *Wildlife Society Bulletin* 19, no. 1.

Paul, William J. 1992. "Wolf Depredation on Livestock in Minnesota: Annual Update of Statistics." Report to U.S. Department of Agriculture, Animal Damage Control.

Peters, Roger. 1975. "Mental Maps in Wolf Territoriality." In Klinghammer.

Peters, Roger P., and L. David Mech. 1975. "Scent-marking in Wolves." *American Scientist*, November–December.

Peterson, Rolf O. 1979. "Social Rejection Following Mating of a Subordinate Wolf." *Journal of Mammalogy*, February.

———. 1984–85. "Ecological Studies of Wolves on Isle Royale: Annual Report." Michigan Technological University.

———. 1993–94. "Ecological Studies of Wolves on Isle Royale: Annual Report." Michigan Technological University.

———. 1994–95. "Ecological Studies of Wolves on Isle Royale: Annual Report." Michigan Technological University.

———. 1995–96. "Ecological Studies of Wolves on Isle Royale: Annual Report." Michigan Technological University.

Peterson, Rolf O., and James D. Woolington. 1982. "The Apparent Extirpation and Reappearance of Wolves on the Kenai Peninsula, Alaska." In WW.

Petrucci-Fonseca, Francisco. 1995. "Managing Wolf–Man Conflicts in Portugal." WH2000.

Phillips, Michael K. 1995. "Reintroduction of Gray Wolves to Yellowstone National Park." WH2000.

———. 1995. "Wolf Restoration Is a Touchstone." *International Wolf*, summer.

Phillips, Michael K., and V. Gary Henry. 1992. "Comments on Red Wolf Taxonomy." *Conservation Biology*, December.

Pickett, S.T.A., and M. L. Cadenasso. 1995. "Landscape Ecology: Spatial Heterogeneity in Ecological Systems." *Science*, 21 July. "Studies of superficially human-free systems can yield misleading results because the structure and function of systems often reflect human influences that are not obvious."

Pimm, Stuart L., Gareth J. Russell, John L. Gittleman, and Thomas M. Brooks. 1995. "The Future of Biodiversity." *Science*, 21 July. "If all species currently deemed 'threatened' become extinct in the next century, then future extinction rates will be 10 times recent rates."

Power, Thomas Michael. 1991. "Ecosystem Preservation and the Economy in the Greater Yellowstone Area." *Conservation Biology*, September.

Primm, Steven A., and Tim W. Clark. 1996. "Making Sense of the Policy Process for Carnivore Conservation." *Conservation Biology*, August.

Promberg, Christoph. 1995. "The European Wolf Network—Coordinating National Wolf Conservation Efforts to a European Campaign." WH2000.

Pyle, Robert Michael. 1995. "Bigfoot Baby Found in Watermelon, Has Elvis's Sneer." *Orion*, summer. On the persistence of belief in nonexistent creatures.

Randall, Dick. 1979. "Wolves for Yellowstone." *Defenders*, August.

Rasker, Raymond, and Arlin Hackman. 1996. "Economic Development and the Conservation of Large Carnivores." *Conservation Biology*, August.

Rasker, Raymond, Norma Tirrell, and Deanne Kloepfer. 1992. "The Wealth of Nature: New Economic Realities in the Yellowstone Region." Bozeman, Mont.: The Wilderness Society.

Ream, Robert R., and Ursula I. Mattson. 1982. "Wolf Status in the Northern Rockies." In WW.

Reed, Susan. 1992. "Wild at Heart." *People*, September 21. A profile of Renée Askins.

Renkin, Roy, and Don Despain. 1991. "Forest Type, Fuel Moisture, and Lightning-Caused Fires." In GYE-1.

———. 1991. "Suckering in Burned Aspen as Related to Above-ground and Below-ground Biomass." In GYE-1.

Ridley, Matt, and Bobbi S. Low. 1993. "Can Selfishness Save the Environment?" *Atlantic*, September.

Romme, William H., and Don G. Despain. 1989. "The Yellowstone Fires." *Scientific American*, November.

Romme, William H., and Dennis H. Knight. 1982. "Landscape Diversity: The Concept Applied to Yellowstone Park." *BioScience*, September.

Ron, Tamar. 1995. "Wolves and Livestock in Israel." WH2000.

Rosenberger, Jack. 1995. "Wolves, Dogs, and Danger." *Animals*, July–August. "While there have been no documented accounts of fatal attacks by healthy wild wolves on people in North America, severe or fatal attacks by wolf-dogs are 'disturbingly common,' according to the Humane Society of the United States. At least ten children have been killed by wolf hybrids since 1986."

Rothman, Russell J., and L. David Mech. 1979. "Scent-Marking in Lone Wolves and Newly Formed Pairs." *Animal Behavior* 27, no. 3.

Servheen, Christopher, and Richard R. Knight. 1993. "Possible Effects of a Restored Gray Wolf Population on Grizzly Bears in the Greater Yellowstone Area." In Cook.

Sharp, Henry S. 1982. "Some Problems in Wolf Sociology." In WW.

Sheldon, J. W., et al. 1995. "Vocal and Spatial Responses of Coyotes to Reintroduced Gray Wolves." GYE-2.

Singer, Francis J. 1991. "Some Predictions Concerning a Wolf Recovery into Yellowstone National Park: How Wolf Recovery May Affect Park Visitors, Ungulates, and Other Predators." *Transactions of the 56th North American Wildlife and Natural Resources Conference.*

———. 1991. "The Ungulate Prey Base for Wolves in Yellowstone National Park." In Keiter, Robert B., and Mark S. Boyce, eds., *The Greater Yellowstone Ecosystem: People and Nature on America's Wildlands* (see book section, above).

Singer, Francis J., and John A. Mack. 1993. "Potential Ungulate Prey for Gray Wolves." In Cook.

Singer, Francis J., Laurel Mack, and Rex Cates. 1990. "Willow Species Abundance, Herbivory, and the Role of Secondary Compounds on the Northern Elk Winter Range." In Singer.

Smith, Douglas W. 1995. "Adjusting to New Sights, Smells and Sounds—In Captivity." *International Wolf,* summer.

———. 1995. "The Founder Wolves." *International Wolf,* summer.

Smith, Douglas W., and Michael K. Phillips. 1995. "Movements and Food Habits of Gray Wolves Released in Yellowstone National Park." GYE-2.

Stachell, Michael. 1995. "A New Battle Over Yellowstone Park." *U.S. News & World Report,* 13 March.

Stone, Richard. 1995. "Taking a New Look at Life Through a Functional Lens." *Science,* 21 July. On the widespread effects of keystone species, particularly top predators, on whole ecosystems.

Sullivan, John O. 1975. "Individual Variability in Hunting Behavior of Wolves." In Klinghammer.

Tear, Timothy H., J. Michael Scott, Patricia H. Hayward, and Brad Griffith. 1993. "Status and Prospects for Success of the Endangered Species Act: A Look at Recovery Plans." *Science,* 12 November.

Terrill, Clair E. 1975. "Livestock Losses to Predators in Western States." In Phillips and Jonkel (see book section, above).

Theberge, John B. 1995. "Does a 75km² Park Protect a Wolf Population?" WH2000.

Theberge, John B., and David A. Gauthier. 1985. "Models of Wolf-Ungulate Relationships: When Is Wolf Control Justified?" *Wildlife Society Bulletin* 13, no 4.

Thiel, Richard P., and Steven H. Fritts. 1983. "Chewing-Removal of Radio Collars by Gray Wolves in Wisconsin." *Journal of Wildlife Management* 47, no. 3.

Thurber, Joanne M., and Rolf O. Peterson. 1993. "Effects of Population Density and Pack Size on the Foraging Ecology of Gray Wolves." *Journal of Mammalogy,* November.

Tilt, Whitney, Ruth Norris, and Amos S. Eno. 1987. "Wolf Recovery in the Northern Rocky Mountains." Washington, D.C.: National Audubon Society.

Tucker, Pat, and Daniel H. Pletscher. 1989. "Attitudes of Hunters and Residents Toward Wolves in Northwestern Montana." *Wildlife Society Bulletin* 17, pp. 507–14.

Turner, John F. 1990. "Wolves and Wyoming High Country." Unpublished essay by the director of the U.S. Fish and Wildlife Service.

Tyers, Daniel, Francis J. Singer, Tom Lemke, and Lynn Irby. 1990. "Ecology of Moose on the Northern Winter Range of Yellowstone National Park and the Gallatin National Forest." In Singer.

United States Department of the Interior. 1994. "50 CFR Part 17, Establishment of a Nonessential Experimental Population of Gray Wolves in Yellowstone National Park in Wyoming, Idaho, Montana, Central Idaho and Southwestern Montana; Final Rules." *Federal Register,* November 22.

United States Fish and Wildlife Service. 1984. "Agency Review Draft, Revised Northern Rocky Mountain Wolf Recovery Plan."

———. 1992. "Alternative Scoping Report."

———. 1993. "Annual Report of the Montana Interagency Wolf Working Group."

———. 1996. "Annual Report of the Rocky Mountain Interagency Wolf Recovery Program."

United States Senate. 1990. "Northern Rocky Mountain Gray Wolf Restoration Act of 1990." Washington, D.C.: Government Printing Office. This was never passed into law, nor did it ever have a chance.

Vales, David J., and James M. Peek. 1993. "Estimating the Relations Between Hunter Harvest and Gray Wolf Predation of the Gallatin, Montana, and Sand Creek, Idaho, Elk Populations." In Cook.

Van Dyke, Fred G., Brenda L. Probert, and Jennifer J. Rozema. 1991. "Vegetation Characteristics of Elk Summer Range in South-Central Montana." In GYE-1.

Weaver, John L. 1978. "The Wolves of Yellowstone." Washington, D.C.: U.S. Department of the Interior, Natural Resources Report No. 14. Proof that there were no wolves of Yellowstone anymore.

———. 1979. "Wolf Predation upon Elk in the Rocky Mountain Parks of North America: A Review." In Boyce, M. S., and L. D. Hayden-Wing, eds., *North American Elk: Ecology, Behavior and Management.* Laramie: University of Wyoming.

———. 1982. "Draft Wolf Management Guidelines and Control Plan." An early recognition that wolf control was going to have to be part of any package.

———. 1983. "Of Wolves and Livestock." *Western Wildlands,* winter.

Weaver, John L., C. Arvidson, and P. Wood. 1992. "Two Wolves, *Canis lupus,* killed by a Moose, *Alces alces,* in Jasper National Park, Alberta." *Canadian Field-Naturalist* 106.

Weaver, John L., Paul C. Paquet, and Leonard F. Ruggiero. 1996. "Resilience and Conservation of Large Carnivores in the Rocky Mountains." *Conservation Biology,* August.

Weber, William, and Alan Rabinowitz. 1996. "A Global Perspective on Large Carnivore Conservation." *Conservation Biology,* August.

Weise, Thomas F., William L. Robinson, Richard A. Hook, and L. David Mech. 1975. "An Experimental Translocation of the Eastern Timber Wolf." Twin Cities, Minn.: U.S. Fish and Wildlife Service. A flop.

Westrum, Ron. 1982. "Social Intelligence About Hidden Events: Its Significance for Scientific Research and Social Policy. *Knowledge: Creation, Diffusion, Utilization,* March.

Whitlock, Cathy. "Long-Term Vegetational Response to Climatic Change and Edaphic Conditions in Yellowstone National Park." In GYE-1.

Wilcove, David S., Margaret McMillan, and Keith C. Winston. 1993. "What Exactly Is an Endangered Species? An Analysis of the U.S. Endangered Species List, 1985–1991." *Conservation Biology,* March.

*Wolf!* Many issues.

*Yellowstone Science.* Many issues.

Yook, Carol Kaesuk. 1994. "Boom and Bust May Be the Norm in Nature, Study Suggests." *The New York Times,* 15 March.

———. 1996. "Ecosystem Productivity Rises with Diversity of Its Species." *The New York Times,* 5 March.

Zimen, Erik. 1981. "Italian Wolves." *Natural History,* February.

———. 1982. "A Wolf Pack Sociogram." In WW.

Zimen, Erik, and Luigi Boitani. 1975. "Status of the Wolf in Europe and the Possibilities of Conservation and Reintroduction." In Klinghammer.

## OTHER

Eicher, Tim. "In the Matter of the Search of the real property of Chad McKittrick and two vehicles, application and affidavit for search warrant." United States District Court, Billings, Montana. May 15, 1995.

Fischer, Hank. "Endangered Species Act Rule 10(j) Reintroduction of Grizzly Bears into the Bitterroot Grizzly Bear Recovery Zone." A proposed alternative for the E.I.S. Draft of March 4, 1996.

France, Thomas M. "Defendant-Intervenor's Reply Brief" in the case of *Wyoming Farm Bureau Federation et al.* vs. *Bruce Babbitt et al.* January 27, 1996.

Great Bear Foundation, Greater Yellowstone Coalition, Idaho Conservation League, Inland Empire Public Lands Council, Predator Project, Sierra Club Montana Chapter, and The Wilderness Society. Reply to Fischer, 1996, above. March 7, 1996.

United States Court of Appeals for the Tenth Circuit. Order. January 11, 1995.

United States District Court for the Court of Wyoming. *Wyoming Farm Bureau Federation; Montana Farm Bureau Federation; American Farm Bureau Federation; Mountain States Legal Foundation, Plaintiffs,* vs. *United States Department of the Interior Secretary, also known as Bruce Babbitt, in his official capacity; Assistant Secretary, Fish and Wildlife and Parks, Department of the Interior, also known as George T. Frampton, in his official capacity; United States Fish and Wildlife Service Director, also known as Mollie H. Beattie, in her official capacity; United States Fish and Wildlife Service Regional Director, Region 6, also known as Ralph O. Morganweck, in his official capacity; Director of the National Park Service, also known as Roger Kennedy, in his official capacity; United States Department of Agriculture Secretary, also known as Michael Espy, in his official capacity; United States Forest Service Chief Forester, also known as Jack Ward Thomas, in his official capacity; Department of Interior; United States Fish and Wildlife Service; National Park Service; Department of Agriculture; United States Forest Service, Department of Agriculture; United States of America, Defendants.* Transcript of preliminary injunction hearings. December 1994.

## CONTINUING INFORMATION

*Defenders*
1101 Fourteenth St. N.W.
Suite 1400
Washington, DC 20005.

*International Wolf*
1396 Hwy. 169
Ely, MN 55731

*Ralph Maughan's Wolf Report*
A frequently updated home page on the Internet, focusing on the Yellowstone and Idaho populations: www.poky.srvnet/~jjmrm/maughan.html

# ACKNOWLEDGMENTS

The return of the wolf to Yellowstone has been the work of people of exceptional distinction, as I hope this book shows. The conservationists and government employees whose collective achievement is now history have given years of long and sometimes anguished days to the wolf with little tangible reward. Their moral courage and strength of character are tonic reminders that there are other kinds of heroes in our time than the powerful and glamorous. Despite the endless demands of their jobs, they have found hours to indulge this writer's importunate needs, and I will never forget their generosity.

My gratitude is especially deep to:

Mike Phillips, Doug Smith, John Varley, and Norm Bishop at Yellowstone National Park, whose devotion to the wolf and to their work is heroic;

Dave Mech of the U.S. Fish and Wildlife Service in St. Paul, Minnesota, whose wisdom, energy, and intelligence make clear why Varley calls him the alpha of alphas;

Ed Bangs, Steve Fritts, and Joe Fontaine of the U.S.F.W.S. in Helena, Montana, who exemplify the passionate truth that shatters the dull-witted myth of the federal bureaucrat;

Hank Fischer of Defenders of Wildlife in Missoula, Montana, the great father of the wolf's return, whose immense store of knowledge I have plundered shamelessly;

Renée Askins of the Wolf Fund in Jackson, Wyoming, who opened to me her hundreds of files and her gentle, fiery heart;

Ed Lewis, Louisa Willcox, Bob Ekey, Ken Barrett, and Mike Clark of the Greater Yellowstone Coalition in Bozeman, Montana, soul-stewards of the great Greater Yellowstone Ecosystem.

Phillips, Smith, Mech, and Bangs reviewed this book in manuscript and saved me from some real bonehead bloopers. Thank you, gentlemen, one and all.

Luigi Boitani, Paolo Ciucci, and Edo Tedesco helped me find my way in the wolf country of Italy. *Ciao, amici, e mille grazie!* No greater pal has wolf or writer ever had than *tu*, Luigi.

Rocky Barker, Michael Milstein, Angus Thuermer, fellow ink-stained wretches, and Ralph Maughan, inkless via Internet—your work saved me a ton of the same. Thanks!

Bill Strachan, Darcy Tromanhauser, Mary Ellen Burd, Kate Scott, Michelle McMillian, and all the rest of the gang at Holt—hurrah!

Molly Friedrich, world's best and most charming agent—roses!

John Weaver, I believe that the world owes to you, more than to any other, the return of the wolf to Yellowstone.

Elizabeth McNamee, my dearest, you have given me life, which was very helpful since a dead guy probably could not have written this book.

# INDEX

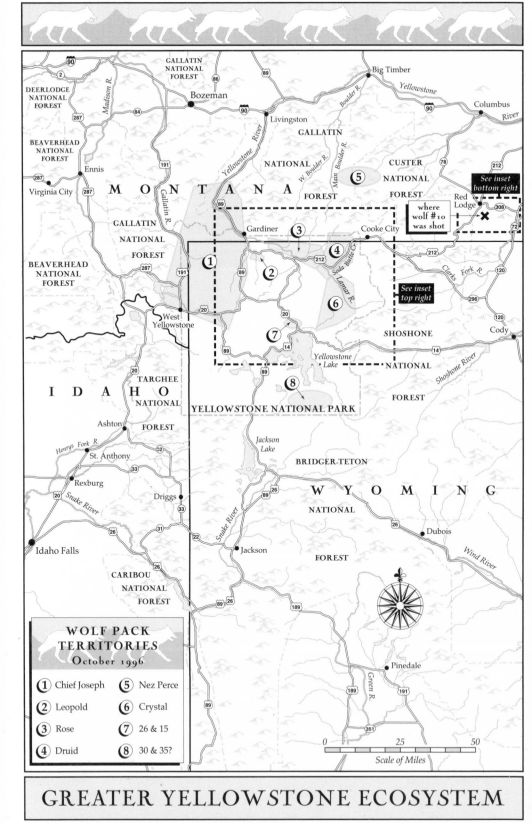

**GREATER YELLOWSTONE ECOSYSTEM**

Map labels (reading across the image):

GALLATIN NATIONAL FOREST
90
2
86
89
Big Timber
Boulder R.
Yellowstone
DEERLODGE NATIONAL FOREST
Madison R.
Bozeman
Livingston
90
84
287
Columbus
River
GALLATIN
W. Boulder R.
Main Boulder R.
CUSTER
78
212
BEAVERHEAD NATIONAL FOREST
191
NATIONAL
⑤
NATIONAL
308
287
Ennis
M O N T A N A
FOREST
FOREST
*See inset bottom right*
Virginia City
287
Gallatin R.
89
Red Lodge
72
GALLATIN
Gardiner
③
*where wolf #10 was shot*
✗
NATIONAL
191
①
②
④
212
212
BEAVERHEAD NATIONAL FOREST
287
89
Cooke City
Soda Butte Cr.
Clarks Fork R.
120
FOREST
20
⑥
296
*See inset top right*
20
Lamar R.
SHOSHONE
Cody
West Yellowstone
⑦
14
120
89
14
Shoshone River
20
TARGHEE
Yellowstone Lake
⑧
NATIONAL
I D A H O
NATIONAL
**YELLOWSTONE NATIONAL PARK**
FOREST
Ashton
32
Jackson Lake
FOREST
Henrys Fork R.
St. Anthony
33
**BRIDGER-TETON**
Rexburg
Driggs
33
89
26
W Y O M I N G
20
Snake River
31
22
Snake River
NATIONAL
26
Dubois
26
Idaho Falls
Jackson
189
FOREST
Wind River
CARIBOU
26
NATIONAL
189
191
FOREST
Pinedale
Green R.
351

**WOLF PACK TERRITORIES**
October 1996

① Chief Joseph   ⑤ Nez Perce
② Leopold        ⑥ Crystal
③ Rose           ⑦ 26 & 15
④ Druid          ⑧ 30 & 35?

0    25    50
*Scale of Miles*